Born to Be King

Born to Be King

Prince Charles on Planet Windsor

//

CATHERINE MAYER

HENRY HOLT AND COMPANY   NEW YORK

Henry Holt and Company, LLC
Publishers since 1866
175 Fifth Avenue
New York, New York 10010
www.henryholt.com

Henry Holt® and ® are registered trademarks of Henry Holt and Company, LLC.

Library of Congress Cataloging-in-Publication Data is available.

ISBN: 978-1-62779-438-1

Henry Holt books are available for special promotions and premiums.
For details contact: Director, Special Markets.

First Edition 2015

Designed by Meryl Sussman Levavi

Printed in the United States of America

1   3   5   7   9   10   8   6   4   2

To Andy, perennially

Contents

Born to Be King

Author's Note

//

IN OCTOBER 2013, A SHORT "TEASER" ON *TIME*'S WEBSITE GENERATED headlines across the world. These headlines quickly described a narrative arc of their own, from the factual "PRINCE CHARLES IN NO HURRY TO BECOME KING"[1] to the sexed-up "PRINCE CHARLES FEARS BECOMING KING WILL BE LIKE 'PRISON'"[2] and through a U-turn: "PRINCE CHARLES 'PRISON' CLAIM DENIED."[3] I had posted the teaser to draw attention to the newly published issue of *Time* magazine, which carried my cover profile of Charles.[4] The teaser pointed to some of the main conclusions of that longer piece: that Charles is a passionate philanthropist, one of the world's most prolific charitable entrepreneurs. He doesn't have the leisure to sit about waiting to be king and is driven by a sense of urgency to get as much done as possible before that day arrives. I wrote: "Much of what you think you know about the Prince is wrong. . . . I found a man not, as caricatured, itching to ascend the throne, but impatient to get as much done as possible before, in the words of one member of his household, 'the prison shades' close. The Queen, at 87, is scaling back her work, and the Prince is taking up the slack, to the potential detriment of his network of charities, initiatives and causes."[5]

Teased or not, the cover story was always bound to draw attention, and not just because Charles emerged as a bit of a charmer, who inspired his friend, the actress Emma Thompson, to the tongue-in-cheek observation that dancing with him was "better than sex." (The quote in my *Time* profile, which launched a first set of lurid headlines, had in fact been truncated for space. Who knows what the tabloids would have made of Thompson's unexpurgated tribute: "He's a great, great dancer. He's the best dancer. Not disco-dancing. Proper dancing. I've never danced with anyone who can actually lead me and I can just relax and go this is great, this is better than sex. He's a very charismatic, virile dancer.")[6]

I had been given remarkable access by the standards of royal press management, which is to say, nowhere near as much as a *Time* journalist might expect from a president or prime minister, but enough to get a strong sense of my quarry and for him to get a sense of me. Before the project could be green-lit, he met me and spoke to me off the record. For six months, I trailed him, came close to learning to remember to curtsy every time we met, listened to his speeches—and his jokes—visited his homes, struggled to keep up with him as he strode across muddy fields, attended a private concert at his Welsh bolt-hole, mingled at multiple events to promote his charities and initiatives, on one occasion dined with him at the Scottish mansion Dumfries House, listened in on one of his private meetings (and inevitably became drawn into the discussion that took place), interviewed a substantial number of people close to him, and eventually sat down in his living room in Birkhall, on the Balmoral estate in Scotland, to an on-the-record conversation with him.

His aides at Clarence House—the name of his London home and the collective name for his staff—agreed to the Prince speaking on condition that this would not be billed as an "interview" and that he could review his quotes prepublication. A few of the most revealing things he said ended up on the cutting-room floor; so did some utterly innocuous remarks. Monarchy moves in mysterious ways. I did not use any rewritten quotes that changed the meaning of the original. About half of the interviewees, particularly those working for the royal households or Charles's charities and initiatives, insisted that I send their comments about "HRH" (His Royal Highness) or "the Boss" for prior approval, and, like the Prince, excised the anodyne as well as the controversial. Other sources opted to remain anonymous.

Similar preconditions were necessary to secure some of the many additional interviews conducted for this book. In January 2014, I returned to

Dumfries House and, as on the first visit, accompanied Charles on a long march around the estate, lasting about five hours while the Prince gave detailed notes to the team overseeing the development of the grounds and various projects on the estate. I seized many additional opportunities to observe him at close quarters, for example in May of the same year accompanying him and the Duchess of Cornwall on their official visit to Canada, interacting with both of them and watching them interact with others.

There is a convention that private conversations with royals are not to be quoted directly. The definition of a private conversation is less than crystalline. One such conversation, between the Prince and a volunteer guide at the Canadian Museum of Immigration at Pier 21 in Nova Scotia, found its way into Britain's *Daily Mail*, prompting a diplomatic spat with Russia. The *Mail* explained its decision to publish on the basis that the volunteer had been standing in the official lineup at the museum.[7] I decided in this book to quote from a few conversations that Clarence House would class as private, for example, between Charles and a collective of Welsh butchers, to give a flavor of the way he speaks and how he engages with people, but I have steered clear of repeating any remarks that would lend themselves to headlines, because they either misrepresented his true views or revealed them all too clearly but without context.

In other circumstances, a biographer could rely on previously published work to fill in the gaps. With Charles, that would be problematic. Many secondary printed sources about royalty are unreliable. So my voluminous reading has been supplemented by multiple interviews with people who know Charles well. One person close to him sent me a heartening e-mail after we spoke, saying that I had clearly come to understand the essence of the Prince. I hope so. I have also drawn on a large body of research about the royals amassed over three decades, most recently authoring four *Time* cover stories and coauthoring a *Time* book, and also as the editor and behind-the-scenes point person for a *Time* cover story on the Queen in 2006 for which I also interviewed Prince Andrew. Two years before that I had shadowed Andrew on one of his trade missions to China and interviewed him in Beijing. I've been delving into the royals since the Diana years. Every encounter with Prince Charles, his family, staff, and friends, quotable or not, has deepened my understanding. Controlled access is better than the only alternative open to the vast majority of biographers: no access.

The Queen has never given an interview, by that name or any other; her children and grandchildren rarely do so. Britain's Freedom of Information Act exempts communications with the Queen, Prince Charles, and the second in line to the throne, William, from public scrutiny (though at the time of going to press Britain's Supreme Court is mulling a challenge to the strictures against revealing the content of some of Charles's correspondence). Palace staff sign confidentiality agreements. Royal press secretaries almost never comment on stories deemed to stray into the ever-narrowing sphere of the purely personal. That policy means some journalists inevitably make honest mistakes based on faulty information from trusted sources cultivated to supplement the meager fare provided by close-lipped royal aides. More unscrupulous reporters see in such reticence a license to fabricate or embroider stories they calculate the palace will find too trivial or intrusive to rebut. There's an assumption, too, that the royals will not sue. So the world is awash with royal nonsense. Inaccuracies and inventions, left unchallenged, are repeated. Repetition gives credence. Once a sufficient number of news organizations has repeated a fiction, it becomes a multisourced fact. News-gathering in the age of aggregation is a giant game of Chinese whispers, in which stories become, like the Prince's eggs, more scrambled with each retelling.

In 2012, Clarence House took the unusual step of publishing on its website a list of "frequently asked questions" about Charles and rubbishing the answers generously provided by the press. "Does the Prince of Wales have seven boiled eggs cooked for his breakfast but eat only one, as claimed in Jeremy Paxman's book *On Royalty*?" the website wondered. "No, he doesn't and never has done, at breakfast or any other time." Paxman, a distinguished BBC broadcaster, had told a story relayed to him by a friend of Charles. After a day's hunting, staff would put out boiled eggs "in an ascending row of numbers. If the Prince felt that number five was too runny, he could knock the top off number six or seven." The story, Paxman added, "seems so preposterously extravagant as to be unbelievable."[8]

Yet it may well have been rooted in fact. Wendy Berry, a former housekeeper at Highgrove, published a memoir of her time in service to Charles in which she described, with pride, serving perfectly cooked boiled eggs to the Prince after he returned from hunting. She put a first batch of eggs on to cook when Charles arrived but, realizing that a member of his party had been delayed, discarded the first batch and started over. There is no suggestion that Charles asked her to do so or knew of the waste, which he would as likely have reprimanded as applauded. His lifestyle, as with much else about him, is riven with contradictions. He lives high on the hog by just about any standard, but combines the showiness of royal life—the banquets, the acreage of cut flowers, retinues larger than most other family members employ—with a frugality absorbed from his parents and austere schooling at the Scottish public school Gordonstoun and more consciously informed by his environmental concerns.

Still the eggs, repurposed as his breakfast-time whim and served as proof of his profligacy, began doing the rounds, joining other half-myths of Charles, the spoiled princeling: that a valet squeezes his toothpaste for him and that he ordered his servant to hold the specimen bottle as he deposited a princely urine sample. Neither of these stories is without a kernel of truth. Michael Fawcett, one of the most compelling and ambiguous members of the Prince's inner coterie, worked for many years as his valet, and after an accident put Charles's arm in a sling, assisted with tasks that would have been difficult with only one hand free. Before and after that brief interlude, Charles has managed such functions, as it were, single-handed. "It's very difficult to fight back," says Elizabeth Buchanan, a former Private Secretary to the Prince. "Because you can fight back [but] how demeaning to have to say the Prince of Wales does not have his toothpaste squeezed. Guess what, if you break your arm funnily enough there are some things you can't do."[9]

The distortions seem harmless, but combine to create a reputation for dissipation that is hard to dispel. Most people believe at least some of the falsehoods in circulation about the royals, not least because some fictions slide into fact. For nineteen months after her wedding, the Duchess of Cambridge—Kate—found herself declared pregnant on a weekly basis. Then reality caught up with invention (though the twins, heralded on the cover of at least three separate magazines, failed to materialize). She gave birth to her son in July 2013; by the spring of 2014, the pregnancy rumors, again involving twins, had been dusted off to be replayed during her official visit to New Zealand. A wine tasting and a white-water boat ride provided Kate with the opportunity mutely to scotch the story, if only temporarily. No sooner had her second pregnancy been announced in September

2014—and although the statement clearly said she was expecting a child—than sources declared the royal womb to be accommodating twin girls.

In the absence of news, editors try to change the narrative to retain interest. For Kate, most often depicted as a blissed-out madonna, a paragon of young motherhood, that meant her March 2014 trip to the Maldives with William—and the couple's decision to travel without George, then seven months old—provided Britain's mass-market *Daily Mail* with an opportunity to test out an alternative story line. "ROYALS JET OFF—INTO A STORM OF PROTEST," declared its print and online editions; "the [couple's] decision sparked a storm on social networking sites Mumsnet, Netmums and Twitter."[10]

It was a manufactured tempest in a child's teacup. Netmums posted an item inviting comment on the royal jolly only at the request of the *Mail*. There had been no discussion before that, and the thread generated little reaction among the website's 1.2 million members. Of forty-two comments in total, only two could be construed as negative. After Netmums protested that the story was inaccurate, the *Mail* deleted the reference to the site from the online article. Had there been outrage on Mumsnet? Not according to Kate O'Donovan, Mumsnet's head of communications, who e-mailed that there were "just over 300 responses, which isn't really a 'storm' by Mumsnet's standards. Not at all unanimous in criticism of the couple, and it's worth noting that about one third of the thread comes after (and so in response to) the *Mail* piece being published."[11] The swell of Twitter reaction also appears to have been triggered by the *Mail* piece that purported to describe it.

This isn't just a function of cynical journalism. The problem for and with the monarchy is that much of what it does, when things are going right, has little news value. Yet the royals need to publicize their work, such as it is, for fear of being accused of laziness and also because much of that work involves drawing publicity to worthy causes or flying the flag for the nations they represent. As a result, there is a constant low-level struggle between the palace press teams, which vainly hope to satisfy reporters with a thin gruel of visits and speeches and photo opportunities, and the media organizations, which have to find something newsworthy in the soup.

In 1985, the *Guardian* dispatched a young reporter to Australia to cover a visit to the country by the Prince and Princess of Wales. Now the editor of the left-leaning *Guardian* newspaper and website, Alan Rusbridger remembers the assignment as "the most awful job I've ever done. . . . It was just sort of humiliating as a journalist. You were bussed from place to place and stood behind a table and something would happen, there would be a ribbon and a pair of scissors and then you would be bussed back and then there would be thirty of you on the bus and your job was to try and concoct something at the end of the day that was not as banal as I've just described it. And it was everything you hated about them and our fascination with them so I just ended up writing four pieces from Australia which were all about what it was like to cover them."[12]

Before Diana came on the scene, most serious journalists were spared such ignominy; their editors abandoned royal coverage to the tabloids, whose intrusions were minor by later standards. "Did you get a picture of my left earhole?" Prince Philip, sailing in Scotland, shouted at a dogged photographer in 1962.[13] Some of the popular press chose to publish a photograph of Philip's left ear with his commentary.

Higher-minded media disdained such trivia. When Anthony Holden, a journalist for the British broadsheet *Sunday Times*, decided the Prince's 1977 trip to Canada might make good fodder for a piece, the startled subject of his interest asked, "What on earth are *you* doing here?"[14] As the only writer trailing Charles, Holden enjoyed near-unfettered access. It was the same story later the same year on a sweep through South America. Holden went on to write three biographies of Charles, at ten-year intervals, each chronicling his increasing disenchantment with the Prince and his media handlers. The feelings were mutual; Holden's second biography revealed strains in the royal marriage that remained largely concealed until the convulsive events of 1992: the publication of Andrew Morton's book *Diana: Her True Story* and the subsequent separation of Charles and Diana. But Holden's biographies also charted the changing challenges of royal media management. No longer might a journalist hope for the ad hoc dinners and head-to-heads with Charles that Holden enjoyed on the 1977 trip. Instead, after Charles's marriage to Diana made royal coverage a commercial imperative for most organizations, the author found himself "in Australia for the bicentennial celebrations of 1988 . . . one of 200 writers and photographers, as many as 70 of whom had flown out from Britain, permitted only to observe the couple from behind ropes, at a safe distance."[15] More than 450 journalists were accredited for William and Kate's 2014 tour of the Antipodes.

Distance has bred distance, of the wrong kind. Monarchy matters but only the republican press consistently acknowledges that fact. Much royal coverage is lobotomized fluff that understands the Windsors only as the cast of a long-running reality TV show—showbiz but not necessarily even showbiz royalty—or conceals an edge of resentment common to all celebrity reporting. Stories are spun from the thinnest of materials.

Relations between royals and reporters haven't always been fraught. For a period in the 1990s, the Prince opened up to his biographer Jonathan Dimbleby, whose book and film have remained key resources for researchers as a result but have never been updated. Now Charles is a born-again virgin—hence his concerns about giving "interviews." It took a sustained campaign to persuade Clarence House, and the Prince himself, that allowing me access to profile him for *Time* might, from their perspective, do more good than harm. I wasn't promising puffery but substance and balance—and that inevitably meant there would be elements in the story they didn't like. My counterargument was that puff pieces don't move the dial on public opinion.

That opinion still owes a good deal to Diana. She understood the power of imagery and the wounds that a well-placed leak could inflict. She, too, cultivated special relationships among the ranks of the media. Her friends, old and new, spread the word about her husband's derelictions. His camp fought back, but without the same skills and hampered by a principal who could never match Diana's luster or her bloodlust. A substantial minority of Britons still supports an idea she boosted in her magnificently dissident 1995 interview for the BBC's *Panorama*: that the succession should skip Charles and pass directly to their son William.[16] Her estranged husband may not actually want to be king, she suggested: "Being Prince of Wales produces more freedom now, and being king would be a little bit more suffocating." "Would it be your wish that when Prince William comes of age that he were to succeed the Queen rather than the current Prince of Wales?" asked interviewer Martin Bashir. "My wish is that my husband finds peace of mind, and from that follows other things, yes," answered the Princess, permitting herself a small smile as she delivered a line that would haunt her husband forevermore.[17]

Eighteen years later, I forgot that smile as I attempted to skewer another widespread myth: that Charles is frustrated by his mother's refusal to die or stand down and let him take what Diana called "the top job."[18] Multiple conversations with insiders—his friends, householders, people working for his charities—had led me to the understanding that the opposite was true. For one thing, the Prince doesn't deal well with death. Despite the comfort his religious and philosophical beliefs should presumably provide, he still mourns, with a startlingly raw grief, his grandmother, his great-uncle Louis Mountbatten, and mentors such as Laurens van der Post—a man of many self-descriptions including explorer and anthropologist and too loose a relationship with the truth to trust his self-descriptions—and Kathleen Raine, a poet. Charles dreads the deaths of his parents.

The Queen's grand age is not only a source of anxiety for the Prince but, before the start of my research for the *Time* piece, had set in train a difficult process behind the scenes at Clarence House, to make space for Charles to shoulder more of the traditional duties of kingship. He was looking at rationalizing his existing commitments and reining in his impulse to intervene. Instead of extending his hand to fresh beneficiaries and new causes, he was under pressure to cut some existing liege men adrift. This ran counter to his usual instincts and also generated considerable bad blood as courtiers turned on each other in the fight for survival. In all of this, Charles put duty before passion. That was why a member of his household compared the Prince to the growing boy in William Wordsworth's "Intimations of Immortality" for whom "shades of the prison-house begin to close" as adulthood nears.

So it was a fair point well made by my informant, but I had reckoned without the acute neuralgia the spirit of Diana still triggers within palace walls. Clarence House swiftly issued a denial of something my piece had not implied because it wasn't true: that Charles was my unnamed source. "This is not the Prince of Wales's view and should not be attributed to him as he did not say these words," said the statement. "The Prince has dutifully supported the Queen all his life and his official duties and charitable work have always run in parallel."

The denial inadvertently gave the story fresh legs and these days resides in the ether along with all the earlier "Charles-doesn't-want-to-be-king" stories, inevitably to be recycled at various points in the future, shorn of context.

Charles does want to be king. He also wants to be much, much more, and that's why he makes such a fascinating subject for a biography.

CATHERINE MAYER
London, December 2014

Introduction

///

If thou pretend'st to be a prince like me,
Blame not an act, which should thy pattern be.
I saw the oppressed, and thought it did belong
To a king's office to redress the wrong:
I brought that succour, which thou ought'st to bring,
And so, in nature, am thy subjects' king.

Almanzor and Almahide, John Dryden

THE PRINCE IS A POLISHED HOST. YEARS OF PUTTING STRANGERS AT ease have endowed him with a repertoire of useful tricks. His bright eyes never glaze. He listens attentively and squirrels away nuggets of information to nourish future conversations. He matches subject and tone to person with perfect pitch and repays confidences with glimpses into his own life—nothing too intimate, just amusing anecdotes or wry tales of the tribulations of parenting or latterly heartfelt paeans to the joys of grand-parenting—to create a sense of connection, of shared experience.

On this particular September evening in 2013, shared experiences threaten to be in short supply. His twenty-four guests hail from France, Poland, Russia, Spain, South Africa, Taiwan, the United States, Uzbekistan, and different corners and conditions of Britain, with little in common apart from the basic fact of humanity and that around half of the people sipping aperitifs in the Tapestry Room at Dumfries House own, between them, an astonishing slice of global wealth. Mischievous members of Charles's staff have coined a collective term for the moneyed classes that he regularly lures to such dinners: "Bond villains."

His aides are adamant that all potential donors are subjected to careful health checks, and this contingent certainly appears more inclined to philanthropy than villainy, aiming not to dominate the world but to help it. Guests turn out to be sponsors of worthy causes, backers of foundations, patrons of music and the visual arts. One man describes himself as an art collector. "Any particular kind of art?" "Yes," he says airily, "art that I like."

At Dumfries House, artworks by old masters hang alongside watercolors by the oldest-ever heir to the British throne. In 2007, Charles scrambled a consortium to buy the Palladian mansion in Scotland, sparing the building a future that might have seen it sprout ungainly wings as a resort hotel and staying an auction that would have dispersed an unparalleled collection of Thomas Chippendale furniture. Under his auspices, the house has become a heritage attraction, and the estate is a seedbed for his charities and initiatives, all of which gobble up money.

So there is no such thing as a free lunch with the Prince, much less a free dinner at Dumfries House, for all that scenes of careless revelry provide the backdrop for predinner cocktails. The mansion's original Flemish tapestries, stitched in the early eighteenth century in the Brussels workshop of Leyniers-Reydams, have been sent away for restoration; in their place hang near-perfect replicas across which Bacchus and maidens and minions cavort with the happy abandon that the previous year landed Prince Harry in the news. ("HEIR IT IS," announced the headline in Britain's largest red-top tabloid, the *Sun*, above a grainy image of a naked Harry cupping his "crown jewels" during a game of strip poker in a Las Vegas hotel.) A few of this evening's guests have already opened their wallets to the Prince's charities. They have been invited to bind them more closely into these organizations. Charles hopes to persuade the rest to follow suit over a visit that includes the dinner, a tour of the house, and, the following day, a vigorous march around the grounds that he leads himself.

Over cocktails he entertains his villains with tamer episodes from Harry's youth. He speaks with obvious pride and affection, and a touch of wonderment. For all his bonhomie, his jokes, and a delight in the absurd that saw him at Harry's thirteenth birthday party laughing uproariously while competing with Emma Thompson in a game in which players donned hats covered in Velcro and used them to try to catch felt-covered balls, Charles is fundamentally serious. His younger son lives in the moment. It's hard enough to master that trick when the future is mapped out years ahead and in hourly increments, harder still for someone of Charles's temperament and experiences.

There's a revealing joke he tells so often that it has acquired a patina of use, like his two favorite pairs of day shoes, buffed and polished and trotted out over decades. His comic timing has always been good. His constricted elocution lends itself at least as easily to humor as to solemnity. (His friends and staffers can't help themselves but mimic his voice and the rictus that pulls down the left corner of his mouth when he is at his most emphatic.) In a parallel universe he might have made a decent stand-up, the funny-looking teenager, his face too narrow a base for the Windsor beak and winglike ears, growing up to exploit the natural comedy in being a man out of joint with ordinary life and turning his bafflement into an amusing routine. Instead, the man who expects one day to reign over the United Kingdom and fifteen other Commonwealth Realms deploys wit to leaven speeches on weighty issues or simply to entertain guests at private functions. These days he's a confident performer, easy in a skin that's come with age to suit him—he turned sixty-six on November 14, 2014. He's dexterous with words, quick with a riposte. He can deliver zingers. But time and again, he returns to this same tired gag.

"If ever you're afraid of being somehow marooned on a desert island—perhaps you're flying a light airplane over the South Seas—always make sure you have in your knapsack a cocktail shaker, one of those collapsible goblets such as they used to issue in the army, a small jar of olives, some cocktail sticks, a phial of vermouth and a hip flask of gin or vodka," he counsels his audience. "If, by misfortune, you do find yourself stranded, like Robinson Crusoe, all alone on a desert island, have no fear. All you have to do is unpack your martini paraphernalia and start to mix the drink."

He pauses, signaling the imminent arrival of a punch line. "I can guarantee that within a minute, someone will jump out of a tree and say, 'That's not the proper way to mix a martini!'"

The joke reliably earns a big laugh, bigger than its payoff would seem to deserve, but then that's the really funny thing about royalty: its members seldom experience the world as the rest of us do because their presence changes it. The Prince knows humanity on its best behavior and at its worst—sycophantic, shallow, sharp-elbowed. He's used to people applauding his every pronouncement and responding to his jokes with great, grating guffaws.

Yet there's a reverse side to the coinage that carries his mother's head. There always seems to be someone poised to leap out of the shrubbery to declare that he doesn't know how to mix a martini. Commentary and criticism have attended him throughout his life like resentful valets. He has never enjoyed the luxury of trying and failing privately. As soon as he began to express opinions, he discovered he was speaking through a bullhorn. As the frail struts of his first marriage corroded, he found himself widely miscast. He had famously semaphored his unease after the engagement was announced, when an interviewer ventured that he and Lady Diana Spencer were "in love." "Of course," said Diana. "Whatever 'in love' means," added her fiancé, his face frozen.

In failing to love the "queen of people's hearts," as Diana would later accurately characterize her public role, Charles appeared a knave as well as a joker.[1] In avoiding the pitfalls of doing little of substance during an apprenticeship to be sovereign that his mother's longevity has stretched over more than half a century, he instead earns censure for doing too much. He's a dabbler, straying into areas of expertise that are not his own. He's a meddler, ignoring constitutional proprieties to intervene in the political process. If he finally accedes to the throne—which he is gnawingly impatient to do—Charles III promises to be as memorable a king as Charles I.

The last point may well prove true, if for different reasons. United with the woman he loves and fondly observing his sons establishing a Camelot of their own, with his charitable empire in full swing and a host of initiatives and campaigns under his stewardship, the Prince is probably more contented than he's ever been. He enjoys life, sometimes. He can be excellent company, in spite, or even because of, the jokes. He has a talent for telling them. A man often mimicked, he is an expert mimic of others. "He's a sort of Rory Bremner," says his godson and cousin, Tim Knatchbull, drawing a comparison with a well-known British impressionist. "He's got the thing where he'll change his face; it's a studied little move. He's got the knack for imitating. You've either got the knack or you don't. The Queen's the same and he's clearly inherited the gene from her."[2]

The Prince is a multilingual polymath, a decent watercolorist, and an expert gardener. The royals are popularly assumed to be horse mad. Charles, however, has a passion for sheep. Emma Sparham, helped by his charity the Prince's Trust to start her own business, met him at a St. James's Palace reception and mentioned the rare breed she keeps, called Soay. "If I was to say the word 'Soay' to 100 people, maybe five of them might know what it is," she said afterward. "He knew exactly what it was, what island they come from and he knows the nature of the animal. He asked if I could catch them because they are renowned for being uncatchable."[3] The Prince keeps flocks at several of his homes, devised campaigns to promote wool and mutton, and scooped the 2012 George Hedley Memorial Award presented by Britain's National Sheep Association in recognition of his outstanding contribution to the sheep sector.

He is kind. He keeps track of the personal circumstances of the people around him, asks after their loved ones, makes an effort to attend events that are important to them. As family members gathered for the funeral of his brother-in-law Mark Shand in May 2014, it was Charles, warm and "extraordinarily tactile," who brewed tea and dispensed sympathy, says Ben Elliot, cofounder of the Quintessentially Group and the Prince's nephew by marriage.[4] Charles organizes surprises and treats for friends and people he admires, such as a joint eightieth birthday celebration at Clarence House for the British playwright Ronald Harwood and *Downton Abbey*'s dowager countess, actor Maggie Smith. He inspires devotion, sometimes more than is good for him. He is loyal to a fault, sometimes to the point of fault. "He's a very human person, incredibly emotionally alert. The radar is very powerful, and he picks up on things," says Ian Skelly, a BBC broadcaster who often helps the Prince write speeches and has also collaborated with him on a startling book. "Because of his background he's spent his entire life trying to work out who's true and who's full of flannel."[5] Unlike the rest of his family, when Charles asks, "And what do you do?" he's keenly interested in hearing the answer.

A compulsive philanthropist, he has founded more than twenty-five charities. "Every one of them is a little pilot project that lights a candle in a dark space," says Lord Sacks, Britain's former Chief Rabbi. Sacks goes so far as to speak of the Prince's "greatness." "I do not go around using that world liberally, I really don't," Sacks adds. "You know why the world doesn't see him for what he is? Because we have very little room for greatness. We're interested in celebrity."[6]

But after a lifetime of being found wanting—the proverbial prophet without honor in his own country—Charles rarely recognizes his own achievements. He is "a glass-half-empty man" in the words of one member of his inner circle, a Prince of Wails. Another person close to him says he has a short fuse. "The royal rage, I call it. Here comes the royal rage." At the darkest points of his life, his despondency has been profound. Even now, in his late-blooming prime, he recites litanies of injustice and in rare on-the-record conversations can't stop plaintive notes from sounding. "Each thing I did you had to meet another lot of people who have all sorts of views of you beforehand, all sorts of prejudices," he confides.[7]

This biography aims to puncture those prejudices to close in on the far more interesting truth. As good a starting place as any must be to identify the mechanisms that occlude that truth. The Prince often blames a toxic press, and he is not wrong. But that toxicity fermented in a complex jelly: amid social change and global strains, at the intersection of republicanism and an avid celebrity culture, in a Britain facing new battles with identity and old struggles with class. Stifling deference gave way to a prevailing mistrust of institutions and public figures. Palace structures have struggled to manage a mainstream media itself in transition and, latterly, in existential crisis. As newspaper revenues have declined, the pressure to produce stories, by hook or by crookery, has increased. Legitimate inquiries must navigate a miasma of half-fact and fiction surrounding the royal households, often without reliable guides and frequently bumping up against official secrecy. The Internet promises a new age of transparency and instead adds to the miasma.

At the center of this confusion, hand in pocket, stands Charles, a man who would in any circumstances prove hard to decode. He is fascinating, flawed as we all are, yet not as we are: a product of an upbringing set apart, conditioned to be different and to believe that difference must be maintained, a native of Planet Windsor. "He identifies with other people's precariousness. In many ways I feel that he's a strange figure in that setup, precisely because he seems to have all of these passions and concerns about issues and people," says Lucia Santa Cruz, his friend since university days. "I think he's one of the most misunderstood figures in history."[8] She may well be right. Charles is hard to understand because we cannot measure him against our own experiences and expectations. He does not always understand us for the same reasons, and that can complicate communications.

He seeks intimacy yet continues with the alienating custom under which many of his friends and all of his staff call him "Sir." (He sometimes signs personal notes "Carrick," a name taken from one of his earldoms.) "There's a competition at Clarence House to see how deep you can curtsy without falling over," says a member of his household. A conspicuous beneficiary of entrenched inequality, the Prince works hard through his charities to redress inequality. He shuttles between stately homes and palaces in a swirl of retainers, yet has installed a wide range of eco-friendly, energy-saving technologies at Highgrove and his other homes. In his search for wisdom, he has sometimes done stupid things and listened to poor advice. He's easier to criticize than to comprehend. "Quite possibly the most creative initiator of charitable projects in the world," as Sacks describes him, he is more frequently depicted as someone without purpose or motivation.[9] A thought leader on the environment, he is caricatured as a man who talks to plants. He works from early morning into the night, combining an increasing burden of royal duty with the voluminous role he has carved out for himself, but is widely assumed to be underemployed.

Born to be king, he actually aims much higher. For himself, he seeks meaning, enlightenment, happiness. For everyone else he is more zealous still. He has set his sights on nothing less than improving the human condition and fixing a battered world. "I only take on the most difficult challenges. Because I want to raise aspirations and re-create hope from hopelessness and health from deprivation," he told me, sitting in his comfortable study at Birkhall on the Balmoral estate.[10] "We talk a lot about the guilt of privilege. Sometimes I think he's driven by guilt," muses Emma Thompson.[11]

It's easy to see why that might be. Birkhall is one of four residences listed on his website and he also has use of other homes in Scotland and Romania as well as access to the family palaces. His publicly declared income in

2013–2014 comprised \$31.5 million from the Duchy of Cornwall, the landed estate founded in 1337 to fund heirs to the throne, plus a further \$3.5 million from the Sovereign Grant, the money provided by the British government to support the Queen, and in some cases her family, in the execution of head-of-state duties. The Prince's Annual Review and the accounts of the Duchy of Cornwall lack fine detail but in the same year revealed official expenditure for his own household of \$19.5 million, another chunk for maintaining sons and daughter-in-law in style, expenditure on capital projects, and a tax bill of \$6.8 million, leaving him with a notional \$4 million to play with on top of any private investment income.

So he's rich—maybe not as stonkingly rich as his Bond villains, but more than comfortable. Some of his critics suggest this means he should fund his own charities. "All the charities are governed and run independently. Whilst HRH is the figurehead, he does not have the funds to keep them all going and it wouldn't be helpful for him to do so," says an aide. "Whilst fundraising is essential to any charity, engaging with businesses, government and the public is of equal importance. If HRH were funding all of these charities privately they would lack credibility and essential buy-in from other sectors."

Clarence House doesn't publish information on Charles's private wealth or the rate of tax he pays on such income. At a briefing about his 2013–2014 Annual Review, his Principal Private Secretary, William Nye, batted away a question. "Let's be clear," said Nye, proceeding to give an answer that fell some way short of that premise. "If [the Prince] had other private income it would be private, so I wouldn't tell you about it. But, to be clear, any income that he has, he pays tax on. There's certainly no income on which he doesn't pay tax."[12]

A similar fog hangs around the monarchy. Buckingham Palace used to say the annual bill to every Briton for the Queen was no more than the price of a cup of coffee, but that was before affluent urbanites became used to shelling out \$4.60 for a venti cappuccino, far more than the 90 cents per head the Palace now reckons the Queen costs. The Palace's calculation seems to be based on dividing her taxpayer funding, the Sovereign Grant of \$58.2 million in 2013–2014, among the entire UK populace instead of just the taxpayers who shoulder the expenditure. Their annual per capita outlay must be closer to \$1.92, or significantly higher if an estimate for policing is included—the sum for guarding VIPs including the royals is thought to be around $206 million a year.

She's not cheap, but the Queen isn't the most expensive head of state either (a distinction one university study awarded to the French; the purely ceremonial German presidency turned out to be only marginally less dear than the UK royals).[13] A British president and his or her apparatus might not prove any more economical. But a president would preside over citizens, not subjects. The real issue about privilege—the reason some people will never accept the monarchy, and the essential injustice that could well induce twinges of guilt in a thoughtful heir apparent—is that the head-of-state role is inherited, not earned.

Nor is the monarch just a figurehead. The Queen holds a constitutional role that is surprisingly substantial. She is the so-called Fount of Justice, head of the Armed Forces, and Supreme Governor of the Church of England; she signs off on legislation and has the power to prorogue Parliament. She advises the Prime Minister of the day and has twice been forced to choose a new premier when the governing party failed to replace its leader. She has mostly adhered to the convention that royals should remain disengaged from politics. Her eldest son does not do so.

Charles seeks to perform the most delicate of maneuvers, "highlight[ing] issues which are of concern to himself and to others in the aim of opening up a public debate . . . over what he sees as vital issues to the health of the nation while avoiding party political issues."[14] His position simultaneously gives him a platform for his views and deafens a swathe of his audience to messages they might applaud from other sources. Nevertheless, with his idealism untempered by the limitations that confront most campaigners, his vision unclouded by the need to seek election or carry board members with him, he has developed into a formidable operator with potent convening powers who has exerted a significant impact across a wide range of fields—indeed far more significant than many of his supporters or his critics recognize. His thinking, similarly unfettered, leads him to wilder philosophical territories than most people beyond his inner circle realize.

The book the Prince coauthored with Ian Skelly and British environmentalist Tony Juniper, published in 2010, opens with a startling sentence: "This is a call to revolution."[15] *Harmony: A New Way of Looking at Our World* is his manifesto. Worried aides did as little as possible to promote

the text because of its unsettling content. Charles had already caused consternation in some corners of Anglicanism in 1994 by suggesting that he
would alter the monarch's title of "Defender of the Faith" to "Defender of
Faith," a comment misconstrued to mean that he subscribed equally to
all religions.[16] *Harmony* reveals the personal creed that underpins and links
his activism in areas as apparently disparate as architecture, integrated
medicine, ecology, education, promoting interfaith understanding, and a
determination to get people eating mutton again. His philosophy blends
perennialism, holism, and other mystically inclined ideas with the nar-
rower faith of the church he expects one day to represent. An edition of
the book rewritten for children and published only in the United States
concludes with another eye-catching phrase: "I intend to be the Defender of
Nature. Will you come and help me?"[17]

A closer read reveals a fundamental and counterintuitive key to its
author. His Royal Highness Prince Charles Philip Arthur George, Prince of
Wales, KG, KT, GCB, OM, AK, QSO, PC, ADC, Earl of Chester, Duke of
Cornwall, Duke of Rothesay, Earl of Carrick, Baron of Renfrew, Lord of the
Isles, and Prince and Great Steward of Scotland, monarch-in-waiting, sym-
bol of entitlement, avatar of the establishment, sees himself as a renegade.

For years he has lobbed ideas into the public discourse and watched
debates ignite. "Because of his position he can be an amplifier of messages
and a conductor of ideas," says his friend Patrick Holden, an organic farmer
and the founding director of the Sustainable Food Trust (and no relation to
Charles's biographer Anthony Holden). "This sense of service goes right to
the heart of the man."[18] The amplification sometimes enables important
ideas to be heard; at other times it proves devastatingly loud. Monarchists
and republicans alike argue that he should be more like his mother, distant and largely silent, a screen to reflect projected ideals of unity and
public service. But Charles will never be, in that respect, like his mother.
He has more in common with his opinionated, idiosyncratic, foot-in-mouth
father, despite documented strains between them. And, in a keen and over-
looked irony, he shares many defining characteristics with Diana, Princess of Wales, whose life—and 1997 death in a car crash in Paris—would
do so much to define public attitudes to the Prince.

"Diana explained to me once that it was her innermost feelings of suffering that made it possible for her to connect with her constituency of the

rejected," said her brother Earl Spencer in his famous funeral oration. Intuitive, compassionate, and volatile, the Prince, like his former wife, has turned his own pain outward, trying, in helping others, to make himself whole. Like her, he is capable of building things up or tearing them down. By instinct and practice, Charles is a king of hearts, compelled to reach out, to try to make a difference. He has recently come to believe that doing so stands not in opposition to his hereditary role—current and future—but offers a way to invest the monarchy with new relevance.

Yet as he increasingly shares his mother's head-of-state duties, he is coming under pressure to sublimate these impulses and passions, to protect the monarchy by joining the forces that deliberately or by accident obscure the scope and scale of his activities and influence. This biography is written in the belief that concealment neither benefits the institution whose future relies on him nor serves the needs of the democracies of which it is a constitutional pillar. If the narrative often reads like comedy, that's because Charles's life serves up comedy at many turns, from the way people behave around him to the way he himself sometimes behaves. He makes jokes and occasionally the joke is on him. As Emma Thompson observes, "there is a deeply absurd aspect to it all, and he's a very intelligent man who's perfectly capable of seeing that."[19]

But this book also has a serious intent. Informed debate around the purpose and future of the monarchy is essential for the health of the democracies in which it is embedded. Counterarguments in support of the monarchy require an understanding of the role of the head of state, the gravitational pull of Planet Windsor, and how the destruction of that celestial body might play out back on Earth. This book attempts to bring clarity to both sides of the debate.

As for the Prince, he deserves to be understood.

ON MARCH 4, 2014, THE OCCUPANTS OF KENSINGTON PALACE—"KP"— forced themselves to act against the grain: they held a soirée for journalists, and not just any journalists, but royal correspondents, benighted souls contracted to spend their days scratching for stories about the House of Windsor. Princes William and Harry, whose dislike of the profession is visceral, looked uncomfortable. William made stilted small talk and escaped as quickly as possible. His younger brother, a flush spreading up from his collar, took a more combative line, interrogating staffers from the *Daily Mail* about the news organization's quick-fire online operation and in particular its paparazzi-driven gallery of short news items, the so-called sidebar of shame. Kate, baby George on hip, mingled easily.

It was an odd event, the grudging quality of the hospitality reflected in its location—a corridor linking some of the administrative offices dealing with the young royals' affairs—and in the meager supply of wine in screw-top bottles. Some of the guests perceived in these arrangements not a potential insult but a positive: that the Duke and Duchess of Cambridge, as William and Kate have been known since their 2011 marriage, and Prince Harry, who in a plot device worthy of a sitcom lives alongside them at KP, are determined to break away from the formality of their grandmother's and father's courts. They are more in tune with the times, so this analysis goes, and thus closer to the people.

Officials articulated this message explicitly before the trio appeared. The Princes had now reached adulthood, William's military career was over, Harry had swapped his helicoptering for an army desk job, and together with Kate they were embarking on lives as working royals. Their aides could not yet be quite sure what form this would take or which causes the Cambridges and Harry might espouse, but the object of the reception was to position their charges as separate brands, integral to the overarching family firm yet distinct from its longer-established leading marques, Queen Elizabeth II and the Prince of Wales. Harry, preparing that week to launch one of his first big solo projects, the Invictus Games, a sporting competition for injured members of the armed forces, made one thing abundantly clear to those of us with whom, in a soldierly manner, he later engaged: he doesn't want to build up a sprawling charitable empire—or large staff—like his dad's. He intends to do things his way.

The problem Harry now faces is one that has defined his father's life: how to turn an accident of birth into a meaningful vocation. Three generations of Britain's monarchy are all out and about performing the royal job—that's eighteen people in total, including the Queen and Prince Philip, Prince Charles, his wife, sons and daughter-in-law, plus Princes Andrew and Edward and Edward's spouse Sophie, Countess of Wessex, Princess Anne, and a raft of names and faces even royal-watchers would be hard put to identify: the Duke of Gloucester, the Duchess of Gloucester, the Duke of Kent, the Duchess of Kent, Princess Alexandra, and Prince and Princess Michael of Kent—all fulfilling an amorphous form of public service defined largely in the doing of it. There are no manuals and, for those loitering in the lengthening line of succession, few predetermined duties. "To be heir to the throne is not a position. It is a predicament," observed Alan Bennett, and it's a line Charles often inserts into his speeches with feeling.[20] His productivity can't be measured by the number of engagements he performs. The Queen still romps through multiple short meetings and events in a day, while her eldest tends to devote larger chunks of time to each occasion. His value is even harder to gauge, like his mum's entangled in wispy sentiments about national pride and identity, but lacking the core function of being head of state that gives hers substance. The success of the royals, collectively and individually, is however more easily tested: through public opinion.

On that basis the monarchy is doing quite well. The Queen heads the Commonwealth, a voluntary association of fifty-three countries, most but not all former British colonies, and reigns as head of state over sixteen of them: the Realms of Antigua and Barbuda, Australia, the Bahamas, Barbados, Belize, Canada, Grenada, Jamaica, New Zealand, Papua New Guinea, St. Kitts and Nevis, Saint Lucia, Saint Vincent and the Grenadines, the Solomon Islands, Tuvalu, and the United Kingdom. (She is also head of state of the Crown Dependencies of Jersey, Guernsey, and the Isle of Man, which are not part of the UK, and of twelve Overseas Territories, remnants of Empire: Anguilla, Bermuda, the British Antarctic Territory, the British Indian Ocean Territory, the British Virgin Islands, the Cayman Islands, the Falkland Islands, Gibraltar, Montserrat, the Pitcairn Group of Islands, Saint Helena, Ascension Island and Tristan da Cunha, South Georgia and the South Sandwich Islands, the Sovereign Base Areas of Akrotiri and Dhekelia on Cyprus, and the Turks and Caicos Islands.)

Jamaica's Premier, Portia Simpson Miller, returned to power in January 2012 promising to make the country a republic; a poll later the same year suggested her compatriots are narrowly against such a move.[21] "This issue still remains the subject of ongoing discussion in Jamaica and no final decision regarding the exact course to be pursued has yet been taken," wrote Diedre Mills, Jamaica's Deputy High Commissioner in London, in response to an e-mailed query in April 2014 about concrete plans to realize Simpson Miller's pledge.

Australians were given an opportunity to break from the Crown in 1999. In a referendum 54.87 percent opted to keep the hereditary head of state compared to 45.13 percent voting to replace the monarch with an elected president. The monarchists still appear to be winning. A Nielsen poll released in April 2014, as William and Kate arrived in Sydney, saw republican sentiment plummet to thirty-five-year lows, with young Australians leading the revival in support for the royals.

New Zealand's Prime Minister John Key instituted a debate about redesigning the national flag as part of a wider discussion about ditching the monarchy, an outcome he believes inevitable if not necessarily desirable. The New Zealand flag has incorporated Britain's union flag since colonization in the nineteenth century. In 2014 came a new invasion. William and Kate arrived on New Zealand shores, streets filled with excited throngs eager to wrap themselves in the flags of Britain and New Zealand, and Key revised his assessment. "I think in my heart of hearts it probably is inevitable [a republic] will happen, but the time frame has moved considerably further out."[22]

In Britain, that prospect looks more distant still. In 1969, when pollsters first began to ask treasonous questions about whether the country might be better off without the Windsors, about 20 percent of respondents answered yes. That number for years held remarkably steady, apart from a few small surges in republicanism fueled by royal missteps and mishaps and skirmishes in the Wars of the Waleses, the bitter conflict that consumed Charles and Diana. In the immediate aftershock of Diana's death, anti-monarchy feelings, which might have been expected to swell, instead plunged sharply. If republicanism failed to flourish, the monarchy lost active support, too. The British Social Attitudes survey (BSA) tracked these developments from 1983, when 86 percent of Britons said it was important to retain the monarchy, through royal doldrums in 2006, when that figure declined to 59 percent. Yet by 2012 the picture had changed again, and dramatically. An Ipsos-MORI poll ahead of the Queen's Diamond Jubilee registered another precipitous fall in republican sentiment, but this time against a corresponding and protracted resurgence in royal popularity.[23] By 2013, a full 75 percent of respondents to the BSA survey believed the monarchy indispensable.[24]

That recovery is remarkable if you consider its context. Politics is in bad odor. Banking and journalism smell worse. Faith in the police and in that most benign of fireside companions, the BBC, is dented. Churches have struggled to adjust to social change, mired in scandal, their pews sparsely populated. And it's the same everywhere you look. Across the globe, trust in big institutions is eroding. Strong government has become an oxymoron in most democratic nations. In the messy aftermath of the Arab Spring and amid the globalization of antiglobalization movements, anger rather than pride more reliably brings people onto the streets.

In Spain that rage burned bright against a monarch who had been revered for his role in returning the country to democracy after the death of dictator Francisco Franco. After King Juan Carlos took an ill-timed holiday in the maul of the Eurozone crisis and saw his daughter Princess Cristina embroiled as a witness in a corruption investigation into her husband's business dealings, support for the crown declined and Juan Carlos abdicated in favor of his son Felipe. (Cristina was subsequently charged with tax fraud; through lawyers both she and her husband, Inaki Urdangarín, denied wrongdoing.) The institution of monarchy is no more proof against the spirit of the age than any other.

Yet crowds still turn out to cheer the Windsors. A million pressed into central London for the 2011 wedding of William and Kate. Tens of thousands squeezed into Wellington's Civic Square and tens of thousands more gathered at Sydney Opera House to glimpse the pair during their 2014 tour of New Zealand and Australia. "I'm a royalist from way back," said an onlooker called Caroline Mumford, waiting outside the opera house. "It's really in my blood, it's about actually seeing Kate, her beauty and her radiance—she's a breath of fresh air. And William, we mustn't forget him."[25]

So often did Kate's photograph grace front pages during the trip that a reader felt moved to write to the editor of the London *Times* on the day his newspaper failed to carry her image. "Sir, Wednesday's paper did not have a photo of the Duchess of Cambridge. I do hope she is all right."[26] Like the mother-in-law she never met, Kate contributes a glamour the Windsor genes never matched, and that means that, like Diana, she sometimes seems to absorb the light rather than refracting it.

The Queen, however, is rarely occluded, whether by shining youth or rain clouds. Sodden throngs huddled along the Thames for her Diamond

Jubilee pageant to witness the monarch, then eighty-six, brave a two-hour sail standing and waving from the prow of a barge, in a numbing downpour that sent six people aboard the accompanying flotilla to hospital with hypothermia. "I have to be seen to be believed," she has said.[27]

In that spirit, the Windsors range widely, touring factories and stores, schools and hospitals; attending events, cutting ribbons, unveiling plaques, working rope lines and rooms full of people, being seen and fostering belief. As the Queen and her consort wind down with age, opting for shorter-haul trips and taking on a lighter palette of public duties, the two generations below them are stepping up to the mark. In October 2013, after tutelage from his father in the intricacies of conducting investitures, including a practice session with a sword specially transported to Birkhall for the lesson, Prince William for the first time stood in for the Queen at a Buckingham Palace ceremony to confer honors. The following month, Prince Charles made his debut presiding in place of his mother at the biennial Commonwealth Heads of Government Meeting.

This was a particularly delicate assignment, part of the extended choreography designed to accustom Commonwealth members to acceptance of Charles as the next head of the organization—an outcome that is not automatic, but will be decided by Commonwealth leaders when his mother dies. The voluntary association of independent countries faces its own challenges if it is to endure much beyond the second Elizabethan age. A reworking of vestiges of Empire as a vehicle for empowerment rather than subjugation, its members are bound by a charter committing them to democracy, open government, and the rule of law. Yet as palace officials watched from behind spread fingers, the Prince found himself conducting the ceremonial opening of a leaders' summit hosted by Sri Lanka, amid international protests against the country's bloody human rights abuses and a state crackdown on the media trying to cover the meeting. It was, says a Clarence House insider drily, "one of the friskier CHOGMs of recent years."

This book will give new insight into Charles's foreign missions and the deployment of royal soft power not just to promote British interests and maintain the Commonwealth, but to tread where government does not dare. To the Dalai Lama and his supporters, the Prince is a champion. He is venerated in Armenia. Romanians embrace him as their own, and not just because Charles claims descent from Vlad the Impaler, the fifteenth-century ruler on whom Bram Stoker purportedly based his fanged fictional character Dracula. "I do have a bit of a stake in the country," jokes the Prince, not infrequently. He owns two properties in Transylvania and lobbies for the preservation of the region's traditional villages.

Middle Eastern royals, unimpressed by the usual ranks of diplomats, open to Charles as an equal: "He's there doing something nobody else can do," said a source during the Prince's February 2014 trip to Saudi Arabia. Charles has been widely pictured stepping his way through a sword dance—"He loves dressing up and dancing," says a friend—but this is not what the source meant. The Prince has been a great supporter of the UK intelligence services. He volunteered to be their first royal patron and came up with the idea of their internal awards scheme, offering a way to recognize good work among professionals whose job means they must hide their lights. Britain's domestic and international intelligence agencies—the Security Service (MI5) and the Secret Intelligence Service (MI6) and the electronic intelligence agency GCHQ, provided a statement for this biography: "His Royal Highness's engagement with the intelligence services is hugely appreciated by the members of the three agencies and warmly welcome." Later in this book I will give exclusive insights into the nature and scope of that engagement. "He's incredible; he's a huge asset," says an official from Britain's Foreign and Commonwealth Office.

Given such rave reviews and his family's buoyant fortunes, you might think that the Prince would sit high in public affections, and he is gaining in approval as he performs more head-of-state duties. Yet polls still show him as a weak link, squeezed between his unassailable mother and the younger generation's allure. He may not be hated, but he's not much loved either, except in republican circles, where he is hailed as a walking, talking argument for an elected head of state. So is Charles really a liability to the monarchy, to democracy, to himself?

Over the following pages, I aim to answer those questions and to look forward to a future more likely than not to see him enthroned. To do so means revealing the Prince in all his complexity, the humanitarian urges that drive him, and the caprices and compulsions that imperil his record. I'll highlight his extraordinary achievements and sometimes equally extraordinary mistakes, explain the culture and influences that produced someone capable of such extremes, and try to delineate the scale of ambitions that mean he will never be content to be just a figurehead. And to answer one question immediately: one reason the mature meat of this story, like the mutton he champions, remains undervalued is that he can be, and not infrequently is, his own worst enemy.

CHARLES LOOKS LIKE THE ULTIMATE INSIDER, BORN WITH A WHOLE canteen of silver spoons in his mouth and, since the death of his grandfather in 1952, only one rung below the very apex of the establishment. Yet that privilege—or life sentence—has doomed him to never feel part of the commonality, but always at a distance, watched and watching. His sense of alienation is palpable. "I try to put myself in other people's position and because I drive about the country endlessly, I've often thought about the lives of people in the places I pass, the streets," he told me.[28] Other members of his family seem more easily to accept their lot. "People say to me, 'Would you like to swap your life with me for 24 hours? Your life must be very strange,'" says his bluff brother Prince Andrew. "But of course I have not experienced any other life. It's not strange to me. The same way with the Queen. She has never experienced anything else."[29]

If offered a life swap for twenty-four hours, Charles would jump at the chance. Instead, he seeks out guides to the planet he can never fully inhabit. Thus it was that in 1985 he arrived at my then place of work, the *Economist*, for a lunch with "people of his age." His request—or command—excluded me. I was too junior and, like him, alien. I wouldn't have breathed easy in the thin air of the fourteenth-floor executive dining room. An American educated in Britain, for the most part at a grammar school and then a redbrick university, I believed in meritocracy—not just that it was a good idea but that we were living it. The scales fell from my eyes after I joined the *Economist*, working alongside men and a handful of women all but a few of whom seemed to have emerged from the same cozy nest of elite schools and Oxbridge colleges. Three decades later, class still mottles British life. The nation's quality press, like many other key institutions, remains overwhelmingly white, male, and privileged, its workforce simultaneously exemplifying and helping to perpetuate structural and cultural impediments to social mobility. One of the most potent arguments against the monarchy is that it acts as guarantor of the dysfunctional status quo.

You have only to watch the political elite groping for connection to ordinary voters and outsourcing their communications to tabloid editors, or spend time around British troops and observe the frequency with which ranks and accents tally, to understand how profound the dysfunction is.

The *Economist* has always been even posher than the rest of the quality press. Back then quite a few of the writers had country piles and owned smoking jackets, sufficiently old-money to look down on the royal family as German arrivistes. Our glass and concrete ivory tower—a piece of new brutalist architecture the Prince surely abhorred—hardly seemed the place to look for clues to the real world. Yet this was in most respects a benign and civilized environment. My colleagues were brilliant, the best of the British—and Charles urgently needed to tap their wisdom.

Four years earlier, a series of events had changed the course of his life: his marriage to Lady Diana Spencer on July 29, 1981, and before that inner-city rioting in England—in April in Brixton, South London, and, just weeks ahead of his wedding, in the Handsworth area of Birmingham, Leed's Chapeltown district, Toxteth in Liverpool, and in Sheffield. "I remember when there were these appalling riots, I just felt 'how can we find ways of giving these characters more opportunity because the whole thing is based on frustration and alienation,'" he said later.[30] (He often refers to people as "characters," an unfortunate phrase that reflects his own alienation.)

That impulse started the process that would transform his rudderless Prince's Trust into an effective interventionist organization that proudly claims to help more than fifty-five thousand young people every year to set up businesses, or move into education, training, or employment. The charity has evolved into the least controversial element of his astonishingly broad and idiosyncratic portfolio of works. In the 1980s, in tandem with its founder, the Trust was figuring out its role in a highly politicized context. This wasn't easy, not least because of the convention that the sovereign—and by extension her heirs—should remain above politics.

In one important respect, the Prince's Trust and Margaret Thatcher's government sang from the same hymn sheet. Both lauded the spirit of enterprise. Still, the state had clearly and comprehensively failed the young people the Trust scooped up and gave practical assistance to in order to develop that spirit. Thatcherites ascribed the failure to a welfare system that cosseted and infantilized; the left ascribed the failure to Thatcherism, which was busily dismantling parts of the welfare system and restructuring nationalized industries that were no longer fit to compete. Britain's manufacturing base shrank while the country's first and as yet only female Prime Minister held power, from 17.62 percent of GDP in 1979 to 15.18 percent when she left office eleven years later. In the same period, the ranks of the UK population deemed officially poor swelled from 13.4 percent to 22.2 percent.[31]

"I was just trying to find ways of reacting to the situation so as unemployment grew—and it was three million or something—and as these traditional industries were shut down, what on earth are we going to find to replace these forms of employment for so many people? It was all taking so long for anything else to spring up so I just thought whatever we could do in a small way would be better than nothing," said Charles.[32] What he could do for others in a small way began to solve in a big way the conundrum that had tormented him for years: how to put his non-job of apprentice monarch to good use. Yet this course was fraught with difficulty for a man literally not of the world, a fact that quickly became apparent to his hosts at the *Economist*.

Michael Elliott, then the *Economist*'s political correspondent (and one of its rare grammar-educated staffers), now president and CEO of the campaigning organization ONE, recalls a discussion that foundered before coffee for lack of common reference points. "Most of the conversation was taken up with an agonized appraisal of the Prince's proper role, together with much royal muttering (conventional wisdom in 1985) that Britain had lost the dynamism for which it once was famous. I begged to differ, and implored the Prince to consider the new, entrepreneurial, street-cred economy being created at that very moment in the clubs and streets, the fashion houses and TV studios and advertising agencies of Soho and Covent Garden. I remember to this day the look of utter incomprehension on the Prince's face as I made my case. Only later did a colleague point out the obvious; that with the exception of visits to the Royal Opera House, it was highly unlikely that the Prince had ever visited Soho and Covent Garden, much less wandered its streets picking up the vital signs of the new Britain."[33]

As Elliott points out, there was only one royal capable of recognizing that new Britain and speaking its demotic language: Diana. The Princess might have helped connect her husband to that reality. Instead, as their relationship festered, she used her gifts to undermine him.

* * *

CHARLES, FOR ALL HE IS AMONG THE MOST EXPOSED FIGURES IN THE world—his progress relentlessly charted from birth through his first day at school, his first drink at a bar, his first girlfriends, his first marriage, the first signs of discord, the first signs that this discord would disfigure lives— remains obscure. "It bothers me that people don't get him, but in the broad sweep of history he absolutely will be seen for who he is," says Elizabeth Buchanan.[34] She's right, but the Prince and all the apparatus around him have long put faith not in transparency but control. "Its mystery is its life. We must not let in daylight upon magic," observed Walter Bagehot, the great Victorian essayist and *Economist* editor, in his analysis of monarchy.[35] Bagehot, who remains a touchstone for constitutional historians—and for palace press managers—defined the role of the monarch in relation-ship to the government as a series of rights: to be consulted, to encourage, and to warn. The monarch-in-training has always felt impelled to exercise the last of these rights with exceptional vigor.

As a teenager looking down from Planet Windsor, Charles saw what man had made and behold, it was very bad, at least some of it. "I couldn't bear the physical aspect of destroying town centers and historical places, digging up all the hedgerows, cutting down trees, making terrifying prai-ries covered in chemicals. All that stuff. I thought this was insanity," he says of his young self.[36]

Even now he is driven by alienation and urgency. Traveling more widely and meeting a greater range of people than most ministers, he routinely shares with those ministers insights gleaned from his encounters via lengthy handwritten letters, dubbed "black spider memos" by Julia Cleverdon, a longtime member of his team, now Vice President of his charity Business in the Community and Special Adviser to his charities on responsible busi-ness practice. Charles writes prodigiously, sometimes dispatching as many as ten memos after dinner, often to staff or ad hoc advisers, and he also keeps journals of his travels. Relying on the protection of layers of official secrecy plus three envelopes, each marked "strictly confidential," according to a former Cabinet minister who received such missives regularly, the Prince expresses himself freely. "I've never had a problem with him," says that former minister. "He is entitled to opinions."

By no means everyone agrees. The reasons, explored in this book, relate both to the constitutional role of the monarchy and, even more so, to the often controversial nature of the Prince's ideas.

Because Charles is a man of the strongest convictions. He now needs the courage of them in a world that has become too porous to rely on secrecy. Half-truths and orphan facts seep almost daily into the public domain. Revelations appear without context. The *Guardian*, under Alan Rusbridger, has been exploring legal avenues to bring much greater scrutiny to bear on the Prince and especially his memos.

Most republicans assume, as Rusbridger does, that familiarity with royalty, and especially with Charles, will breed contempt—that his mystery is his life. Exposed for who and what he is, this royal joker will break the consensus that sustains the Crown. They may be right. To know the Prince is not necessarily to love him, whatever love means. He has admirable qualities, an arsenal of jokes, and a cupboard full of vulnerabilities that explain much of what he does, while not giving him a free pass. He means well. He cares. He spends his life trying to contact the world in order to save it. He is "a man who has no ambition but to make a difference for the better and to do good," in Buchanan's view.[37] He is also complex, difficult, more than occasionally intemperate, not infrequently wrongheaded, and on some issues plain wrong. This biography attempts to draw a balance among those flaws—and the flawed outcomes they sometimes produce—and the closely woven skeins of positive influence and good works that, like Charles's letters, remain routinely hidden. There is murk around our understanding of the role of the head of state, the meaning of neutrality, and whether Britain's king of charitable endeavor is suited to become Britain's King. Let daylight in.

CHAPTER 1

His Life in a Day

//

EVERY ONE OF THE SIX-THOUSAND-PLUS RESIDENTS OF TREHARRIS, in South Wales, appears to have decanted onto the sidewalks lining either side of the narrow street outside the butcher's shop, Cig Mynydd Cymru. Inside the small premises, an officer from the Metropolitan Police Service's special protection unit, SO14, completes his inspection. Despite the potential security risk, he asks the proprietors to leave the back door gaping wide. "Keep it cool," advises the officer. "He likes it as cool as possible."

Eight-year-olds Ben and Ryan, swinging from the crowd barriers, wonder what other demands the Very Important Person about to arrive in their midst may make. They are aware that the visitor has special powers. "He bosses people around," says Ben. Ryan—"fully Welsh, no English whatsoever," he proudly declares—expands on the theme. The VIP "tells people what to do and if they don't, he'll behead them," he says. When the Prince's car pulls into view, both boys holler and whoop and the whole crowd, young and old, applauds and waves Welsh flags, demonstrating the sense of local ownership that has always underpinned the strength of the Windsors' global brand. The last Welsh Prince of Wales, Llywelyn ap Gruffudd, died in 1282. Sentiment against the English Crown still flares in some parts of the country, but Treharris lays on a royal welcome.

This is a typical day for Charles, which is to say, it bears little detailed resemblance to the day before or the day after, but in outline appears numbingly similar, a production line of public engagements and sidebar meetings, small talk, the brief sanctuary of the car, then out again to wave and smile and entertain.

On this particular date, July 3, 2013, the third day of his annual summer visit to Wales ("Wales Week"), he has risen early at his whitewashed farmhouse Llwynywermod. ("'Llwyn' rhymes with ruin," a helpful member of his household e-mails. The double L, technically known as a "voiceless alveolar lateral fricative," sounds "like throat clearing." Y is pronounced "uh"; "werm" and "od" are as you'd expect.) Most mornings Charles undertakes a series of exercises originally devised to keep the pilots of the Royal Canadian Air Force in fine fettle and practiced by the Prince to alleviate his bad back. "Occasionally," says Julia Cleverdon, "in the royal train you hear a frightful bump."[1]

He will have consumed a small breakfast, likely "a few grains," according to a staff member, and not a boiled egg culled from a long row of boiled eggs. This will keep him going until dinner. He never eats lunch if he can help it, and the people who work with him quickly learn to carry hidden food supplies for themselves. He'll also have drunk enough water to sustain him but not so much as to require unscheduled pit stops. "He knows exactly how to hydrate his body to just the right degree," says his godson Tim Knatchbull. "It's an incredible talent. As it is to be most of the time—not all of the time, but most of it—an incredibly affable human, happy to listen, talk and be interested. Everyone's always telling him 'you've got to move along here' but he'll get interested and find someone to talk to and do everything at a leisurely pace."[2]

During the first engagement, touring the series set of the BBC sci-fi series *Doctor Who* at Roath Lock Studios in Cardiff with wife Camilla, the Prince has chatted with other alien species, Ood and Sontaran, and been persuaded to use a voice modulator to address a Dalek in a Dalek voice. "Exterminate!" he called out, laughing, "Exterminate!" But much of the conversation revolved around the succession. The reigning Time Lord, actor Matt Smith, is preparing to make way for a new Doctor Who, and Charles seemed keenly interested in the choreography of the handover.

Smith won over doubters after taking over the role in 2010 from a popular predecessor, David Tennant. His successor has big shoes to fill.

It's a predicament familiar to the Prince, who has spent more than sixty years preparing to take over from a popular predecessor. The Queen has lumbered her son with two huge problems. In reigning for so long so successfully, she has fixed public expectations about what sovereignty means. If Charles outlives his mother—and the "if" is not inconsequential; the Queen appears in robust health again after a brief illness in 2013 and her own mother lasted to 101—he will inevitably attract criticism simply for not being her. If he does become King, he'll only have at most one or two decades in which to make the role his own.

In the eternity of the meantime, the Queen has consigned her son to a destiny that is both inescapable and nebulous, like a Sontaran force field. Most jobs come with descriptions and clear parameters. Being heir to the throne has none of these attributes. It is an open-ended contract and, like everything about Britain's unwritten, fluid constitution, is defined by conventions and precedents and how the incumbent decides to play it.

"A FEW PEOPLE ARE LUCKY ENOUGH TO KNOW EXACTLY WHAT THEY want to do. They've got the talent or whatever it is. There's no problem," says Charles. "But there's a hell of a lot of others who don't really know and may not be obviously academic, who suffer from low self-esteem. I see it absolutely everywhere." His shoulders rise and fall. This isn't a shrug of acceptance but an involuntary shudder. "That's one of the reasons I wanted to make a difference to people's lives," he concludes.[3]

The Prince the people of Treharris are about to meet appears confident to the point of smoothness. He seems to know exactly who he is and why he's on this planet. Yet his youth was scarred by self-doubt and lack of direction, and he still grapples with big existential questions. Like many philanthropists, in helping others, Charles has found a way to help himself.

Many years ago he embarked on a chivalric quest of his own devising, seeking meaning, enlightenment, and happiness. Capturing any of these grails—and he's still trying, though happiness is finally in his grasp—depends on his ability to reimagine the possibilities of princedom. In attempting to do so, he has roused fire-breathing dragons and has more than once breathed fire himself, scorching instead of debating. He has appeared at times a heroic King Arthur, defending core values, at other moments a figure of fun, Don Quixote tilting at wind turbines, which he once called "a horrendous blot on the landscape,"[4] only later to recommend their use in *Harmony*, though he still prefers the offshore variety.

A late developer, as a young man Charles often appeared to have little more idea than Ben or Ryan about what being a Prince of Wales might actually entail, but his instincts were always to push at the limitations of his position. Just as his own sons are intent on establishing their own specialisms and styles, he yearned to do things differently from his parents.

"I want to consider ways in which I can escape from the ceaseless round of official engagements and meet people in less artificial circumstances. In other words, I want to look at the possibility of spending, say, 1. <u>three days in one factory</u> to find out what happens; 2. <u>three days, perhaps, in a trawler</u> (instead of one rapid visit); 3. <u>three or four days on a farm</u>," the thirty-year-old Charles wrote to his Assistant Private Secretary in 1978. He tends to be emphatic in written communications, underlining key phrases and drizzling exclamation points throughout his texts. "I would also like to consider 4. <u>more visits to immigrant areas</u> in order to help these people to feel that they are not ignored or neglected and that we are concerned about them as individuals."[5]

He never did escape the ceaseless round, and although he spends more time on average at each engagement than the Queen, he packs serial appointments into every grinding day. His dream of immersion in real-world experiences remains mostly that, a dream, though he has dipped briefly into other lives. "He's lived in a croft on the outer Hebrides," says Elizabeth Buchanan. "He's been on hill farms, he's been on trawlers, he's been on fishing rigs down in Cornwall. He's been in the inner cities all over the country, inner cities everywhere."[6]

Charles also does quite a lot of things that his mother does, supporting the armed forces and the charitable sector by holding honorary positions and patronages, conducting around half of all investitures, officiating at events, listening politely to speeches, secretly scrunching his toes in his shoes to stay awake during languorous passages, or ranging across the United Kingdom and the Realms to meet as many people as possible, to be seen and believed. He defines this royal role as supporting his mother in acting "as the focal point for national pride, unity and allegiance and bringing people together across all sections of society, representing stability and continuity, highlighting achievement, and emphasizing the importance of service and the voluntary sector by encouragement and example."[7] Yet there are fundamental differences to his mother in approach and content. The aspirations of his 1978 memo foreshadowed the way he has used his position not as the Queen uses hers, to maintain the status quo, but to campaign for change.

Until recently, he accepted that encroaching kingship must necessarily curtail his activism. His charities and causes would take a backseat once and if he ascended the throne or in the case of regency, if his mother grew too infirm to continue as acting head of state. One of his former Principal Private Secretaries, Michael Peat, set out the nature of that change as part of a response issued in March 2007 to the makers of a hostile documentary about the Prince: "It hardly needs saying that the Prince of Wales, of all people, knows that the role and duties of the heir to the throne are different to those of the sovereign and that his role and the way he contributes to national life will change when he becomes King. In other words it is misconceived and entirely hypothetical to suggest that problems will result if the Prince of Wales fulfills his role in the same way when King. He will not."[8]

Charles has already started to cut back commitments in order to take on more of his mother's work. That process also involves an attempt at closer integration with Buckingham Palace, inserting some of his staff into its structures in anticipation of that transition. None of this has been easy for Charles. His independence is hard-won. The mounting pressures emanating from Buckingham Palace have therefore helped to spur him to a reappraisal: perhaps becoming King might in some respects enhance his role as a change-maker rather than bringing it to a close. This is not only because the convening power of a king is surely greater than the convening power of a prince. The most thoughtful member of the royal family, Charles has been pondering long and hard about how the monarchy can best serve its subjects.

This royal train of thought has deposited him in uncharted terrain. Throughout his adult life, people (and most woundingly his father) have dismissed the things he has chosen to do—whether trying to help the socially excluded or save rain forests or preserve dying skills—as time fillers, eccentricities, indulgences. He has come to believe that such activities are not only compatible with his status, but could be integral to royal duty, to reasserting the relevance of the Crown.

ALL ROYAL VISITS WITHIN THE UK ARE PLANNED BY PALACE AIDES IN conjunction with local officials. In the Commonwealth Realms, each government takes the lead. On foreign soil, British diplomats negotiate itineraries with the national authorities. But no matter how the details have been finessed, each schedule for Charles is designed in his distinctive image.

So in a single day, Wales will get to see how multifaceted its Prince is, from the joker-royal, game for a laugh on the *Doctor Who* set, through more serious—and controversial—incarnations as the day progresses until evening when he transforms again, this time into a generous host. All of these Princes are more confident and comfortable than the troubled spirit that first visited these parts after being made Prince of Wales at the age of nine and returned here as a lonely student and later as a lonelier husband and later still as a widower. This is the Charles of Charles-and-Camilla, finally settled with the woman he calls "my dearest wife"—and that epithet is clearly true in both senses. When they are together, they are solicitous of each other, exchanging secret smiles, fleeting touches of the arm and waist. When they are apart, her influence is still tangible to those who knew him before. He has close relationships with his sons and has grown fond of his daughter-in-law and she of him. His grandson delights him. The royal barometer is more often set to fair than rain.

At the end of the Cardiff studio tour, he and the Duchess part company, better to distribute the largesse of their time. He heads to the nearby Prince's Trust Cymru headquarters, newly opened with the aim of helping at least some of the growing ranks of young unemployed—in Wales standing at more than one in four—into training or work. Camilla, who has been developing her own spread of campaigning interests, departs for Porthcawl in Bridgend, to meet a group of activists working to establish an outpost of the homelessness charity Emmaus in the seaside resort hit by sagging visitor numbers and the impact of the economic downturn on an area that never recovered from the closure of the South Wales coalfield in the 1980s.

Such destinations impart a flavor that some palates define as dangerously political. To ask teenagers about their experience of seeking employment in a jobs drought or men and women sleeping rough about how they came to live on the streets is to discuss policy failures as well as personal turbulence. A 1986 documentary followed Charles on a visit to a Prince's Trust project at a holiday camp in Great Yarmouth. As the camera watches him watching a group of kids perform a version of the Pink Floyd track "Another Brick in the Wall," they unexpectedly insert a lyric aimed at the Thatcherite credo of the time: "We don't need no jobs creation / We don't want a fascist nation." The voice-over is deadpan: "Where a politician might have decided this was an appropriate moment to move on, the Prince chose to stay and talk to them."[9]

In visiting the butcher's shop in Treharris, the Prince pursues another of his agendas. All the Windsors are more "country" than "town," brought up to enjoy rural pursuits such as stalking and shooting, to take a hand in estate management, and most at ease when the glow of sodium lamps recedes into the distance. "I'm a countryman—I can't stand cities," Charles once said.[10] In a commentary the Queen provided for the 1992 documentary *Elizabeth R*—the closest she has ever come to giving an interview—she talked about her involvement with the Sandringham estate and stud farm: "I like farming. I like animals. I wouldn't be happy if I just had arable farming. I think that's very boring."[11] She lives and breathes—and breeds—horses, as her mother did before her and her daughter now does.

Charles used to take an interest in horseflesh (though never as keen as his fascination with sheep). He gave up polo, the sport he described as his "one great extravagance," aged fifty-seven, only after almost as many injuries. He stopped riding out with his local hunt in Gloucestershire after foxhunting with dogs was banned in 2004. But there is much else that binds him into rural life on a daily basis, not least the Duchy of Cornwall, which under his stewardship has diversified and expanded, buying more than twelve thousand hectares of agricultural land from the Prudential insurance company in 2000 to take its total footprint to around fifty-three thousand hectares in twenty-three counties and increasing its capital account from $742.5 million in 2004 to $1.4 billion in the financial year ending April 2014.

The Duchy is Charles's golden goose—and an albatross. Any male who is first in line to the throne automatically becomes Duke of Cornwall. The Duchy operates to generate profits for such heirs, and though it now does so in a thoroughly modern way, as a property developer and landlord, it retains original period features. It is exempt from capital gains tax and it is not subject to corporation tax because it is not legally a corporation. The income enables the Prince to maintain a laboratory for his ideas; the anomalous status of the Duchy fosters resentment against antique privilege.

It is yet another factor that sets Charles apart from most people, yet it also created his connection to constituencies that feel themselves ill represented by metropolitan politicians: foresters, gamekeepers, hedgelayers, small farmers such as the founders of the butcher's shop in Treharris. In securing his own rural base—the Duchy purchased Highgrove House in Gloucestershire and the nearby Duchy Home Farm in 1980—the Prince consummated his love affair with the land. At Highgrove he redesigned the gardens, telling a documentary team in 1986, "I love coming here. And I potter about and sit and read or I just come and talk to the plants."[12] It was one of his jokes but it lumbered him with the label of plant whisperer, especially after the satirical British TV show *Spitting Image* depicted his latex alter ego inviting a potted fern to his fortieth birthday party.

Duchy Home Farm under the Prince's direction became a model of organic husbandry. Modern agriculture tends to produce repetitive vistas pocked by ugly buildings. At Duchy Home Farm improbably glossy rare-breed cattle graze certified organic fields demarcated by verdant hedgerows. Barley and wheat grow upright—the unmodified strains, unlike higher-yield varieties, strong enough to support their crowns of grain. Mixed varieties of cabbages flourish in beds laid out almost as prettily as the gardens at Highgrove, fronds of cavolo nero mimicking the three feathers of the Prince of Wales's heraldic badge.

It's a working farm, but also a showcase for sustainable methods that it's hard to imagine anyone else would have found the time or resources to establish, especially more than thirty years ago. "He was in the vanguard of [environmental thinking] but he came at it from his unique perspective," says the Sustainable Food Trust's Patrick Holden. "Given that no person on the planet has travelled more widely, he's been a witness to the destructive impact of humanity on the environment at first hand and feels obliged to do something about it."[13]

In 1990 the Prince again moved ahead of the pack, founding one of Britain's first organic brands, Duchy Originals, under the aegis of his charitable foundation. His farm supplied some of the oats for the brand's first product: oaten biscuits. The line expanded to encompass more than two hundred organic brands sold by a variety of retailers, swelling the coffers of the foundation until economic downturn and strategic weakness turned the tables, making Duchy Originals dependent on financial sustenance from the foundation. But the Prince isn't a man who easily relinquishes his initiatives. When trouble brews, his favored response has been to regroup and rebrand, sometimes sustaining enterprises that would never survive without his involvement, at other times producing stronger organizations. In 2009, an exclusive licensing and distribution deal with Waitrose effectively outsourced the management of the brand to the supermarket.

Three years after the launch of Duchy Originals, Charles took pleasure in seeing ground broken on another project: Poundbury, often described as his model village but actually an extension to the town of Dorchester, on Duchy land and, like Duchy Home Farm and Duchy Originals, both prototype and platform, in this case for community architecture, traditional crafts, and walkable, mixed-use, mixed-income, low-carbon development. Its quaint streets are explored in a later chapter.

"The difference between the Prince and an elected politician is the time horizon," says Fiona Reynolds, the former Director-General of the National Trust—the Prince is its Patron—who also worked with him during her stints at the Council for National Parks and the Council for the Protection of Rural England. "An elected politician is always thinking about the next three to five years; tomorrow afternoon can be a long way off in politics. Whereas he is unashamedly thinking about the long term, and in fact it's his duty as heir to the throne to think about the long term. Although what he's often said has been controversial, he has been positioning things precisely where politicians are very unlikely to be. . . . He has moved the debate forward in a number of ways; he has made respectable the very notion of climate change which 20 years ago was seen as an extraordinarily distant and contentious issue."[14]

Charles made his first public speech on the environment at twenty-one, warning of the need to "discipline ourselves to restrictions and regulations . . . for our own good."[15] In the intervening years, his ambitions, and his rhetoric, have ripened. "My greatest fear is that we're busily wrecking the chances for future generations at a rapid rate of knots by not recognizing the damage we're doing to the natural environment, bearing in mind that this is the only planet that we know has any life on it," the Prince says, urgent and unblinking. "It is insanity in my humble opinion to destroy this miraculous entity floating around in space that is linked with the extraordinary harmony of the universe."[16]

His profound environmental concerns twine with a determination to preserve and safeguard traditional rural life and these, in turn, connect to his other causes and activities, all of which find expression not only in patronages of existing causes—which number more than four hundred in total—but in charities and initiatives that he sets up.

Much of this activity takes place below the radar, to the frustration of the Prince and his aides. "When I was Private Secretary, people would say to me, 'What has the Prince done for us?' And I'd say, 'Well there's the Prince's Trust.' And they'd say, 'Oh yes, that has helped a lot of people to get off the unemployment queue and realize their potential,'" recalls Clive Alderton. "Then they'd say, 'He doesn't really do very much,' and I'd say, 'He did hundreds of royal engagements last year,' and it would be five hundred or more, and they'd say, 'Oh, that's really very good.' And I'd see that *Monty Python* scene about 'What have the Romans done for us?' playing out in my mind."[17]

There are many Pythonesque notes to the Prince's existence. At times he could be one of the prophets from *Life of Brian*, addressing a slack-jawed crowd, or Brian himself, thrust into a public role he never sought. His quest and the jostling of the knights around him recall *Monty Python and the Holy Grail*. Though the Prince employs professionals of a high caliber, the underlying structure of Clarence House is of a court, with all the intrigues and rivalries that entails.

What little organizational logic there is to the Prince's portfolio has been applied after the fact. For more than forty years, he has spotted what he sees as gaps in the voluntary sector, often on the basis of single conversations, and sought to plug them, grafting onto the creaking structures of his court the massive apparatus of Britain's widest-ranging professional charitable empire.

The Prince has no hesitation in exporting his ideas and obsessions abroad, to Commonwealth countries or places like Romania for which he simply feels an affinity. At home, he also sees it as his job to "promote and protect the country's enduring traditions, virtues and excellence," whether through interfaith work or patronages or a focus on rural Britain that he feels is otherwise lacking. Cig Mynydd Cymru (the name translates as "Welsh mountain meat"), the little butcher's shop in Perrott Street, is the kind of enterprise he wants to see thrive, a cooperative formed in 2006 when local farming families came together to figure out if they could market quality meats at affordable prices. Only John and Celia Thomas from Penrhiw have followed the Prince's lead to take their herds organic—and risk the price premium that entails in a low-income region—but all of the meat on sale is traceable and distances are short between pastures, slaughterhouses, and customers.

Waiting for the Prince's arrival amid the hum of chiller cabinets full of beef, chicken, duck, lamb, pork, and, of course, mutton, and a tempting display of crusty pies and Welsh Scotch eggs, John Thomas expresses gratitude for the Prince's advocacy on behalf of small-scale and traditional farming. "He has promoted mutton, which has been a neglected meat for many years. He has done a great deal for farming, and recently for wool, which is a neglected byproduct of the farming industry," says Thomas. The Prince in his estimation is doing a good job, whatever the job might be. "Rather than struggling to find a role, he's found a very practical role and he's to be admired for it."

FINALLY THE ROYAL VISITOR ARRIVES, PUSHING INTO THE BUTCHER'S shop through a pandemonium of cheers. He's wearing a suit with a patched pocket and one of his ancient pairs of shoes. He still affects the severe parting of his hair, low above his left ear, he's maintained since childhood. "I've fought him tooth and nail for years. I just want him to move it, up or bloody down, somewhere, because it's always been in the same place," says Emma Thompson.[18] The bald patch that had already started to show by the time of his first marriage has now expanded to a tonsure. He looks more monk than the figure he has become: the knight errant of the Realms. Camilla calls her husband a "workaholic" and not just because of the hours he keeps. At this moment, using his position to do something he believes in— something he believes is doing good—he is giving in to an apparently benign addiction. Although he quickly buckles down to business, such as it is, he will overrun the time allotted in his schedule for this stop because he is fascinated.

He can talk to anyone but feels most at home with country people such as his hosts at the shop and with the teenagers he met earlier at the Prince's Trust in Cardiff. He quizzes Thomas and other members of the collective about marketing and pricing, and tells them about a training scheme for butchers at Dumfries House, teaching them how to cook the products they sell. Graduates of the course are reporting a 20 percent sales increase, says the Prince, because they are able to suggest recipes to their customers and tempt them into trying different meats and cuts. "You need to know exactly what the constellation of the animal should be." Then he's off on another tack, about whether there's any demand for the flesh of old ewes and talking about his "mutton renaissance" again. "I'm trying to tell everyone just how marvelous mutton really is."

The Prince plays the old ham at the butcher's, entertaining his audience and mugging for the camera produced to immortalize the occasion. "If the photographers weren't interested, that would be the time to start worrying," the Prince said in 1982.[19] This was a brave declaration from someone who had always disliked media attention, even before that attention soured. Aged fourteen, he walked into a bar and ordered a cherry brandy. It was the sort of escapade that for other teenagers would have brought few if any consequences, and he only did so to take shelter from crowds who had recognized him. Unfortunately for Charles, a journalist inside the bar recognized him, too, and filed a story. The incident made headlines, the licensee and the barmaid who served him faced charges, later dropped, the Prince had privileges at school revoked, and, worst of all, he saw his royal protection officer sacked from the squad for allowing the princely misdemeanor.

But the Prince endures, and even encourages, press coverage about his official and charity work because he understands its utility. "One must grimace and bear it," he says.[20] When the Welsh butchers offer him a plate of faggots, tasty meat patties formed from chopped pork and offal, he adopts an expression of comical alarm: "Which bit of the animal is this? Don't tell me it's the bits nobody else wanted." Asked to bite into a beef burger by the photographer, he declines, laughing. "Forgive me, I'm not going to do my wide-mouthed frog for you."

For most working royals, there are two main aims to such visits, at home or abroad: to provide a boost to their hosts, in terms of positive reinforcement and publicity; and to promote the monarchy, by being seen and believed. Like most things the Windsors do, there's little hard information available to measure impacts scientifically by balancing business or funding generated against the disruption and costs incurred. The Prince's Duchy of Cornwall income covers his and Camilla's official activities and those of his sons and daughter-in-law, but not the bill for the upkeep of Clarence House or for official travel, which amounted in total to $2.55 million in the year to April 2014, drawn from public funds. Wales Week in 2012 incurred two transport bills of over $16,000 each. In 2013 none of the individual journeys breached this threshold so were not itemized. They included a variety of different transport methods including a helicopter journey for Camilla to Porthcawl. There's an additional cost to taxpayers for security. A request to the local Merthyr Tydfil County Borough Council about the expense of policing the Prince's visit to Treharris produces only the figure for the road closures ($24) and the installation of the crash barriers ($240).

Without a complete rundown, it's tough to judge value for money, and even then many of the benefits are intangibles. Celia Thomas of Cig Mynydd Cymru e-mailed: "We all thoroughly enjoyed the visit and meeting the Prince of Wales, and everyone is still talking about it. We have made a poster with some of the lovely photographs taken on the day, which is proudly displayed on the wall of the shop. We found the Prince so easy to chat to and he showed a genuine interest in what we are doing. He even asked about our shop refurbishment when he was talking to Dai Havard, our MP, the other day. There certainly was a huge benefit to the shop and a huge boost to morale."

At the time, the wider populace of Treharris also appears delighted. Ben and Ryan, who get to meet the Prince when he goes on a short walkabout, pronounce him "a-mazin'," and he departs with spoils: a Styrofoam box of choice cuts, a raft of fresh information about farming in Wales, and a set of questions and follow-up actions arising from the conversation, all immediately entrusted to an aide. But the publicity will disappoint. Only local newspapers pick up the story.

By contrast, William and Kate's trip to Australia and New Zealand the following year will generate worldwide saturation coverage, including daily transmissions of images of beauty spots. The bill for the nine-day New Zealand leg tots up to some $781,500 and is met by taxpayers at the destination, like most official travel by royals to the Realms. Tourism chiefs in Australia and New Zealand proclaim the publicity beyond price. For the monarchy it certainly is. "I'm officially no longer a republican," tweeted Patrick Gower, the political editor of the Wellington-based TV station 3 News. The journalist may not have been entirely serious, but his compatriots, like their Australian counterparts, succumbed to the charm offensive in droves.

The Prince cannot hope to match the poster children of the monarchy, and not just because of his greater age. Charles knew what it was to be overshadowed from the moment he married Diana. On the couple's 1983 perambulations around Australia, he ran his wife a poor second. "So infatuated was the crowd at every walkabout that as [the royal couple] got out to work the crowd, an involuntary moan would rise from that part of the crowd which turned out to be nearest to the Prince and furthest from the Princess," recounts Jonathan Dimbleby.[21] It is an experience already familiar to his son William, cast in the shade by Kate's dazzle, but there the similarity ends. William is proud of Kate as Charles never was of Diana, and the Cambridges work as a team in a way the Waleses never managed. William is more easily photogenic than his dad, too. "Never forget that William is a Spencer," says a Buckingham Palace official. "William and Harry are rock stars around the world," says former British Prime Minister John Major, who became the boys' financial guardian after Diana's death.[22] The Princess lives on in her sons.

"I HOPE THIS ISN'T AN ANTICLIMAX. I CAN ONLY IMAGINE IT MUST be," says the Prince as he arrives at Ebbw Fawr Learning Community to find that some of the people gathered outside the new state school have been waiting since early morning for a glimpse of royalty. It's a refrain familiar to anyone who has heard him give speeches. "I am immensely grateful to you all for taking the time to be here this afternoon—even if it's only out of curiosity!" he has said more than once.[23] "Ladies and Gentlemen, I am enormously impressed to find so many of you here this evening prepared to consider the role of investors and, in particular, pension funds in the move to a sustainable economy. I can only take it as a compliment to four of my charities which operate in this area—unless, of course, you are all here out of curiosity as to what I might say next!" he tells another gathering.[24] "Well, Ladies and Gentlemen," he greets another group, "I'm so glad I've got this opportunity to join you all this afternoon. I had this dreadful thought that all I had done was to stop you doing all sorts of other things you'd much rather be doing!"[25]

Self-deprecation may be a good icebreaker, but the Prince's insecurities are real. Excitement and affection greet him wherever he walks a rope line or works a room, yet for the glass-half-empty Prince, the crowds might always be bigger and the coverage better. Though he observes William and Harry with intense paternal pride, the emotion is marbled with a little jealousy and a wider vein of frustration, not because he begrudges their popularity but because of what he could do with such backing. Unlike his more charismatic sons and glistening daughter-in-law, over and above being a royal, he is a missionary with urgent messages to impart. There are bigger issues at stake than just the survival of the monarchy.

His visit to the butcher's shop Cig Mynydd Cymru has been slotted into the schedule to flag up the dangers of industrialized farming, the imbalances created by ill-thought-out subsidies, the perception he sets out in *Harmony* that "modern high-tech agriculture" risks turning "farming into an arms race against Nature, excluding everything from the land except the highly bred crops designed to be resistant to powerful pesticides and grown using industrial production methods." (The Prince invariably refers to nature with a capital N, and as "she" or "her," in conscious opposition to mainstream culture. The Enlightenment "objectified" nature, he complains. "'She,'" he writes sadly in *Harmony*, "became 'it.'")[26]

At his next stop he zeroes in on another preoccupation: inequality. He has come to Ebbw Fawr to launch the first Wales-based program run by the education charity Teach First. In partnership with the Welsh government, Teach First plans to recruit highly skilled graduates to work in schools located in impoverished areas, giving additional assistance to six thousand disadvantaged pupils each year. The Prince strolls through the school connecting easily with the dignitaries who have turned out in Sunday finery to meet him and more easily still with the pupils.

Teach First defines its mission as ending inequality in education. "How much you achieve in life should not be determined by how much your parents earn," declares its website. "Yet in the UK, it usually is." The Prince is the charity's patron. He sees no contradiction between its mission and his position. Indeed the phrase resonates. He believes that who your parents are should not restrict how much you can achieve—even if you're the Prince of Wales.

BACK AT LLWYNYWERMOD, IT'S NOT MUCH OF A STRETCH FOR Charles to imagine himself in a parallel universe, living out his days as a gentleman farmer. His residence in Carmarthenshire is large but by no means palatial, rustic rather than grand, with lime plaster walls and slate roofing. Like increasing numbers of rural landowners, he even rents out rooms—when he's not in residence—to paying guests.

Like them, the Prince is transient, arriving for at most a few consecutive days. To simulate homeliness, he always brings with him certain essentials: framed photographs of Camilla and his children, his canvases and paints, and a cushion, more than once paraded by the British press as a symbol of indulgence but better understood as a support for the Prince's troublesome spine if not as his version of a security blanket. As a schoolboy sent away to board from the age of eight, he poignantly wrote of missing his "homes."[27] As an adult, he has accepted a life of permanent homesickness, shuttling between houses that he inhabits but, apart from two cottages in Romania, doesn't strictly speaking own. His regular haunts include Llwynywermod, Highgrove and Tamarisk on the Scilly Isles (all property of the Duchy of Cornwall); Dumfries House (owned by a trust); family residences such as Birkhall (which he rents from his mother) and the other mansions on the Balmoral estate as well as Sandringham; and Crown properties such as the complex on the Mall that incorporates the Prince's London operational base, since 1988 St. James's Palace and, from 2002 onwards, expanded to encompass neighboring Clarence House.

Until Queen Victoria moved to the larger, uglier Buckingham Palace just down the Mall, sovereigns resided at St. James's Palace. These days the elegant Tudor building, commissioned by Henry VIII and once home to Anne Boleyn, is a frequent setting for conferences, meetings, and receptions. Prince Charles may not command front pages as younger family members do or bring out crowds in equivalent numbers, but what he lacks in mass appeal, he makes up in convening power. He has received a startlingly diverse range of guests, from the Australian pop star Kylie Minogue to the Dalai Lama, often shunned for fear of offending China. (Pope Francis declined to meet the exiled Tibetan leader in December 2014.) Charles's guests have included people who are still at the top of their game and figures whose moment has since passed or shaded into notoriety. He welcomed the British DJ Jimmy Savile as a frequent visitor, unaware of his habit of inappropriately touching the palace secretarial staff (Savile turned out to be a prodigious pedophile and sex offender), and in 2002 gladhanded Bashar al Assad at St. James's Palace.

Few people reject an invitation from a future king. If this means the Prince has sometimes kept dubious company, it also grants him extraordinary access and a platform. He used his 2013 Advent reception, attended by the Archbishop of Canterbury and other prominent religious leaders, to highlight the suffering of Syrian Christians in the civil conflict that Assad's brutality helped to trigger. He holds regular powwows with business and industry, pushing his interlinked agendas of sustainability and community engagement. He recalls, with gratitude, the advice of the politician and diplomat Sir Christopher Soames—the father of one of his close friends, MP Sir Nicholas Soames—who first alerted him to the ease with which he might expect to bring high-level participants together. "That is a piece of advice I have never forgotten and I've developed and pursued and I've found over and over again," says the Prince. "And right, there may be advantages in my case because I haven't got a particular axe to grind and people notice that I suppose, when you get people round a table you discover that frequently it's the first time they've all sat round a table. You think, this can't be possible. They must've sat and talked. These are people you'd think would form a sensible integrated approach. Not a bit of it." He takes pride in his facility at "getting business people, government and agencies to sit down with NGOs, who normally they might never have talked to, except they shout across a huge chasm."[28]

In 2009, a clutch of world leaders and prominent figures pulled up gilt chairs around one of his capacious tables for a summit of his Prince's Rainforest Project (PRP): eight elected premiers—Australia's Kevin Rudd, France's Nicolas Sarkozy, Germany's Angela Merkel, Guyana's Samuel Hinds, Indonesia's Susilo Bambang Yudhoyono, Italy's Silvio Berlusconi, Japan's Taro Aso, and Norway's Jens Stoltenberg—plus then US Secretary of State Hillary Clinton, four British Cabinet ministers, President of the European Commission Jose Manuel Barroso, Canadian Minister of Finance Jim Flaherty, Secretary-General of the United Nations Ban Ki-Moon, Gabonese Defense Minister Ali Bongo Ondimba, Saudi Arabian Foreign Minister Prince Saud Al-Faisal, and World Bank President Robert Zoellick.

The Prince had established the PRP two years earlier, focusing its efforts on identifying the economic drivers of deforestation and suggesting possible alternatives. The international community was mulling a market mechanism akin to carbon credits to make trees more valuable alive than dead, but the Prince worried that the scheme would arrive too late and do too little. He used the 2009 summit to float the idea of an emergency bridge. His intervention led to the formation of a secretariat by the Norwegian and British governments that in turn kicked off an intergovernmental process. The following May in Oslo, thirty-five donor countries agreed to an investment of $4 billion over three years into projects to reduce carbon emissions.

The Prince continues to drive his environmental campaign, presiding over further summits at St. James's Palace and taking the podium at high-level conferences. His PRP lives on, renamed the International Sustainability Unit, and entrusted with a broader remit that looks at bringing agriculture and forestry into harmony rather than competition, sustainable fishing, and resilience, particularly food and water security. Few of the summit attendees retain the same portfolios or even hold office. As of December 2014 Merkel is the only elected leader who attended the summit to remain in power. The Prince's constancy comes at a price. He has no democratic mandate, nor is there a mechanism for voting him out. It is one of his greatest strengths as a campaigner and the reason why some people will never accept his right to campaign.

AT A PUB IN THE MARKET TOWN OF LLANDOVERY, ANOTHER GROUP of people convened around a table by the Prince embark on a game without fixed end. The players include off-duty protection officers, drivers, and aides, members of the retinue that accompanies Charles on most of his travels, road-weary veterans whose devotion to the Prince can be measured in the numbers of days they spend away from home and the breadth of their knowledge of pub games. This particular contest sees each player alternately exclaim "fuzzy duck" or "ducky fuzz," or at least try to. If someone fumbles the phrase, often producing an obscenity and a double measure of amusement, he or she takes a deep drink and the direction of the game reverses.

The entertainment earlier in the evening at nearby Llwynywermod has also provoked hilarity, if not so predictably. The Prince and his Duchess conclude their day in Wales by hosting people from the locality and further afield to an evening of Welsh folk songs and dances. The guests who take their seats in Llwynywermod's converted barn reflect different strands of the couple's interests: cultural figures, assorted flavors of civic worthiness, business leaders who may prove good for donations to the Prince's charities, and a few real friends—Patrick Holden, who farms in the area, attends with his wife. At first everyone is transported by the music of the truest of voices harmonizing a cappella, harp and fiddle, and blackbirds nesting in the eaves, late in fledging, that fill every interlude in the program with more singing. After two summer carols comes the first clog dance, then four more carols and a harp solo.

At the second clog dance, *Pedwarawd clocsio*—a clogging quartet—Camilla's shoulders begin to shake. The royal hosts sit in the front row, backs to most guests, who perhaps assume the beauty of the music has moved her. As she struggles to conceal her tears, it becomes apparent that the dancing display, as athletic as aesthetic, has indeed made her cry, with suppressed laughter. The Prince touches her hand, restraining or comforting, and his shoulders shake, too. Her tears—and mascara—continue to flow.

It isn't the most regal of behavior, not something you can imagine the Queen doing. For the public, this is proving a positive, and for the Prince it has undoubtedly always been part of Camilla's attraction. Warmth, spontaneity, and humor have been scarce commodities in his life, from his earliest years.

He is at his most serene in her company, yet on this evening in Wales, as most nights, he will not follow her straight to bed, but instead sits down to his paperwork. It's what he does. "I keep trying to get him to have more than one gin," says Emma Thompson. "Have another, I keep screeching."[29] But there are always letters to read and more to write. The black ink scuttles across the virgin sheets, urgent and insistent.

Any understanding of the Prince must flow from an understanding of the institution that created him and which he serves. Concern about his questing extends beyond republican circles and the tea tables of staunch traditionalists. In the corridors and back rooms and private apartments of Buckingham Palace there is mounting anxiety as the Queen's reign enters what one Clarence House insider calls "its inevitable twilight." In defining his role as heir apparent, the Prince has signaled a redefinition of the monarchy. Some courtiers—and the sovereign herself—fear that neither the Crown nor its subjects will tolerate the shock of the new.

The Queen set the terms by which her son is judged—and so often found wanting. Yet her reign speaks to the importance not of staying still but of maintaining the illusion of unbroken tradition, perfect continuity. The next chapter examines that reign and her role and the private person so rarely glimpsed. The biggest test of her change management will come with her passing, determined by decisions beyond her control yet still bearing her stamp. How the Prince inhabits kingship—and how firmly—will owe much to the Queen, not just as a role model but as a mother, and to Prince Philip, the father he fears and whose approval he still seeks. His parents schooled Charles in duty and tried to give him a grounding in the real world, recognizing that the monarchy must mirror the experiences of its peoples. His upbringing of lonely privilege and public school privations left him flailing. The roots of his activism and awkwardness, his urgent need to make sense of the world and to improve it—the drivers for his Princely quest— lie deep in the strangest of childhoods.

CHAPTER 2

Mother Load

//

YOU KNOW SHE'S NEAR BECAUSE, LIKE A WICKED QUEEN IN A FAIRY
tale, she's preceded through palace corridors by slavering hounds.
There are four of them, Holly and Willow, Candy and Vulcan, two corgis
and two dorgis, the offspring of a morganatic union between a corgi and a
dachshund. One of the dorgis seems fond of the salt naturally secreted by
human skin and sets with rough tongue to licking any ankles left uncovered, growling if interrupted. Her owner proves at least as intimidating,
tiny, flinty, and near impossible to read. Elizabeth II has spent more than
eight decades perfecting her poker face.

In the course of her life, the world has convulsed and shuddered like a
werewolf under a full moon, pushing out a new coat and fangs, the old
familiar lines disappearing under a mass of phenomena that to many of
her generation seem monstrous. When Princess Elizabeth was born in 1926,
the British Empire extended across a quarter of the globe. By the time
she ascended the throne, the relics of empire were crumbling, leaving a
difficult legacy in the former colonies and at home in a nation that no longer felt sure of its identity, place, or purpose. Britain had won a war but
risked losing itself.

The new head of state handled these transitions with the inscrutability
she had cultivated from the moment her uncle's traumatic abdication pushed

her to the top of the line of succession. With this same lack of expression she has presided over social and cultural revolutions harnessed to new technologies that shrank the physical world while amplifying its tumult and confusion. She watches, apparently impassive, as the peoples of her Realms adopt peregrine ways of speaking, dressing, thinking, and behaving, native to their age groups and globalized cultures or imported as populations diversify. At the time of her accession just over 4 percent of the British population was foreign born; that total now stands northward of 12 percent, a figure that does little to reflect the thrilling heterogeneity of British cities or the tensions accompanying that transformation. In 1952, most women married, like the Queen, at twenty-one and like her quickly popped out a first child. Only 35 percent of them worked, as she did (and none of those working worked as she did). Female participation in Britain's labor force has risen to 71 percent. When she took the driving seat of the family business, just a quarter of households owned cars. Now only a fifth do not. During her reign churchgoing has sharply declined. The average age of congregations has risen heavenward, mirroring changes to the wider population as fewer people marry or stay married or raise large families or have any children at all during life spans that have lengthened by thirty years since the beginning of the twentieth century. Britons, like their Queen, are becoming grizzled.

Hers are the gray hairs of unique experience. She has held weekly audiences with twelve Prime Ministers and accepted the resignations of eleven of them, starting with Winston Churchill. She discussed the Suez Crisis with Anthony Eden; the Falklands War with Margaret Thatcher; the first Gulf War with John Major; Kosovo, Sierra Leone, Afghanistan, Iraq, and the War on Terror with interventionist Tony Blair; and with David Cameron Libya and the decision forced on him by a rebellious Parliament to stay plans for military action against Syria. Major, who served as Prime Minister from 1990 to 1997, describes the audiences as "a hugely valuable resource . . . In politics you have to be careful what you say, however close the person is to you. But with the Queen there need be no such inhibition." The weekly discussions, he says, "are like a confessional with a particularly trusted priest."[1]

The Queen has twice been forced to use her prerogative to choose Prime Ministers, in 1957 and again in 1963 before the Conservative party instituted a formalized process of selecting a leader, both times passing over a prominent candidate, Richard Austin (Rab) Butler, to appoint respectively Harold Macmillan and then Alec Douglas-Home, who renounced an earldom and lesser peerages to serve as plain Sir from the benches of the House of Commons. Butler had pioneered Britain's free school system and supported the postwar Labour government's introduction of the welfare state; he referred to some of his own Tory colleagues as "Colonel Blimps." In appointing Macmillan, the Queen overrode the advice of her outgoing Prime Minister, Anthony Eden, but conformed to the urgings of his predecessor Winston Churchill and other Conservative grandees. By selecting Douglas-Home, she appeared to favor a man not only of the unambiguous right but of the aristocracy over the more charismatic, left-leaning Butler. Constitutional historian Vernon Bogdanor argues that she had little real choice and that the decision "cannot be said seriously to have misrepresented Conservative opinion at the time."[2] "Prime Ministers, who've seen the Queen at close quarters often for many years, would not be able to tell you with any certainty what her party political views are," says John Major.

If the Queen conceals her political instincts like a hand of cards, her personal likes and dislikes, played almost as close to her chest, are ecumenical. Her favorite Prime Ministers both rose from the lower middle classes: Labour's Harold Wilson and Major, a Tory. There was no love lost between her and Thatcher or real connection between her and Blair. These views have filtered through the accounts of palace observers and the Prime Ministers themselves. The Queen has never again been forced to make her preferences public. The Conservative party adopted a mechanism for choosing its leaders without the need for royal intervention, and Britain's first-past-the-post electoral system until 2010 reliably produced emphatic outcomes that the monarch simply affirmed when the pre-selected leader of whichever party emerged with the largest number of parliamentary seats made his—or, in 1979, her—way to Buckingham Palace.

Ahead of the May 2010 general election, with polls predicting electoral stalemate, there was speculation that the Queen might be forced once more to intervene in the selection of a Prime Minister. "We're told the monarchy is 'value for money,'" wrote Graham Smith, director of the antimonarchist group Republic. "Well now's the time for the monarch to earn her crust. If she ducks the responsibility she confirms once and for all that she is constitutionally pointless, a political eunuch stranded by the tide of modern democratic principles our leaders try to apply to a feudal system." He added: "If the Queen has written herself out of the script for fear of making the wrong decision what we're left with are shadowy deals and secret memos that will shape the way in which our next prime minister is chosen without the benefit of public scrutiny. Whatever the outcome of this election, we need the appointment of the prime minister to be conducted in the open."[3]

The Queen did not, in Smith's terms, earn her crust. For five days the incumbent Prime Minister Gordon Brown hung on in the hopes of forming a coalition with the Liberal Democrats until they opted to enter government with David Cameron's Conservatives. The Queen remained aloof from all the negotiations. A palace source suggests this represented not the abdication of her constitutional role but its practice, steadying nerves through the fact of her existence during the transition from one political reality to another that occurred without unrest on the streets or major jitters in the financial markets.

Graham Smith did see one wish partially fulfilled. Within months, the new coalition had published a draft of the Cabinet Manual, a document setting out the guidelines that had been used in formation of the government. In his introduction to the finalized text, Cameron cited a "desire for a political system that is looked at with admiration around the world and is more transparent and accountable. . . . For the first time the conventions determining how the Government operates are transparently set out in one place. Codifying and publishing these sheds welcome light on how the Government interacts with the other parts of our democratic system."[4] Downing Street officials warned that the manual should not be mistaken for the beginnings of a written constitution, but it remains the only official publication of the modern era to attempt to define in writing the role of the monarch.

It does so in one pithy sentence that doesn't so much prescribe what a monarch should do as describe what the Queen has done: "The Sovereign is the head of state of the UK, providing stability, continuity and a national focus," the document declares. That is the job the Prince expects to inherit. Supporters of a republic would prefer to replace the hereditary system with elected heads of state, each poll pitting different visions of Britain against each other. That might prove bracing. It would not be comforting. "You don't have an election and a dispute as to who the next monarch is, with half the country thinking the wrong person has been elected, as you do with a republic," says John Major.[5]

In remaining on show, apparently immutable, as everything changed around her, the Queen may have provided a guidepost in unfamiliar land-scapes and a nucleus of unity at a time when most impulses favor disintegration. The European project is fracturing. The concept of Britishness has stretched thin. Both ideas are coming under increasing strain as nationalist and populist movements gain strength in befuddled response to globalization. While Scotland contemplated a rupture with the rest of the United Kingdom, leaders of the campaign for independence assured voters that shuffling off the yoke of Westminster need not mean losing the Queen or the reassurance of stability the Crown provides. Though the monarch devoutly hoped Scots would opt to stay in the union, and despite the urgings of members of her close family to intervene, she kept her own views guarded, going no further than to express the wish that Scots would "think very carefully about the future." Her aides went to "great lengths to communicate the Queen's own unimpeachable position," says a palace insider. After the September 2014 referendum, in which 55 percent of voters opted to retain Scotland's place within the sovereign's still-United Kingdom, Buckingham Palace released a statement by the Queen. "As we move forward, we should remember that despite the range of views that have been expressed, we have in common an enduring love of Scotland, which is one of the things that helps to unite us all," she said.

Such gestures of reconciliation come naturally. Sources say she found it harder to accept the apologies of the Prime Minister who was caught by film crews during a trip to the UN General Assembly in New York later the same month boasting about calling the Queen to convey the referendum result. "The definition of relief is being the Prime Minister of the United Kingdom and ringing the Queen and saying, 'It's all right, it's OK,'" Cameron told former New York Mayor Michael Bloomberg ahead of a business meeting. "That was something. She purred down the line." While nobody in the palace rejected the idea that the result secretly pleased the Queen, officials were irritated by the breach of protocol that revealed her private thoughts. John Major cannot recall a similar lapse, he says. "However far back you go, Prime Ministers will talk generically but they will not talk specifically. If they did, then you lose the value of the private audiences with the monarch."[6]

Cameron's description of the Queen purring drew snorts of incredulity. Around Prince Philip she is sometimes, disconcertingly, kittenish, but to most people—and certainly Cameron—she remains unyielding and literally and figuratively unstrokeable. To touch the Queen is an act of lèse-majesté.

In commanding respect, she has also gained public affection. She may be owed a debt of gratitude, too. Far-right parties have been making significant gains in some countries, as voters lash out at mainstream politicians they don't trust and immigrant populations they find convenient to scapegoat for economic hardships. The French National Front won almost a quarter of the vote, more than any other party, in May 2014 European elections. Its close equivalent in the UK, the British National Party, lost the one seat it held in the European Parliament, as another anti-immigration, Euroskeptic party, the United Kingdom Independence Party—UKIP—surged to claim twenty-four seats. UKIP shares many hallmarks of far-right parties and gives succor to the central mythology that foreigners and outsiders threaten national cultures and prosperity. Its leader, Nigel Farage, drew fire—and, presumably, hard right votes—by suggesting Britons would be right to be concerned if Romanians moved in next door to them.[7] But his party has also made a show of expelling or disciplining representatives for expressing "unacceptable" views, such as the Henley-on-Thames councillor David Silvester, who perceived in severe flooding in England God's response to the same-sex marriage bill. Such views may play well with a narrow band of the electorate, but are seen by the UKIP leadership and less partial observers to mitigate against the party's chances of continuing to capture a wider vote and solidifying its position as a serious electoral force.

There are many reasons why Britons may be less susceptible than some other Europeans to an unvarnished far right, not least its lucky habit of producing incompetent far-right leaders. Richard Chartres, Bishop of London and close to the Prince since they attended Cambridge University together, believes that Britain's constitutional monarchy and its staunch Queen have also helped to immunize the population against far-right populism. "One of the things that the monarchy has done in this country very much is keep the right wing respectable," he says. "If you look at all those countries where the monarchies collapsed after the First World War, one of the consequences was a visceral street rightism, which has flourished in a vacuum of iconic figures who could sum up national pride. One of the things that the Queen has done is she's occupied that space. She's also offered a kind of reassurance and continuity at a time when our place in the world is dramatically reduced."[8] A nagging question for those who see the Queen as a bulwark against extremism and disintegration is this: will her son be able to fulfill that role?

IF THE MAN OF GOD'S ARGUMENT FOR SAVING THE QUEEN IS UNPROV-able, the fact of her steady presence in public life is undeniable. "Apart from my sister, she is the only other person who has been a total constant in my life ever since I came to consciousness. The Queen was there, and that's an incredible rock I think to have in your life," says the actor Helen Mirren.[9] After a career spanning four decades, Mirren accepted the role that would snag her an Oscar in 2007 and lodge her almost as indelibly in the public imagination as the character she played. The movie *The Queen* dramatized and sought to explain in human terms Elizabeth II's greatest misstep: her failure to read the national—and global—mood in the wake of Princess Diana's death. As the sovereign grieved in private, anger against the Windsors built like suppressed sobs. Finally the Queen let herself be persuaded to display her sorrow on television. "We have all been trying in our different ways to cope. It is not easy to express a sense of loss, since the initial shock is often succeeded by a mixture of other feelings: disbelief, incomprehension, anger—and concern for those who remain. We have all felt those emotions in these last few days," she said.

It was enough but only just. Such mistakes have been few and far between, and they have always been similar to each other in nature. The Queen appeared austere and uncaring in 1966 when she waited six days before visiting Aberfan in South Wales after a landslide of coal waste buried its school, killing 116 children and 28 adults. She missed the funeral in Lockerbie of a ten-year-old victim of the terror attack on Pan Am Flight 103 over the Scottish town. "At a time of national mourning, we rightly and naturally turn to the Queen for our lead," wrote columnist Jean Rook in the *Daily Express*. "Broken-hearted Britain watching TV needed to see their

equally grieving monarch." Buckingham Palace provided a frigid expla-
nation: the Queen does not attend memorial services or funerals.[10]

The Queen scrapped that convention and has adjusted as far as she is
temperamentally able to a world that needs to see her grief to believe it.
She also relaxed into motherhood, enveloping her second batch of children, Andrew and Edward, with a warmth denied to Charles and Anne.
She loved her first- and second-born, but in the early years of her reign
focused on her duty as sovereign to the exclusion of much else.

Charles in particular learned early in life to equate duty with denial
and denial with destiny. That he was born to assume the crown, the
Prince said, "dawned on me with a ghastly inexorability."[11] When he was
just one year old, his mother spent six weeks away, and on her return took
four days to catch up with administrative affairs—slipping in a quick trip
to the races—before rejoining her son. After she acceded to the throne,
such separations became more protracted. In 1953, she toured the Commonwealth with Philip for six months. When Charles boarded the royal
yacht, excited finally to see his parents after their long absence, he tried to
join the dignitaries lined up to greet them. "No, not you, dear," said the
Queen.[12]

This book explores a character shaped by nature and nurture and perhaps just as much by the absence of nurture. Charles was born into a
unique set of circumstances and an odd environment. He was also the
product of an age that warned against showing children too much ten-
derness for fear of spoiling them. His mother may appear changeless, but
she has always reflected the times—and moved with them.

THE WINDSORS WOULD LIKE YOU TO BELIEVE THAT THE THINGS THEY DO
are things that have always been done, but that is just a case of smoke and
gilded mirrors. The dynasty rebrands and refreshes itself constantly and
carefully, and sometimes weathers more radical reinventions, too. The premier symbols of Britishness refer to themselves as "European mongrels,"
says Prince Andrew, and that's about right, though the most concentrated
element of the Windsor line is German, with a leavening of Danish blood.[13]
In 1917, as European powers slid toward war and British antipathies to all
things German deepened, King George V quietly exchanged his family

name Saxe-Coburg-Gotha for Windsor, the reassuringly English-sounding name of their castle in Berkshire. He urged Prince Louis of Battenberg, his cousin and married to one of Queen Victoria's granddaughters, to anglicize his surname, too. Battenberg, who had carved out a high-flying career in the Royal Navy, rising to First Sea Lord by the time war with Germany appeared inevitable, complied. It wasn't enough to save his job, but it spared royal embarrassment, not least when in 1947 his grandson Prince Philip of Greece and Denmark took British citizenship and adopted the clunky new family name, Mountbatten, just before marrying the future Elizabeth II and gaining a new title, Duke of Edinburgh.

Most changes to the institution of monarchy during the Queen's reign have barely rippled the surface, "imperceptible" in the words of one courtier; yet in their totality they've been profound and transformative. Everything is the product of instinct, not analysis or training. "I didn't have an apprenticeship," she once said. "My father died much too young and so it was all a very sudden kind of taking on and making the best job you can. It's a question of maturing into something that one's got used to doing and accepting the fact that here you are and it's your fate. Because I think continuity is very important."[14]

Unlike her long-serving heir, she benefited from only a few years of formal preparation for assuming the throne after her father's unexpected elevation to kingship. This consisted of on-the-job experience and lessons from Henry Marten, the Vice Provost of Eton College, who instructed her in constitutional history including the works of Walter Bagehot.

A more vivid history lesson came courtesy of the Luftwaffe. In September 1940, a German bomber scored a direct hit on Buckingham Palace. "We heard the unmistakable whirr-whirr of a German plane. We said 'Ah, a German' and before anything else could be said there was the noise of aircraft diving at great speed, and then the scream of a bomb," wrote Elizabeth's doughty mother, Queen Elizabeth. "It all happened so quickly that we had only time to look foolishly at each other, when the scream hurtled past us, and exploded with a tremendous crash in the quadrangle." The letter ends with a postscript, key words underlined in the family tradition. "Dear old BP is <u>still standing</u> and that is the main thing."[15] Her daughter understands that no edifice, however storied or solid-looking, is invulnerable. She has dedicated her life to keeping the monarchy standing.

In 1947 the Princess celebrated her twenty-first birthday in South Africa, during a royal tour that failed in its objective of revitalizing support for the pro-British General Jan Smuts, but launched the young Elizabeth as a future sovereign and gave a foretaste of the high solemnity with which she would approach the role. In a broadcast from Cape Town, she said, "This is a happy day for me; but it is also one that brings serious thoughts, thoughts of life looming ahead with all its challenges and with all its opportunity." She spoke of the "terrible and glorious years of the Second World War" and looked forward with others of her age group to being "able to take some of the burden off the shoulders of our elders who have fought and worked and suffered to protect our childhood."

"There is a motto," she said, "which has been borne by many of my ancestors—a noble motto, 'I serve.' Those words were an inspiration to many bygone heirs to the throne when they made their knightly dedication as they came to manhood. I cannot do quite as they did. But through the inventions of science I can do what was not possible for any of them. I can make my solemn act of dedication with a whole Empire listening. I should like to make that dedication now. It is very simple. I declare before you all that my whole life whether it be long or short shall be devoted to your service and the service of our great imperial family to which we all belong."

In 1952 that earnest service started in earnest with her father's death. Elizabeth was just twenty-five. Her daughter, Anne, not yet three years old, was deemed too young to attend the coronation. Charles, aged four, his hair already severely parted, rested a weary head on his hand as he watched his mother crowned. Ahead of the ceremony, she had undertaken practice sessions wearing sheets pinned together to give her a sense of the robes she must maneuver into Westminster Abbey and wore the imperial state crown around Buckingham Palace to try to accustom herself to its weight. "It goes on, the ceremony, for quite a long time, so you can end up with a terrible headache," the Prince explained. "So I remember my mother coming up, when we were being bathed as children, wearing the crown. It was quite funny. That's a vivid memory, I must say."[16]

The new Queen found herself in charge of a palace system stocked with courtiers, who occupied positions as she did, by dint of heredity. She preserved some of the picturesque pomp and the florid job titles—she still employs a Mistress of the Robes; the Master of the Horse rides alongside her carriage at ceremonial occasions; she is serenaded every morning at 9:00 a.m. by the Queen's Piper, though she once confessed that the sound of bag- pipes had long since palled—but she has stocked key roles with profession- als. The Keeper of the Privy Purse may sound ceremonial, but the title incorporates management of both the private and public revenues of the Queen, responsible for intricate budgets and for defending them to par- liamentary committees. The incumbent since 2002, Sir Alan Reid, used to be a senior partner at the auditing and accountancy firm KPMG.

In 1957, a television crew came to Sandringham to film, for the first time, the Queen's Christmas message. "I very much hope that this new medium will make my Christmas message more personal and direct," she said. "It is inevitable that I should seem a rather remote figure to many of you, a successor to the kings and queens of history; someone whose face may be familiar in newspapers and films but who never really touches your per- sonal lives. But now at least for a few minutes I welcome you to the peace of my own home." She has continued to look for ways to bridge the gap between herself and her subjects. In 1958, at the urging of her husband, she quietly retired the custom for debutantes to be presented at court, opening her doors instead to a wider range of guests, often nominated by external organizations such as charities or selected as representatives of identity groups: women in business, Irish living in Britain, the Asian community. She holds multiple audiences, not just with Prime Ministers but with other senior figures of the British establishment, and travels around meeting as many people as can be filed past her. The number of bedecked and behat- ted guests turning up to her garden parties tops thirty thousand per year. "She likes a rapid throughput," says an aide.

IN THE YEARS BEFORE DIANA'S DEATH THE QUEEN SIGNED OFF ON SIG- nificant changes in the way the monarchy interfaced with the rest of the state, advised by the so-called Way Ahead Group, a body of senior aides and royals that formed in recognition that the monarchy urgently needed to do some strategic thinking. On November 20, 1992, toward the end of a dismal twelve-month run that saw publication of Andrew Morton's revelatory book about Diana and the marriages of three of the Queen's four children collapse, flames gutted Windsor Castle, causing $58.5 million of damage and burning away the notion that Britons would unquestioningly shell out to maintain the trappings of their monarchy. John Major's government, wrestling unsuccessfully with recession and the aftermath of a currency crisis that had just tipped sterling out of the European Exchange Rate Mechanism, announced that it would foot the repair bill, provoking outrage. "It was a bump in the road," says Major now. "Even in the most difficult moments of the 1990s, there wasn't a millisecond when the monarchy was in any real danger from the point of view of people up and down the country. It is deeply rooted . . . You don't dig it up quickly."[17]

The senior royals feared nevertheless that Britons might go in search of shovels. Four days after the fire, the Queen made a speech at Guildhall to mark the fortieth anniversary of her accession. "There can be no doubt," she said, "that criticism is good for people and institutions that are part of public life. No institution—city, monarchy, whatever—should expect to be free from the scrutiny of those who give it their loyalty and support, not to mention those who don't."[18]

Yet the mechanisms for funding royalty had been kept deliberately opaque. A 1972 amendment to the Civil List Act for the first time inserted a requirement for the Treasury to review the Queen's spending, but set the reviews at ten-year intervals. More frequent scrutiny, the law stated, would not be "consistent with the honor and dignity of the Crown"; daylight is dangerous. MPs were forbidden from asking questions about the royal finances except during the review period.

Monarchs from George III onward surrendered the assets of the Crown Estates to government in return for official expenses and annuities through the Civil List, later augmented by grants from various government departments. In addition, the monarch enjoyed a substantial—and tax-exempt—private income from the Privy Purse, mostly generated by the Duchy of Lancaster, an estate held in trust for the monarch and constituted along similar lines to the Duchy of Cornwall. Before the Windsor fire, the Queen had already held discussions about making voluntary tax payments, as Prince Charles already did, giving the Treasury 50 percent of his Duchy of Cornwall income in advance of his first marriage and 25 percent after that happy day.

Each review of the Civil List invariably drew headlines about "pay rises" for the Queen. The Prince had tried in the 1980s to head off criticism by exploring ways of fundamentally altering the financial arrangements between government and the royal households. His imagination was caught by a proposal to retire the Civil List and return the Crown Estates, and their income, to royal care. The idea wouldn't fly, and not only because the costs of the monarchy by now exceeded the revenues from its hereditary lands. A self-financing monarchy would no longer be beholden to Parliament, becoming more remote, more royal, in effect more powerful.

The Windsor fire precipitated a compromise. The government announced that the Queen intended to pay income and capital gains tax on her private income and also to slash the numbers of royals living on handouts from the state by financing them herself. Charles echoed the move, opting to pay the maximum rate of income tax on his Duchy revenues. The Queen also implemented a cost-cutting program, agreeing that her court would live on a static budget for the next two decades. Still protests against the plan for a taxpayer-funded restoration of Windsor Castle smoldered. After the failure of a private fund-raising initiative for Windsor Castle that attracted only $40,000 in donations, the Queen found the money for repairs by opening Buckingham Palace to tourists. Around half a million visitors from across the Realms and beyond tramp through the state rooms every summer, producing a useful revenue stream and opening up a narrow strip of royal life to public view.

The Way Ahead Group eventually disbanded, but only after the practice of strategic thinking had been incorporated into the fiber of palace organization. That has meant continuing small-scale reforms and a few more eye-catching measures. In 2011 the Queen signed off on a new system for financing herself and future heads of state to a formula agreed to by the coalition government whose birth pains she had observed the previous year. The Sovereign Grant consolidated the grants and sources of income previously paid to the monarch via the Civil List and government departments, making the arrangements a tad less impenetrable and holding its custodians a touch more accountable and giving the Queen a smidgeon more of the independence the Prince had sought.

Guests and the tourists paying to visit Buckingham Palace enter a stage set, constructed and maintained to project majesty. Look closer, and you'll find cracks in the edifice of monarchy, not so much metaphorical fissures as palpable decay that in 2007 sent masonry crashing from the roof, narrowly missing Princess Anne as she got into her car, and two years later dislodged a chunk of stone that came close to felling a police officer on duty. In March 2012 the Public Accounts Committee flagged up the statistic that 39 percent of royal properties stood, precariously, in need of remedial work. The committee's chairwoman, MP Margaret Hodge, criticized the Queen's household. "I expected to see a better performance," she said. "They've got to get a bit real."[19]

NOBODY WHO HAS SEEN THE BACK CORRIDORS OF BUCKINGHAM Palace would assume the royal household to lack a sense of harsher realities. Away from the public areas, thick carpeting gives way to worn runners along corridors that branch into a series of domains: working offices, working kitchens, the engine rooms of an international corporation, and beyond those, staff bedrooms, guest suites, and royal apartments. The geography of the palace reflects the topology of the Queen's life. Nobody can say for sure where the sovereign's public duty ends and her private sphere begins. Paperwork and retainers follow the Queen like corgis. No royal home ever feels truly homely, but Buckingham Palace is the bleakest. Surrounded by more than eight hundred employees and a clutter of unwanted gifts and excess furniture, stacked Wellington boots and dog hair, the Queen, Prince Philip, and a shifting population that at times includes their children Anne, Andrew, and Edward and cousin Princess Alexandra, carry out their odd sort of work and their odder form of living.

"Most people have a job and then they go home and in this existence the job and the life go on together," the matter-of-fact Queen tells viewers of *Elizabeth R.* "Because you can't really divide it up; the boxes and the communications just keep on coming and of course in modern communications they come even quicker. Luckily I'm a quick reader so I can get through a lot of reading in quite a short time. . . . I do rather begrudge some of the hours that I have to do instead of being outdoors."[20]

That is a rare complaint. Mostly the Queen just gets on with the business of being Queen, accepting the lack of freedom and restriction of personal space that entails and expecting her children to knuckle down to their fate with similar resignation. She planned to invite the Home Secretary of the day to attend the birth of Charles just as an earlier Home Secretary in 1926 had paced the halls of her parents' house in Bruton Street during her own difficult delivery. She had grown up understanding that such invitations were part of a tradition dating back to 1688 when opponents of James II circulated a rumor that he had substituted an imposter child, smuggled in a warming pan into the palace, for his stillborn heir. Sir Alan Lascelles, her father's Private Secretary, brought her the welcome news that the custom, like so many royal traditions, had been fabricated, in this instance spun to permit officials to cluster "in the private apartments of royalty daily, and particularly at moments of special significance such as births, marriages and deaths."[21]

So on November 14, 1948, baby Charles drew his first breath in Buckingham Palace without a Home Secretary present to attest to his bona fides. He often seems like a cuckoo in the royal nest—superficially more at odds with his parents than like them—but nobody has ever challenged his heritage: it's clearly visible in his features, his expressions, his habit of clasping his hands behind his back just like his father. What he never learned to do is wear a mask, as his mother does.

If you cannot hide, you can at least hide your feelings. The impassivity that defines the Queen's public image is not feigned, but it is assumed. Even in the compromised privacy of her family circle, she gives little away and with her husband has created a family culture that prizes restraint and approves of stoicism. Friends remember that her corgis got into a fight with Princess Anne's dogs. A dog died. Neither the Queen nor Princess Anne mentioned the incident, to each other or the rest of the family.

Her staff learns to look for fractional signs of displeasure: is the Queen's mouth a little more downturned, the presence a degree more glacial? From behind the mask, she misses very little. Her micromanagement is legendary. She knows things about palace life—about what members of the household have been up to—that can only come from bat-like hearing and preternatural powers of observation. She pays attention to the smallest details. A 2014 trial into allegations of bribery and phone hacking by employees of Rupert Murdoch's *News of the World* heard that the monarch had reprimanded police on guard at Buckingham Palace for eating snacks put out for guests; a witness claimed she had drawn lines in the bowls to monitor levels.[22] Praise—and her transfiguring smiles—fall like desert rain.

Her foil and consort, support and center of the most hidden of public private worlds, the Duke of Edinburgh is their most frequent recipient. He still brings out a softer side to the Queen. He has never publicly commented on rumors of his infidelity, though he once inquired of a relative, "How could I be unfaithful to the Queen? There is no way that she could possibly retaliate."[23] Whatever the royal couple's arrangement, the marriage works, as a loving relationship and a professional partnership. "Regardless of whether my grandfather seems to be doing his own thing, sort of wandering off like a fish down a river, the fact that he's there—personally, I don't think [the Queen] could do it without him, especially when they're both at this age," said Prince Harry in 2011.[24]

Penniless and stateless, Philip wasn't an obvious choice to marry the future head of a reigning royal house, though his candidacy was buoyed, or burdened, by support from his uncle Louis "Dickie" Mountbatten. "I have come to the conclusion that we are going too fast," King George VI, father of the prospective bride, warned Mountbatten in response to the latter's unrestrained enthusiasm for the project.[25] Mountbatten's ardor burned so bright that Philip wrote to his uncle pleading for a little space: "Please, I beg of you, not too much advice in an affair of the heart, or I shall be forced to do the wooing by proxy."[26] Elizabeth needed no encouragement. It may have been the only time in her life that she allowed heart to rule head, putting her own desires before duty. Courtiers thought she was making a mistake. Philip seemed to them uncouth, lacking in polish. Her suitor might speak the King's English, but he lacked a filter between brain and mouth. He still does.

His gaffes have become legend. "Are you running away from something?" the Duke asked expatriate Brits in Abu Dhabi. He compared schoolgirls in red uniforms to "Dracula's daughters" and suggested Nigerian President Olusegun Obasanjo, in national dress, looked "ready for bed." "Damn fool question!" he told a journalist who asked if the Queen was enjoying an official trip. To another solicitous inquiry—"How was your flight?"—he responded, "Have you ever flown? It was just like that." He has racked up as many sexist and racist comments as a rogue UKIP candidate. "You're not wearing mink knickers, are you?" he asked a female fashion writer. He warned a British student in China, "If you stay here much longer, you'll go home with slitty eyes." His popularity may owe something to the misplaced notion that statements that offend against political correctness are a sign of authenticity. Yet he is authentic, in the sense that he never seeks favor by falsifying his views, though he often conceals them in public. A modernizer—at least by the standards of the family he married into—his most significant role has unfolded behind the scenes, supporting and encouraging his unflappable wife, and overseeing the raising of their children.

Philip grew up with a surfeit of surnames, Schleswig-Holstein-Sonderburg-Glücksburg, and a paucity of security. A year after his birth, on June 10, 1921, on Corfu, his uncle Constantine of Greece was forced for a second time to vacate his throne. Losses in a war with Turkey hardened sentiment against the royals, who had been imported from Denmark a generation earlier. Military rebels executed the general of the Greek army and came close to meting out the same punishment to the King's brother, Prince Andrew, who had commanded troops in the disastrous conflict. Instead they dispatched him into exile with his fragile wife, Princess Alice, and their four daughters and only son, Philip. Their youngest daughter, Sophie, married first, in 1930, to a German aristocrat who died as a high-ranking SS officer in an air crash in Italy in 1943. The three elder girls wed within months of each other in 1931, all making alliances with German nobles. The matrimonial flurry coincided with a deterioration in their mother's mental state. Consigned to a sanatorium, Princess Alice moved in and out of institutions, diagnosed at one point with schizophrenia, but eventually recovering sufficiently to found an order of nuns. Her husband washed up in the South of France, beached first by the pleasures of the region and then by the outbreak of World War II, which erected political and logistical barriers between members of a family already divided by emotional conflict.

From the age of nine, Philip commuted between far-flung relatives and schools in Paris, England, Germany, and Scotland, the last two institutions shaped by Kurt Hahn, a visionary—and eccentric—educator. Philip arrived at Salem in southern Germany just as Hahn, a Jew who spoke out against the Nazis, departed for the safety of Britain, where he swiftly found in a vacant eighteenth-century estate called Gordonstoun a more secure plantation for his ideas. Philip followed him there in 1934.

The school in the far northeast of Scotland imposed a Spartan physical regimen on pupils—a later alumnus, novelist William Boyd, wrote that "if Borstals or remand homes were maintained in similar conditions, there would be a public outcry"—but looked for its educational ethos to Athens and Plato's *Republic* rather than to Sparta.[27] "Hahn followed Plato in defining virtue in the individual as a harmony or balance between the various faculties of the psyche, more simply expressed in public-school jargon as the ideal of the 'all-rounder,'" noted Robert Skidelsky. "'What do you do with the extrovert?' Hahn was asked. 'I turn him outside in,' was the reply. 'And with the introvert?' 'I turn him inside out.'"[28] Hahn's regime failed to turn the outer-directed Philip inward but confirmed the future husband of the Queen in the belief that the best way to transform boys into men is to set them challenges. That idea underpins the Duke of Edinburgh awards scheme he founded in 1956 at Hahn's behest and informed the educational route Philip charted for all three sons.

The Duke has always relished challenges and has a record of rising to them. He became "Guardian" or head boy at Gordonstoun and captained the school cricket and rugby teams. At Dartmouth naval college, he won distinction as an outstanding cadet. Serving aboard the HMS *Valiant* as a midshipman during World War II, he earned a mention in dispatches for his part in the Battle of Matapan, a 1941 skirmish off the coast of Greece that sank five Italian vessels. By the end of the war, he had transferred to the British Pacific Fleet, participating in the landing on Iwo Jima and serving aboard one of the escort ships that accompanied the USS *Missouri* and HMS *Duke of York* to accept the Japanese surrender.

His wife's sudden elevation scotched his promising career and landed him, like all Windsors apart from the Queen, with the predicament of prominence without predefined purpose. At Matapan he wielded the spotlight, turning it on enemy ships. As the royal consort he is caught in it, always at the edge of its circle, trailing two steps behind the woman on whom it is trained. She learned to give away nothing in its full beam. In Philip she found a mate whom experience had taught to deny his feelings even to himself.

TWO PEOPLE SHORT ON SELF-DOUBT AND LONG ON COMPOSURE, THE Queen and Prince Philip have always been self-sufficient, sustained largely by each other and the odd martini. (The Duke's preferred way to mix the drink is inevitably at odds with Charles's; Philip likes the "lemon mixed with the drink, only a little bit of vermouth, triple the gin steeped on the ice and left for 10 minutes.")[29]

Their eldest son remembers his childhood as a series of tests, upsets, and discomforts. He was shaped as much by adversity as by positive example: through the absence of his parents but also friction with his father. As the Queen grappled with her new role as head of state, the Duke of Edinburgh had taken charge of child rearing, approaching the problem—and Charles in his father's estimation has always been a problem—with his usual direct-ness. The Duke noted that Charles was a sensitive child—so unlike his robust little sister Anne—and drew the conclusion that the best, and kind-est, course of action would be to toughen him up. The toughening-up pro-cess sometimes looked like mockery. When the child flinched, it provoked the father to poke harder.

The dynamics of the relationship have barely altered. In much of what Charles does—his passionate conservationism, his commitment to helping young people, even in his hobby of painting—he emulates the Duke of Edin-burgh and reflects their common heritage as products of Kurt Hahn's school-ing. Yet communications between them are congested and the approval he craves is rarely bestowed. Brickbats fly when he least expects them. In a 2008 television interview, his father took a sideswipe unprovoked by any line of questioning. "Organic," he said. "It's not an unmixed blessing and it's not an absolute certainty that it's quite as useful as it sounds. . . . You've got to be emotionally committed to it but if you stand back and try to be open-minded about it, it is quite difficult to really find where it's been a real benefit."[30] Viewers will have known that Charles has been banging the drum for organic farming since the 1980s. Less obvious was that in the mouth of the irascible Duke, "emotionally committed" is a scathing criticism. It also describes the way his son approaches every project and cause he espouses.

After the death of Sir Christopher Soames, the Prince sent a letter of condolence to his bereaved friend Nicholas. "I have minded so much for you and thought so much of you during these last few days while you had to watch your father gradually slip away before your eyes," he wrote. "I kept thinking that it might have been my father and I can imagine all the thoughts and feelings that you were probably experiencing, both before and after he died. Relationships with fathers can be such complex ones—I remem-ber we often talked about our own relationships with our own respective fathers and how they've not been easy always. . . . So often, I supposed, one must long to have got on better or to have been able to talk freely about the things that matter deeply, but one was too inhibited to discuss."[31]

That inhibition has always been two-sided, generational. The Queen and her consort are not only the products of their own demanding upbringings but of the wider spirit of the postwar period. "These professional naval officers and military officers trooped home having watched their buddies have heads blown off and limbs blown off and tried to settle back into civvy street," says Tim Knatchbull.[32] The survivors' impulse was to put a brave face on things, whatever the cost.

Knatchbull knows the Queen not as a distant head of state but a dear and supportive cousin and friend of the family. His father, Lord Brabourne, grew close to the Queen and the Duke of Edinburgh after marriage to Mountbatten's eldest daughter, Patricia, now Countess Mountbatten of Burma. Both couples produced their first children in the late 1940s, raising them, says Knatchbull, according to "a prototype of childhood and parenting from the previous generation, from the Empire and India."[33] By the time the couples turned their attention to their youngest children—Prince Edward, Timothy Nicholas Knatchbull, and his identical twin Nicholas Timothy, all born in 1964—the sensibility they applied to the process had changed. In place of the earlier parenting that Knatchbull equates with the regimented "Preobrazhensky March," a piece of music that often accompanies displays of Russian military muscle, Knatchbull and his twin and their cousin Edward were nurtured to the more relaxed rhythms of the Beatles era. "The Queen and Prince Philip and my parents were very clever, hip, savvy, intelligent, interested, forward-looking people, interested in young people, interested in the revolutions going on across Europe, the cultural revolutions, the social revolutions, and rather in sympathy with them and regarded by their peers as being avant garde because of how quickly they adopted some of the new ideas of the Swinging Sixties, including new ideas of parenting, which is that you spend masses of time with your kid. Which is what Prince Edward got. Which is what I got."[34] Which is what Charles did not get.

In 1979, Irish republicans detonated gelignite they had concealed on the fishing boat Knatchbull's family used when staying at Classiebawn Castle, Mountbatten's Irish holiday home. Knatchbull was gravely injured. His parents defied doctors' predictions to pull through but remained hospitalized for months. Everyone else aboard died: Knatchbull's grandfather

Mountbatten, his grandmother Lady Brabourne, a fifteen-year-old local boy called Paul Maxwell, and Nicholas, Knatchbull's twin.

During Knatchbull's long convalescence, the Queen invited him and one of his sisters, Amanda, to stay at Balmoral. They found her in "almost unstoppable mothering mode."[35] "The Queen is extraordinarily animated when it comes to care and detail and motherliness and economy and domestic matters and that isn't understood," says Knatchbull, sitting in his West London office, shrapnel scars faint but visible. "People assume she's a lofty figure and head of state but no, actually she's first and foremost a home-maker and therefore a caregiver to the people in the home."[36]

Her youngest sons, Andrew and Edward, benefited from that well-concealed motherliness. She has easy connections with her grandchildren and other family members such as Knatchbull. Princess Anne, her father's favorite, has always been at least as stalwart as her parents. Charles drew a shorter straw, the first child and the neediest, just three when his mother ascended the throne. He suffered another misfortune, too. Instead of growing up in the palace, tended by private tutors and shielded from curious eyes, Charles became a royal guinea pig, the first heir to the throne to attend school. The change, like most of the careful recalibrations of Elizabeth II's reign, made perfect sense. The monarchy must evolve, stay in touch with the people. The strategy produced a Prince of Wales avid to understand his future subjects and to be understood, but only partially equipped to succeed in either endeavor.

Nor has he ever developed the thicker skin his father hoped for him, especially where Philip himself is concerned. In 2012, when the Diamond Jubilee tour brought the Queen and the Duke of Edinburgh to Burnley in northwest England, Charles seized the moment to lay before them some of the fruits of his labor. Six of his charities had been working to regenerate Weaver's Triangle, a derelict area in a town that has frayed with the decline of the cotton industry. "No other group of charities could have played the same role or achieved as much as the Prince's Charities," enthused a 2011 evaluation report, published by the Cass Business School at City University London. As the royal trio traveled by barge to Weaver's Triangle, Philip's voice cut through the excitement. "I can't think why you want to save all these terrible old places," he said. Of all people, the Duke really should have known the answer.

CHAPTER 3

A Prince Among Men

//

C HARLES IS A PASSIONATE GARDENER, OF IDEAS AND INITIATIVES AS
well as gardens. "These things have grown like topsy over the years, as
I've seen what I feel needs to be done," he says of his charities. "I couldn't
do it all at once. I couldn't at Highgrove just do the whole garden in one or
two years. Bit by bit you go round."[1]

The landscapes he creates, whether figurative or physical, bear marked
similarities. Though he recognizes the necessity for pruning to maintain
healthy plants and sustainable organizations, he shies from too stark an
approach. "We ask before we cut anything," said Suzie Graham, one of two
head gardeners at Birkhall.[2] Charles's impulse is to create refuges, for other
people and for himself. "All my life I have wanted to heal things, whether
it's been the soil, the landscape or the soul," he explained in the introduction to one of seven books about Highgrove that have sprung up as a result
of his green fingers.[3]

His gardens are full of hiding places, paths that twist unexpectedly, and
rustic shelters. "The eye should be led; you want to think 'I wonder what's
around that corner?' Little follies are terribly important, too, as they give
a focus to reach or sit in once you get there," he ruminated.[4] Most of the
follies encircle seats just large enough for a prince and his cushion. At Highgrove he also installed a larger sanctuary of stone, clay, and barley straw,

equipped with a wood-burning stove and built to geometric principles he considers sacred. The phrase inscribed above the wooden door in Pictish—the language of a tribe of ancient British farmers, ruled by kings—means "Lighten our darkness we beseech thee, oh Lord."

For his sixtieth birthday he took delighted possession of a new folly, a thatched summerhouse nestling on an island in the Muick, the tributary of the River Dee that cuts a path through Birkhall's grounds. On a sparkling September day in 2013, he should really be enjoying its seclusion or indulging in another experience his youth too seldom provided, the opportunity to spend quality time with close family. He has come to Birkhall for a short break. William and Kate have brought baby George to visit. Camilla is pottering upstairs. But here is the Prince, closeted in his living room with a journalist, while aides paw the carpet outside, impatient to bend his ear ahead of a lengthy meeting scheduled the next day with the heads of his charities. He continues to respond just as Gordonstoun programmed him to do: the more stressful his own life, the more hemmed in by duties and deadlines, the more he volunteers to take on additional responsibilities. It's a debt to Kurt Hahn—or a curse—that Charles freely acknowledges.

School taught him that sitting back wasn't an option, he says. "I always feel that reflection and discussion should lead to practical action." He leans forward. "I also feel more than anything else it's my duty to worry about everybody and their lives in this country, to try to find a way of improving things if I possibly can."[5]

"PLUS EST EN VOUS"—MORE IS IN YOU: GORDONSTOUN'S MOTTO reflects the school's abiding ambition to mold students into individuals who aren't simply academically proficient but socially engaged. Its founder took guidance from Plato, who wrote that "the whole of education should be directed to the acquisition of such a knowledge as will teach a man to refuse the evil and choose the good," and sketched out a map toward achieving that end that started with physical exercise or "gymnastic."[6] Pupils endured a lot of gymnastics during the Prince's incarceration at the school, cold runs, cold baths clouded with the effluvia of previous occupants, but their academic lessons didn't look much different from those of other British private schools—such institutions are confusingly known as public schools—of the time. The heir to the throne studied literature and classics, wrestled with algebra, and marveled at the burst of radiance created by holding magnesium strips in the flame of a Bunsen burner. There were few other sources of brightness. "It's such hell here, especially at night," he scrawled in a private letter. "I don't get any sleep practically at all nowadays. . . . The people in my dormitory are foul. Goodness they are horrid. I don't know how anyone could be so foul. They throw slippers all night long or hit me with pillows or rush across the room and hit me as hard as they can, waking up everyone else in the dormitory at the same time."[7]

Many former pupils of Britain's elite boarding schools recall similar experiences. The changes in attitude to parenting that redefined family relationships in the 1960s—the transition to a more nurturing culture that Tim Knatchbull describes—took far longer to percolate into the public school system. Children as young as seven were routinely dispatched into the care of institutions that, like the parents who sent them, believed that a little adversity built character. By daylight the teaching staff imposed discipline, but at night and in unseen corners of the schools a second layer of enforcement kicked in as fellow pupils acted out their own difficult assimilation by picking on kids yet more vulnerable than themselves.

Charles was an obvious target. "It was a point of honor to make physical contact with the Prince of Wales [during school games]," remembered one of his contemporaries at Gordonstoun. "And the more violently the better."[8] That wasn't the sharpest source of his misery. At Charles's first school, Hill House in London, a brief ferment of press coverage, stemmed by obliging editors at the request of Buckingham Palace, marked him as an outsider. He carried the embarrassment and discomfort to his next schools, boarding from the age of eight, first at Cheam, an English preparatory school his father had briefly attended. His attempts to blend in, never entirely convincing to himself or his supposed peers, bit the dust at the end of his first year when they sat together to watch the closing ceremony of the Empire and Commonwealth Games. With no prior warning to her son, the Queen announced that she had elevated him to his hereditary title: Prince of Wales. Soon afterward, paraded in his new principality for the public, he found himself mobbed by crowds who in an excess of patriotic zeal broke through barriers. The same status that threatened to overwhelm him with mass attention ensured he remained profoundly isolated. Classmates shunned his company for fear of being accused of sycophancy.

Cheam introduced its emissary from Planet Windsor to the business end of another British institution: corporal punishment. Palace officials had insisted he should be treated as other boys. The school authorities may not have been able to force other children to follow this instruction but they took it seriously enough to twice administer beatings to the heir to the throne for his part in dormitory fights. At Gordonstoun, the regime of punishment reflected Hahn's unusual educational vision. The cane was part of the headmaster's arsenal—by the time Charles arrived in 1962, Hahn had retired, leaving a man called Robert Chew at the helm—but symbolic and ritual sanctions played a larger role. Boys earned promotion through stages defined by uniforms and so-called training plans detailing their non-academic tasks and activities. After the Prince's infamous cherry brandy incident, Chew demoted his royal charge to "new boy," stripping him of the rank he had painstakingly earned and adding to Charles's anguish.

The school aimed to instill a sense of personal responsibility in each student. Pupils filled in forms every night to assess themselves against a series of goals they helped to identify. Hahn had devised his teaching methods to counteract social ills he feared risked squandering the promise of younger generations in listless self-indulgence. He listed these "diseases" in a treatise written the year Charles came to Gordonstoun: "decline of fitness and physical health: in particular due to the modern methods of motion, e.g., car, train, and elevator; decline of initiative and the spirit of adventure: easily to be recognized as 'spectatoritis,' an 'illness' brought about by the new media, e.g., radio, film, and television; decline of imagination and recollection: especially fostered by the restlessness of modern people and their increasing fear of silence, loneliness, and seclusion; decline of carefulness and thoroughness: primarily caused by the dwindling importance of the crafts and by the increasing inclination to look for quick results and easy solutions; decline of self-discipline and renunciation: chiefly furthered by material affluence and the easy access to alcohol, cigarettes, and pills; decline of compassion and mercy: in particular encouraged by the diminished community life and the expanding subjectivism, individualism, and egoism."[9]

Long before the rise—and slump—of the couch potato, Hahn had spotted in the Weimar Republic signs that the social and technological changes that to much of the world appeared as progress might carry downsides. Gordonstoun today is a markedly kinder institution than when Charles was a pupil, coeducational and closely attentive to student welfare, but the school still demonstrates commitment to its founding ideals by maintaining a student-run fire brigade, mountain rescue team, lifesavers, and coast guard watch that provided rare glints of enjoyment in the young royal's gloomy days.

As the boy clutched his coverlet against the onslaught of bullies, so the adult clings to the positives retrieved from Gordonstoun. He did not send his own sons to the school—William and Harry experienced the softer climes of Eton College—but in his charitable endeavors, in the ceaseless campaigning, the relentless fund-raising, Charles continues to put into practice the central tenet of the education his parents chose for him. "At the end of the day it was very good for you. It wasn't a holiday camp. But on the other hand it did build a character," he says. "And I do think character-building is vital. It's another reason I've been trying for years to try and ensure this is still possible within the education system and as part of the extracurricular aspect of education."[10]

The Queen and Prince Philip are not infrequently discomfited by the child their genes, parenting, and educational choices produced. "He always says, 'If they didn't want me to do things and have ideas, they shouldn't have sent me to a Kurt Hahn school,'" says an aide.

THERE WAS ONE MAGNESIUM BURST OF LIGHT TOWARD THE END OF his school days: six months at Timbertop, a school in the middle of the Australian bush run to Hahnian principles. Though at least as rugged as Gordonstoun, baking hot rather than icy, the culture suited Charles, and distance from many of the things that troubled him, not least his own parents, enabled him to develop a veneer of assurance. Back at Gordonstoun, to his own surprise as well as his father's, Chew made him head boy. Charles also became the first royal to take A-levels, school-leaver qualifications similar to SATs but roughly equivalent in standard to Advanced Placement examinations.

His B in History and C in French might not have suggested an academic bent, much less recommended that he study among the eggheads and bluestockings of Cambridge University, but in this, as in other key decisions, the Prince had no say and the Queen expressed no view. She sat silent at a Buckingham Palace dinner in 1965 as guests including the Prime Minister of the day, Harold Wilson, the Archbishop of Canterbury, and senior members of the military and academia, but excluding Charles, hashed out a plan that saw him head to Trinity College, Cambridge, and then, just as he threatened to settle, to University College of Wales at Aberystwyth for a term to learn Welsh ahead of his investiture as Prince of Wales. The idea was to mollify Welsh nationalists; the Prince's own desires took a backseat.

To a BBC interviewer he said: "As long as I don't get covered in too much egg and tomato, I'll be all right."[11] He joked, nervously, in a first televised interview with David Frost: "I don't think I can sort of rush in and declare the whole place a republic or home rule for everybody, you know." Did the Prince consider his childhood an advantage or a disadvantage? Frost asked. "Well it's a disadvantage I suppose in the sense that one is trying to lead as normal a life as possible at school and at Cambridge," replied Charles, steepling his hands. "But it's not a disadvantage because it's not. . . . If you're leading a more sheltered life, you know, because obviously one's been brought up . . ." He tailed off, spread the hands, tried again. "It's a very . . . It's a sort of dual upbringing that one has to try to do, and I think that perhaps that I've gone to school and university and everything in a much more normal way than any of my predecessors did has been an experiment in royal education. And of course it has been slightly difficult and there have been disadvantages at moments when I've regretted it but I think one gets over this."[12]

It would take him half a lifetime to do so. He fitted into university a little better than school but he always felt conspicuous, never at ease. "He was immensely distracted by the fact that he had to go off and be invested and so it was a very difficult life," says Richard Chartres, a fellow undergraduate and close friend, now Bishop of London. "He's a person of high intelligence which I think is often denied by people. He got a really very good degree when you realize the distractions that he had to cope with. [Charles graduated with a respectable but not exceptional lower second class honors degree.] But he was a bit young for his age, perhaps. Not so knowing." He adds: "I was struck by things that continue to be the case with him.

Elaborate courtesy, the real desire to put people at their ease and a sense of humor and memory of what you said. We had great conversations about witchcraft I remember. . . . Very very agreeable, courteous person who never threw his weight around or presumed. He was very good news, very good news indeed."

Lucia Santa Cruz, the daughter of the Chilean ambassador, met the Prince at a Cambridge dinner party thrown by Rab Butler, for whom she worked as a research assistant. The Conservative politician, twice passed over as Prime Minister, had by now become a Lord and the Master of Trinity. "Charles was very mature intellectually insofar as his interests and his curiosity and maybe not so mature emotionally, which is understandable because he had been submitted to very few experiences personally in terms of friends and relationships," she says.[13] That duality would endure for years.

Never certain of his father's approval or his mother's affection, Charles has tended to form bonds with older men and women, and even in friendships with people closer to his own age, the child prince is still visible. He looks up to the preternaturally confident Richard Chartres, unfolds in the serene presence of Patrick Holden, relaxes with the buoyant Nicholas Soames, blossoms around the vibrancy of Emma Thompson or, indeed, his dearest wife Camilla, and has employed more than a few warm, enveloping women over the years: his longtime adviser Julia Cleverdon; Martina Milburn, who runs the Prince's Trust; and his former Private Secretary Elizabeth Buchanan, for example. He enjoys the company of people who respect his position but don't stand on ceremony. In return, he has learned to overcome the reserve that was the legacy of his parents' generation and class even before its magnification in palace culture. "The fact that Prince Charles is such a kissy man is brilliant, because how the hell does he stand up to all the pressure on him not to be kissing his sons or even his cousins or godchildren. But I grew up with that relationship with him and it continued," says Tim Knatchbull.[14]

Two older family members provided the young Prince with much-needed measures of surrogate parenting and a range of formative influences. The Queen Mother was the most nurturing presence in royal circles, gladly looking after her grandson when her daughter traveled and becoming one of his mainstays as he grew older. The Prince credits his grandmother with inspiring his love of the arts and music. She supported him through turbulences, but rarely gave sharp advice. "That was not her style," explained the Queen Mother's official biographer, William Shawcross. "She never liked to acknowledge, let alone confront, disagreeableness within the family. It was a characteristic which had earned her the nickname 'imperial ostrich' among some members of the [royal] household. She thought her role was not to try and change people's courses but to be an anchor."[15]

Nevertheless, her disapproval could be as palpable as her daughter's and she imbued her grandson with a "tremendous sense of duty," according to Nicholas Soames, who recalls watching the Queen Mother stand "ramrod" straight as she realized members of the public were watching her. "When you're on parade, you're on parade."[16]

In his great-uncle Louis Mountbatten, Charles found a father figure who closely resembled his real father. Mountbatten had dash, raffish charm, and a compelling backstory as a statesman, war hero, the last Viceroy of India, and its first Governor-General when it became an independent dominion. Unlike Philip, he rarely crackled with contempt, spoken or unvoiced, toward Charles. And unlike the Queen Mother, Mountbatten doled out advice—vigorously. The mentoring started in earnest in 1972, when Charles's naval career stationed him in Portsmouth, not far from Mountbatten's Hampshire house, Broadlands. Mountbatten's advice on women and marriage would prove disastrous, but he gave better counsel on being a royal, frequently warning Charles against any behavior that recalled another of the Prince's great-uncles, the feckless Edward VIII, known to the family as David, whose self-indulgence led to "his disgraceful abdication and his futile life ever after."[17] He told the Prince off for proposing a sudden change in his travel plans that would have inconvenienced other people. This was "unkind and thoughtless—so typical of how your Uncle David started."[18] This useful reprimand came in April 1979, just a few months before Mountbatten's assassination.

The loss of Mountbatten made him want to die, too, Charles wrote in his diary: "In some extraordinary way he combined grandfather, great-uncle, father, brother and friend."[19] The fates were kinder in respect of the Queen Mother, who lived to 101. Yet when she died in 2002, just a few weeks after the death of her daughter, Princess Margaret, the Prince fell into despair. Despite his belief in an afterlife, the comfort his faith should bring, and a wider philosophy that sees death as a necessary part of the ecosystem, Charles never quite relinquishes his grief. He fills his domains with little shrines and memorials; he goes into his gardens not to talk to the plants but to the deceased. He tries to keep the Queen Mother, Mountbatten, Laurens van der Post, and a host of other departed spirits alive in his heart even if there is one persistent, shape-shifting ghost called Diana he would sometimes prefer to forget.

A 1998 MOVIE CENTERS ON TRUMAN BURBANK, A SALESMAN WHO turns twenty-nine before he discovers that his life is a fiction spun for a reality television program, *The Truman Show*. He reacts by rebelling against the unseen director and then opting out of the show. Charles has lived a version of that story, always observed, but, unlike Burbank, painfully aware of the fact. He never walked off the set, despite the temptation, nor did he rebel consciously. Yet by embracing duty and simultaneously redefining it in terms provided by his parents and his education, he created a narrative strand for the Windsor Show that its directors didn't anticipate and couldn't control.

To be fair, there weren't many other options available to the young royal. Worthy precedents and inspirational role models were in short supply. Since the eighteenth century, male heirs to the throne had welcomed their fate not as a challenge but as an invitation to make hay while the sun still shone on their predecessors. "There's a long history of relationships between Princes of Wales and actors," says Emma Thompson. "Not just actresses, not just the rude relationships as HRH would say, though," she jokes. "God knows I've tried, I've tried—he wasn't having any of it."[20]

It's a familiar theme among friends and members of the Prince's household. "If he had been more frivolous and less hardworking he may well have been more popular," muses Richard Chartres. "But actually when you think of the possibilities of frivoling in such a position they're considerable."[21] "He could do what most of his predecessors did—he could be sitting on a beach in the Caribbean with fast cars and fast women and fast horses and fast boats and everything else and living off the money of the Duchy of Cornwall, and be very comfortable," says Elizabeth Buchanan.[22] "HRH has every right to sack all of us and go round the world on a yacht," says Andrew Wright, Treasurer to the household of the Prince and Duchess and also Executive Director of the Prince of Wales Charitable Foundation. "Over the last forty years he could have said, 'I'll spend all of that money on myself and do the odd engagement just to keep my profile up.' "[23] "He works like a Trojan," says his former Private Secretary, Clive Alderton. "That's one of the reasons people close to him buy into him. If you have £19 million [$30.5 million] a year, you could choose to have quite an easy time of it. I think the UK and other Realms are fortunate to have someone who didn't choose the easy road."[24]

Would press and public look any more kindly on a Playboy Prince than they do on the Perturbed Prince who inhabits the space? George, Prince of Wales, later Prince Regent and King George IV, became the butt, almost literally, of gloriously savage caricatures that mocked his rotund backside and pilloried his extravagant lifestyle. A century later, Queen Victoria's eldest son, Edward, known as Bertie, earned a similar treatment and the malicious nicknames "fat Edward" and "Edward the caresser" during his fifty-nine years as heir apparent, the longest such apprenticeship before Charles's.

Bertie's many mistresses included theater stars Lillie Langtry and Sarah Bernhardt, the aristocratic Lady Randolph Churchill (great-grandmother to Nicholas Soames), and Alice Keppel, who endured a second, postmortem bout of notoriety during the breakup of the Waleses' marriage as Camilla's great-great-grandmother. His accession as Edward VII, far from intensifying the criticism, helped to dissipate it. After Victoria's long and increasingly somber reign, his evident enjoyment of life represented permission to wider society to loosen up a bit.

Yet the louche conduct of a Prince of Wales has also accurately predicted failure as King. Mountbatten was right to hold up Charles's great-uncle David as an example to avoid. "For some years after I joined his staff, in 1920, I had a great affection and admiration for the Prince of Wales," wrote Sir Alan Lascelles, former Private Secretary to the man who would reign as Edward VIII for only 325 days. "In the following eight years I saw him day in and day out. I saw him sober, and often as near drunk as doesn't matter; I traveled twice across Canada with him; I camped and tramped with him through Central Africa; in fact, I probably knew him as well as any man did. But, by 1927, my idol had feet, and more than feet, of clay.

"Before the end of our Canadian trip that year, I felt in such despair about him that I told Stanley Baldwin (then Prime Minister, and one of our party in Canada) that the heir apparent, in his unbridled pursuit of wine and women, and of whatever selfish whim occupied him at the moment, was going rapidly to the devil and would soon become no fit wearer of the British Crown. I expected to get my head bitten off, but he agreed with every word. I went on: 'You know, sometimes when I am waiting to get the result of some point-to-point in which he is riding, I can't help thinking that the best thing that could happen to him, and to the country, would be for him to break his neck.' 'God forgive me,' said SB. 'I have often thought the same.'"[25]

Edward VIII didn't fulfill their wishes and tumble from a horse. He fell further than that, abdicating the kingship and responsibility. His marriage to a divorcée meant he could not remain on the throne. His specter still haunts palace thinking, and not without reason. He showed up the danger to the institution from members who put desire before duty. Some of Charles's harshest critics within the palace accuse the current heir to the throne of similarly selfish behavior. It's not that they blame him for choosing Camilla over Diana. They feel he puts his more cerebral passions—his charities and initiatives—before his duller royal job. They are a long way from being persuaded of Charles's evolving view: that campaigning and kingship can be synthesized.

Yet if a Prince with a purpose inevitably creates controversies, purposeless royals are often liabilities. Charles not only grew up schooled on stories of his great-uncle David's disastrous reign and more disastrous departure but grew older watching his younger brothers flounder. Despite the similarities among the siblings, the shared genes, their Planet Windsor sensibilities, and Gordonstoun education, the alchemy that created in Charles a compulsion to make a difference seems absent in Andrew and Edward.

MILITARY SERVICE TENDS TO SUIT ROYALS; INSTITUTIONALIZED FROM birth, they are comfortable inside a system where everybody knows their rank. The comparative anonymity of uniform also affords them their best chance at blending in, and even then it's only a partial pass to real-world experience. "For me [being stationed at Camp Bastion] is not that normal because I go into the cookhouse and everyone has a good old gawp, and that's one thing that I dislike about being here," said Prince Harry, during one of two deployments to Afghanistan as Captain Wales of the Blues and Royals. "Because there's plenty of guys in there that have never met me, therefore look at me as Prince Harry and not as Captain Wales, which is frustrating. Which is probably another reason why I'd love to be out in the PBs [patrol bases], away from it all. It's as normal as it's going to get. I'm one of the guys. I don't get treated any differently."[26] The remarkable dysfunction of a war zone offered Harry a simulacrum of the commonplace.

In choosing to serve Queen and country, he and his older brother, William, followed a path well trodden. Their father and Windsor uncles all spent time in uniform. Only Prince Edward failed to qualify, reportedly to the implacable fury of his father, dropping out in 1987 after only a few months of his training to be a royal marine. "Edward has been put through a terrible ordeal and has no one to speak for him," said Romy Adlington, who had apparently got to know the Queen's youngest and most tender son during his undistinguished studies at Cambridge and has been described in press reports as a former girlfriend. "As one of his closest friends, I want the public to know he is a normal human being who has to make an important decision. He doesn't have the same responsibility as his brothers, yet he still can't go off and do what he wants. He has often asked me: 'What's it like to go for a walk alone in the park? How does it feel to be able to walk into a shop without everyone staring at you?' That's all he wants to be able to do."[27]

Charles's naval career lasted longer—five years—but despite the action-man tag, defense chiefs never risked putting him in the line of danger. "I had a yearning for some sort of action—some sort of constructive, <u>useful</u> naval operation where perhaps a medal could be won," he confided in a letter.[28] That wish would not be satisfied and though he earned pilot wings, he could not fully spread them, restricted to the safest craft and deployments. He proved a proficient pilot, an indifferent seaman, eventually promoted to captain of a minesweeper. His officers appreciated his command, less because of his naval skills than his kindness. They also marveled at his lack of confidence.

Prince Andrew has never appeared troubled by questions about his

abilities, or by many questions at all, though he describes himself as insa-
tiably curious. With no small irony, insiders say he owes his self-assurance
to the mothering of the Queen, who indulged her second son as she never
did her older children and continues to shield him. He took easily to the
Navy and benefited from greater leeway to serve than his big brother, as
the "spare" rather than the "heir." Returning from the Falklands War, he
found himself greeted less like a veteran than a pop star. "Is it his cheerful
charm, his naturalness, his exploits as a helicopter pilot in the Falklands
or his roguish reputation with beautiful girls? Or a combination of these
that go to make Andrew the most charismatic of the young royals?" This
was Andrew Morton in 1983, nine years before the journalist produced a
more substantial piece of writing. "His arrival on the scene has given a
new meaning to the initials HRH. With Andrew they stand for His Royal
Heartthrob."[29] The only direction for His Royal Heartthrob after such
adulation was down. Consigned to a desk job in 1997 and from 2001 out of
the Navy as a "full-time working member of the royal family," as Buckingham Palace describes him, the Prince soon acquired a less flattering
nickname, "Air Miles Andy," reflecting the widespread perception that he
was rather more skilled than his elder brother at frivoling—and spending
taxpayers' money to do so.

For nearly a decade after leaving the military, Andrew performed a role
of sorts, as Britain's Special Representative for Trade and Investment, dispatched on missions by the British government to foster business links
abroad. On one such trip in 2004 the Duke of York—Andrew has worn
the title since marriage to Sarah Ferguson—arrived in Beijing to find a banner festooned across the entrance to the hotel: "WELCOME TO THE
DUCK OF YORK." He roared with laughter. He approached everything in
China with similar good cheer, putting in long hours and apparently achieving results for a number of British enterprises, not least in the "the agricultural sector where we want to be able to produce a lot of genetic semen
and stock for the [Chinese] pig trade," as he said at the time.[30] Royal life
has never been as glamorous, but to be royal in the twenty-first century is
to operate as a salesperson for all manner of products and concepts.

The Duke's royal status opened doors in the People's Republic that might
not have yielded to mere ministers. Whether his advocacy for Britain can

secure deals worth more than the considerable cost of his travel is a moot point, not least since he stood down as trade envoy in 2011, explaining on his website that he wanted to "evolve the role that I perform with the Government and business, resulting in a more diverse portfolio of activities that reflects these changes." In reality, it had become difficult to deploy him as an official standard-bearer for Britain after press revelations about his links with Jeffrey Epstein, a US financier with whom Andrew continued to frivol after Epstein had served a jail sentence for soliciting prostitution with a minor. The friendship between the royal and Epstein came under the spotlight in 2011 when Sarah Ferguson fell for the wiles of Mazher Mahmood, an undercover journalist posing as a Middle Eastern businessman. Reportedly some $8 million in the red, the Duchess of York offered to facilitate access to her ex-husband for a fee. The ensuing scandal exposed the Yorks' ties to Epstein, who had given the Duchess money toward clearing her debt and introduced the Duke to young women, including Virginia Roberts, who alleged that Epstein had paid her for sex when she was just fifteen. A photograph taken when Roberts was seventeen shows Andrew with his arm around her. He denied any impropriety, but retreated to a lower-profile role.

The Duke still undertakes royal engagements, still puts on a cheerful front, but, says a palace insider, he's something of a lost soul. "It was his tragedy that they didn't let him stay in the Navy," says the source. Charles's friend Nicholas Soames chimes with that opinion: "Where he was really happy was in the Navy and he should never have left it because he was jolly good at it."[31]

Yet Andrew had probably given as much as he could to the military. He was good at the practical side of the job but no strategist; his value as a recruiting sergeant—and young royals are among the forces' best recruiters—had expired. When he left the Navy, he once said wistfully that he would like to have learned a trade—perhaps, he mused, become a plumber—but he wasn't allowed to do so.

THE DREAM OF REAL-WORLD EXPERIENCE OFTEN CROPS UP ON PLANET Windsor, but the prospect of a royal turning up to fix your leaking closet flange or rod your drains remains remote. Where there's muck there's brass, and where there's brass there's the possibility of being spattered with accusations of exploiting royal connections for profit.

When Sophie, Countess of Wessex, married into the royal family, she sought to continue her career in public relations. A 2001 exposé by Mazher Mahmood in the *News of the World* brought her time in the commercial world to a close. She and her business partner had been lured by the false prospect of business in the Middle East into touting the advantages of hiring a member of the royal family. "When people find we're working for you, the chances are you'll get people interested: Oh gosh, they've employed the Countess of Wessex's PR company," Sophie told Mahmood, whom she believed to be a prospective client.[32]

Her husband, Prince Edward, the youngest of the Queen's sons, also stumbled in the commercial world. As *People* magazine correctly anticipated when he quit the marines, "anguished as his decision was, the greatest trial for Edward lies ahead. Put simply, he doesn't have a job anymore, and his prospects aren't at all bright."[33] Edward didn't share that assessment. Since royalty is sometimes viewed as a branch of show business, he saw no reason he could not reinvent himself as showbiz royalty. By the time he stepped down as joint managing editor of Ardent Productions in 2002, the television company had certainly made an impact, turning out few programs and no critical or popular successes, but forced to apologize after apparently breaching an agreement by the rest of the British media to avoid dogging Prince William during his studies at St. Andrew's University. "They're a sad joke in the industry, really," an anonymous television executive told the *Guardian*. "As time has gone on, their incompetence has become more and more obvious. There have been very small examples of vanity TV companies before, but not on this scale. Any company, in any industry, that had burned through that much share capital without making a profit would've been closed down by its investors years ago."[34]

The limits of Edward's instincts for light entertainment had been laid bare mere months after he left the Marines, by the most bizarre public relations sally in the Windsors' history. He cooked up *The Grand Knockout Tournament*, a celebrity revival of a game show called *It's a Knockout*, held in front of a plywood castle at an English theme park, pitting four teams against each other headed by himself, the Yorks, and Princess Anne. It was, unfortunately, the only show Edward ever masterminded that drew a mass audience, eighteen million in the UK and eventually some four hundred million worldwide. Charles and Diana gave the proceedings a wise, wide berth. Stuart Hall, the presenter of the original game show and coconspirator with Edward in devising the tournament, set the contestants to slapstick challenges and periodically thrust his microphone at the team captains for sound bites. "What are we going for? Gold, gold, gold!" bellowed Edward, but his team only scraped into third place. His sister, by contrast, described her tactics as "cool, calm and collected." "All this quasi-excitement doesn't matter a damn to you then," said Hall. "No, we're the strong, silent types," replied Anne.[35]

Her team—and Save the Children, the charity whose standard she carried as its president since 1970—emerged the winners. Of the Queen's children, she is the only one to have tasted success on a regular basis and managed the awkward straddle between royalty and real life with anything approaching ease. Her participation in the tournament marked a rare lapse in her strong and largely silent dealings with the world that saw her cap her career as an equestrian competitor by earning a gold medal at the 1971 European Eventing Championships and two silver at the same contest in 1975 as well as competing at the 1976 Olympic Games in Montreal. "If it doesn't fart or eat hay, she isn't interested," her father quipped, but having a particular skill and an unremitting focus helped Anne to find and maintain direction where her brothers could not. She continues to work with horses, breeding them at her Gatcombe Park estate and holding several horse trials there including the annual Festival of British Eventing. She designs eventing courses, for Gatcombe Park and external clients, and runs the estate as a working farm, all the while managing her royal engagements and charitable patronages with brusque efficiency.

Her children have been spared a similar balancing act. Anne declined royal titles for them, enabling son Peter and daughter Zara to live as subjects of the Crown, rather than its representatives. Peter is a banker; Zara an equestrian who has at least equaled if not surpassed her mother's considerable achievements. There are already signs that the royal first cousins have been handed a rougher deal. Andrew's website states that his eldest daughter, Princess Beatrice, "works full time in business"; younger daughter, Princess Eugenie, is described as "pursuing a career in the art world."

She has moved to New York, which may give her some respite from media attention, but although both princesses are also patrons of charities, it is their social engagements that are fodder for the tabloids. Edward and Sophie's children, Lady Louise Windsor and James, Viscount Severn, born in 2003 and 2007 respectively, are likely to face similar difficulties and dilemmas.

William and Harry, meanwhile, must make choices that long ago set a previous heir and spare on widely divergent courses. William knows how limited his career options are, but is essaying a compromise, becoming an air ambulance pilot for a charity based in East Anglia. Harry is eking out his military service at a desk job as he plots his next moves. Both brothers understand that traditional royal duties—cutting ribbons, launching ships, supporting grandmum by keeping mum—may not be enough to sustain popularity or their own sanity. Today's Royal Heartthrob is potentially tomorrow's hapless royal headache. Their father has carved out another option, but after watching His Royal Humanitarian struggle with his critics and his own self-doubt, the boys are seeking a third way.

In this they are also guided by their mother's example, both in terms of what they would hope to achieve and the remorseless attention they are determined to escape. They were too young when she died to grasp the true dynamics of their parents' relationship, the dysfunction each brought to the marriage, or the ways in which its collapse played out in private and in the media. She has been dead for more than seventeen years, but her influence still pervades every corner of royal life.

CHAPTER 4

The Knave of Hearts

//

T HEY ARE BOTH NATURALS; THEY HAVE RHYTHM, POSTURE, NEAT footwork. He mastered the moves at an early age—everyone in his family learns ballroom dancing and Highland reels. On the dance floor he has discovered one of the few environments where he can express himself freely. His wife studied ballet, and harbored fleeting ambitions to continue to a professional level. She's taller than her husband, even in her stocking feet, but the difference isn't jarring. Once buttery, with plump cheeks and ample décolletage, she has become, like him, spare. Her asymmetrical turquoise-colored evening gown exposes one fleshless shoulder and a jutting collarbone. As the band strikes up Stevie Wonder's paean of wonder "Isn't She Lovely?," the pair begins to whirl. Fellow guests at the Southern Cross Hotel in Melbourne stay seated, applauding the display and cheering small flourishes that see the man spin his partner like a ballerina. It's a polished performance but also a strange, strained one. The couple wrestles around the room, the sum of two graceful presences oddly graceless. There's no chemistry. Charles and Diana may be in step, but they are not in harmony.

They first danced for the cameras two years earlier, also in Australia. Then there was a spark in the marriage, and the Prince grinned as he steered Diana through arc turns. By the time of their 1985 tour, the Waleses find themselves acting out cheery story lines for their gullible audiences. Their union has already met its dynastic goal, producing an heir, William, and a spare, Harry. The Prince and Princess dote on their sons but barely tolerate each other. They live separately for much of the time. Within a year, both of them will have committed adultery. Diana believes Charles has already done so, from the outset of their marriage. This detail and other claims and counterclaims will become the subjects of countless studies: articles, books—fact, fiction, and genres in between—plus documentaries, movies, and art projects, as well as diverse legal investigations. The Internet will provide a platform for everything from solemn tribute sites to the wackiest of conspiracies. Interest gutters but always flares again.

If it seems extraordinary that a relationship severed by divorce in 1996 and more permanently by death the following year should still mean something to so many people, that is because the union intended as a symbol and guarantor of tradition became, in its unraveling, an agent of change. The nuptials had done more than provide light relief from the fractious reality of recession and a government determined to push through harsh reforms; 21.7 million Britons and as many as 850 million viewers worldwide sat glued to their sets to watch what the Archbishop of Canterbury Robert Runcie with unintended acuity termed a "fairy tale" in his address to the congregation. This was an event of significance not only to its principals and to the interlocking institutions of the establishment they represented, but to a global constituency that found in their story a unifying ideal. The failure of that ideal is still playing out.

The Prince is an activist and provocateur. His greatest ambition is to drive change, but he certainly never imagined or hoped that his first marriage would contribute toward a more skeptical society or encourage a fiercer media. These changes appall him and impact him. Diana haunts him.

So although old history, this period of his life remains active history, the prism through which much of the world perceives the Prince. He was born in 1948 but his most enduring public persona emerged during his mother's "annus horribilis," 1992, with the publication of Andrew Morton's portrait of Diana in June and the formal announcement of the Waleses' separation by Prime Minister John Major to the House of Commons in December.

The Prince on show today, the one closely observed for and in this book, has developed a veneer of assurance and below it the stirrings of real confidence. It is easy in the company of this Charles to accept the most firmly rooted interpretation of his first marriage: of a substantially older man who chose a child bride for dynastic rather than romantic reasons, recoiled as she cracked under the strain of public and palace life, betrayed and cold-shouldered her. Many aspects of the tale hold true, yet there is a missing piece that, once slotted into the image, subtly alters it. This doesn't excuse the pain the Prince caused Diana but it helps to make sense of what happened. Twelve years and seven months separated the couple, a gulf between their generations. But Planet Windsor operates on a different calendar to earth. In human years Diana's bridegroom was almost as unformed as she was herself, barely out of his teens.

As nicholas soames shakes with laughter, the towers of paperwork on his desk threaten to topple. The idea tickling him is that he and his childhood friend might have been more sophisticated than their contemporaries because they had the run of palaces. "We were not experienced men of the world. Absolute balls, that is. It's just so funny, all that. It's an absolutely preposterous idea. Charles was at Gordonstoun, which he hated, and I was at Eton, and we saw each other in the holidays and we lived an incredibly simple, straightforward—OK, we were very lucky—but we lived a very simple life," says Soames. "The idea that this was wonderfully glamorous. . . ."[1] When the Conservative Member of Parliament for Mid Sussex grimaces, which he does frequently during a long and discursive conversation at his Portcullis House offices, his resemblance to his maternal grandfather Winston Churchill is inescapable.

Soames has remained close to the Prince since they met as twelve-year-olds, apart from a period of exile when the Prince tried to mollify Diana by cutting ties with old friends. "I'm sixty-six tomorrow," Soames says. "I'm sixty-six years old. It's a lifetime. And for two years in the middle of that lifetime I didn't see him at all. For two years he was married to Princess Diana. He was kept under lock and key."

The slip about the length of the royal marriage—which in legal terms endured for more than fifteen years, and in public perception from wedding day to disintegration achieved a stretch of at least a decade—is revealing.

It was during the first years of the marriage that the Prince made consistent efforts to please his wife and find equilibrium within the relationship. During that period, says Soames, the Prince "was just trying desperately, in my judgement. He was desperately trying to make it work and was trying quite rightly to make every concession to make that happen."

Diana always viewed Soames as an enemy, and she had reason to do so. He was one of only a handful of friends of the Prince to question the wisdom of their engagement and to remain immune to her charm offensive. His loyalty to the Prince is boundless and a touch bromantic. "He's absolutely amazing," says Soames at one point. "I'm not just holding a candle for him. He just is." To supporters of Diana—and after all these years, the world and royal circles still divide into Diana and Charles camps—Soames's testimony is too partial to be valuable. Yet his fervor tells its own story about how the Prince has lived much of his life, surrounded by people who feel moved to fight his cause. More than that, Soames is a mirror image of Charles, the sort of person the Prince's background and breeding might have been expected to produce, hearty and largely uncomplicated. "His pleasures were those of the countryside," says Soames. "I didn't go to university; I went straight into the army; but the Prince went off to Cambridge and I should think Cambridge was a very sophisticated life for him. He wasn't sophisticated in the sense you understand it. His manners were sophisticated and he had sophisticated tastes, I suppose, but he wasn't sophisticated in the ways of the world in any sense at all."

Soames illustrates his point with an anecdote. In 1970, he became equerry to the twenty-one-year-old Prince, and the two men traveled together. "We went to the most marvelous places. We stayed with this woman. She was a very famous actress called . . . Jesus Christ!" Soames strikes his forehead. "I can't remember what her name was. I've never laughed so much in my life. We stayed in rooms in her house. She was a friend of Lord Louis [Mountbatten] and Prince Philip's. Would it be Merle Oberon? We stayed in her house and everything was electronic. You'd never seen anything like it. You pressed a button and the curtains opened. I remember thinking 'this is way above our pay grade.' It was like playing with a dodgem set."[2]

The Prince who found electric curtains exciting found pretty young women electric, though there would always be rumors about his sexual preferences, not least because dating him turned out to be a chaste experience. It was hard enough for him to meet potential girlfriends, much less "sow his wild oats and have as many affairs as he can," as Mountbatten urged the Prince in a letter to do.[3] A bleak childhood that simultaneously entrenched the idea of his social superiority and instilled a sense of deep inferiority had left Charles ill equipped for a relationship of equals. His position gave him almost no chance of learning unobserved.

Girls expecting to meet the Prince of press reports—a dashing action man, "fearless, full-of-fun Charlie" as one alliteration-loving hack dubbed him, the world's most eligible bachelor—discovered a starkly different reality.[4] As a student and later a naval officer, the Prince possessed neither freedom of spirit nor of movement. The isolation that had dogged his schooldays endured. Lucia Santa Cruz, one of few close friends forged at university—and never, she says crisply, a girlfriend, despite misleading reports—recalls that when the Prince returned from a six-month deployment in the Navy, he wrote to ask her to meet him when his ship docked. He had nobody else to welcome him home. "Everybody was being met by somebody and I felt so sorry," she says. "I was already engaged and it was quite difficult because of what the press were saying [about their relationship] but I thought, 'I can't let him down.' That was an instance of how precarious his emotional support was, really."[5]

Diaries and bleak letters written during that period chart a series of encounters more comical than romantic. At a nightclub in Acapulco, he sat rooted to his chair, summoning up the nerve to ask "a lonely-looking girl" to dance, only for her to turn him down "in a terrifying American accent."[6] According to Jonathan Dimbleby's biography, when the Prince's ship arrived in Hawaii, the royal tremulously accepted an invitation to accompany two women to their apartment only to realize that the naughtiness they had in mind consisted in persuading him to smoke a joint. His protection officers and local police waited outside. He made his excuses and left.

Back in Britain, his opportunities for meeting women were even more circumscribed. Friends, and the ever-attentive Mountbatten, tried to help out by organizing group outings and parties with potential candidates for royal romance. One of these candidates—who prefers to remain anonymous—joined the Prince in the royal box at a theater with several other young hopefuls. She and the Prince exchanged only a few words, but the next day he called and haltingly asked her out. This was an era when a first date more usually involved a trip to the cinema or a visit to a pub. Charles issued an invitation to lunch at Windsor with the Queen and Prince Andrew followed by a polo match.

Subsequent dates followed a similar pattern, hemmed in by protocols and the Prince's worries about the press. "He was very concerned about the effect the unwarranted attention would bring to me," says his former flame. "But there was no preparation, then or at any time, no advice from courtiers [regarding] travel plans and avoiding press, which was odd considering they were the enemy." Finding time in the Prince's schedule, planned to the minute months in advance, added a further layer of difficulty. Nothing could be spontaneous. Dinner parties were staid affairs. "People would be having fun, relaxing, smoking out of the windows, but then before he arrived they'd stub out cigarettes and stand to attention." Guests, including this girlfriend—by now accorded that label by Prince and press—addressed him as "Sir," bowing or curtsying as he entered the room. She once thwacked her forehead on the princely chin, bending the knee as he leaned forward to kiss her. She doubts he was aiming for her mouth. Throughout the not inconsiderable time as his official squeeze, they rarely kissed on the lips, much less spent a night together.

THE DISTORTING CULTURE OF PLANET WINDSOR MAGNIFIED THE proprieties of the time. The sort of gels deemed suitable to be royal girlfriends must also fit the bill as suitable future wives. The Prince should leave them untouched and intact. Mountbatten advised his great-nephew that a man of his standing should "choose a suitable, attractive and sweet-charactered girl before she met anyone else she might fall for. After all, [your] Mummy never seriously thought of anyone else after the Dartmouth encounter [with Prince Philip] when she was 13!" He added this helpful insight: "I think it is disturbing for women to have experiences if they have to remain on a pedestal after marriage."[6] Royal girlfriends who failed to meet these criteria quickly learned how icy the Queen and her courtiers could be.

Sexual experience was to be gained with experienced women, preferably married. Lady Dale Tryon, an Australian married to an English peer, was widely reported to be just such a paramour based on the testimony of her friends and the journalists she contacted while promoting her fashion business, Kanga. This was her nickname, devised, she let it slip, by Charles. The logistics of affairs, usually more complicated for the parties involved than premarital dating, were for the Prince a little easier to manage than his official love life. The landed gentry regularly hosted house parties and would welcome the wandering heir as an overnight guest. He was holidaying with Kanga and her husband at their lodge in Iceland when he heard the news of Mountbatten's murder.

Such relationships introduced the Prince to warmth and intimacy, but only in small portions. He never had to negotiate with his lovers, beyond figuring out plans for assignations. (An illicit recording of a telephone conversation in 1989 between the Prince and Camilla, then Mrs. Parker Bowles, contains a detailed discussion about which friends' house they might use for a meeting, the likelihood of encountering traffic on the possible route, and even which route to take.) Liaisons came with ready-made boundaries: they started from the premise that they could never be acknowledged; the demands the women might make on him were limited.

Failure to observe these rules carried risks. By the time Kanga died in November 1997, not yet fifty, she no longer belonged to the Prince's inner circle. Crippled by an unexplained fall from the window of a rehabilitation clinic called Farm Place where she had gone to try to shake an addiction to painkillers, she had later been detained under the Mental Health Act. Four months before her death from septicemia, she had spotted Charles at a polo match, attempting vainly to reach him in her wheelchair. Officials blocked her route. A source says he did not see her. He may never have done so clearly.

Only Camilla has ever been able to be fully herself around the Prince because she has nothing to hide from him. Robust and cheerful, she entered the relationship free from neuroses and, ironically, from any expectation of being his Queen. Lucia Santa Cruz brought the couple together in 1971. "My father was Ambassador in London for five years and then he came back to Chile," says Santa Cruz. "I stayed on and Camilla and I lived in the same building. She was on the ground floor, I was on the second floor. Although I'd known her before, we became very, very close because I was left on my own and she was amazingly kind and generous. We saw each other every day. I never did forget the first Christmas I was on my own: I spent it with her family. They made a pillow full of presents."

When it occurred to Santa Cruz that her friend might be a good match for the Prince, she wasn't thinking like a courtier. Camilla Shand was sixteen months older than Charles and wouldn't have passed Mountbatten's pedestal test. The Prince wasn't her first boyfriend. She had been passionately involved with one of his friends, Andrew Parker Bowles. She once donned leathers and rode a motorbike in the US. She smoked and drank and enjoyed life rather too visibly for comfort. But Santa Cruz correctly anticipated that Camilla would appeal to the Prince. "I always thought that he needed more emotional life," she says. "And I thought that Camilla was such a human, down-to-earth, warm person that she would be a very good addition to his life. I thought, 'She's someone who's going to appreciate him, in spite of his position' and that was his greatest need. To be appreciated for what he was in spite of what he represented. Anyway, he was coming for a drink or to pick me up and I said 'Can Camilla come up?'"

The rest is—mostly inaccurate—history. A media legend grew up that Camilla had walked up to the Prince on the polo field and introduced herself with brazen wit: "My great-grandmother was your great-great-grandfather's mistress, so how about it?" A similar joke was made at the first meeting, but not by Camilla. Santa Cruz presented Camilla to the Prince, "and I said 'Now you two watch your genes' because of Alice Keppel."[7]

With Camilla, the Prince would eventually develop his first—and, arguably, only—truly adult relationship combining love and passion, respect and equality, plus a sense of humor that often leaves both of them guffawing and weeping. Camilla is "rude and raunchy," says Emma Thompson, approvingly.[8]

Charles and Camilla enhance and complement each other. It seems obvious they should have stayed together and spared everyone, especially their spouses, considerable aggravation. But the Prince hadn't begun to learn to be a good partner to anyone. He had few measures against which to judge his feelings for Camilla. Still lacking in confidence, choosing her would have meant overriding his family, the Buckingham Palace apparatus, and his own belief that in doing so he risked damaging the monarchy he had been brought up to serve.

"It was out of the question for [the Prince] to marry Camilla because she was older, and there was this idea that you had to be a virgin and with no past that the press could do anything about," says Santa Cruz. "Lord

Mountbatten had been very firm about that and he had a lot of influence over Prince Charles and so [the Prince] went away to the Navy and then Camilla started seeing Andrew again and married him. Emotions are complicated and she had this kind of obsession about Andrew. The other thing was out of the question, and she thought she shouldn't keep [the Prince] in this involvement because his duty was to marry and procreate."[9]

The Prince convulsed in anguish when he heard the news, but he did nothing to intervene. Mountbatten responded to the Prince's distress by intensifying his campaign to promote his own granddaughter Amanda Knatchbull, sister of Tim, as a prospective royal bride. Those closest to the Prince have not always easily distinguished their interests from his, and Mountbatten wished to bind his dynasty, already intertwined with the Windsors through Prince Philip, yet closer to the monarchy.

Amanda Knatchbull, more than eight years Charles's junior, rejected his offer of marriage when eventually he made it. She had seen enough of his life to know what being Princess of Wales might entail. Mountbatten didn't live to see the Prince walk up the aisle with a woman who in every respect fulfilled the marital prospectus he had laid out, nor would he witness the toxic fruits of his advice.

To this day, the Prince apparently maintains the denial he issued in Jonathan Dimbleby's 1994 film about him: that he did not resume his relationship with Camilla until after the irretrievable breakdown of his relationship with Diana. This seems to him an important point—a point of honor. Despite everything that has happened, a source says he still doesn't realize that it is also semantic. Whether or not he and Camilla consummated their passion in the early years of his marriage to Diana, they never entirely relinquished it. There were, as Diana observed, three people in her marriage.

Lady Diana Spencer had accepted the Prince's proposal in the belief that she was in love with him and he with her, no matter that he publicly queried what "in love" might mean. She had scant understanding of the process that had selected her or the life that awaited her. Yet only five months after getting engaged, she already suspected her fiancé's commitment. During a joint interview broadcast on the eve of their wedding she averred that

Charles had been "a tower of strength" as she learned to deal with the unfamiliar pressure of media attention. "Gracious!" he interjected, instinctively
rejecting such undeserved praise. "I had to say that because you're sitting
there," she shot back, smiling but perhaps not joking.

Her answers also betrayed a blankness about the future. She had plotted every second of her three-minute walk down the aisle of St. Paul's Cathedral but not a single moment of her subsequent reality. "After the marriage
how do you see your role developing, Lady Diana, as Princess of Wales?"
one of the interviewers asked. "Well I very much look forward to going to
Wales and meeting everybody," she replied, stumbling over her answer. "But
my life will be a great challenge."[10]

It already was. Behind the scenes, both bride and bridegroom grappled
with swirling anxieties but separately persuaded themselves that to bolt
would prove more damaging than to continue the pageant. Curled ven-
omously amongst a pile of wedding presents and cards, Diana had discovered a bracelet bearing the initials "GF," intended for Camilla. (A piece of
jewelry for Kanga escaped her notice.) Diana already recognized in Camilla
not a potential friend but a rival. The Princess told Andrew Morton that
the initials stood for "Gladys" and "Fred," supposedly Camilla and Charles's
pet names for each other; Charles's biographer Jonathan Dimbleby reported
that the letters stood for "Girl Friday," the Prince's sobriquet for Camilla.
Both versions are plausible, the first reflecting the Prince and Camilla's
shared sense of humor, the second the Prince's reliance on Camilla.

Since Gladys and Fred first met there have been few areas of Fred's life
not susceptible to advice from Gladys. She has been his sounding board
even in matters that directly concerned her and therefore should have
excluded her counsel. He consulted her as he dithered over marriage to
Diana and then got cold feet ahead of the ceremony. He shared with her
the manifestations of Diana's distress, much of it caused by Diana's justi-
fied jealousy.

He courted Diana only briefly before the engagement, itself just five
months long. He didn't understand her at all or recognize the baggage she
carried from an upbringing as difficult in its way as his own. The more he
sensed that she was not the jolly country girl he had assumed, the more she
revealed her vulnerabilities and began to succumb to the eating disorder
that would dog her for much of the rest of her life, the more he struggled

with the prospect of marriage. Family members and most friends encouraged him to get a move on, though there were dissenting voices, including that of Nicholas Soames. On the eve of the wedding, the Prince, says a member of his inner circle, "was desperate. 'I can't go through with it. . . . I can't do it.' I always told him afterwards that if it had been a Catholic marriage, it could have been declared null. Because he wasn't really [committed], because she started with the bulimia and everything before the wedding."

THE BRITISH ROYALS AND THEIR ADVISERS BELIEVE—AND THEY'RE probably right—that their hereditary monarchy relies for its survival on the inertia of tradition. For as long as the show continues without obvious hiccups, low-key but offering occasional excitements such as weddings and births, most subjects of the Crown seem content. Ruptures spark questions. Older courtiers—and the Queen herself—shudder at the memory of the national soul-searching that attended Edward VIII's abdication to marry the American double divorcée Wallis Simpson. His face had already been printed on coronation memorabilia when he signed away his birthright on December 10, 1936. Forty-four years later the prospect of redundant souvenirs proved sufficient to persuade a fearful Diana to go through with her looming marriage. After she found the bracelet for Camilla, she contemplated calling it off. "I went upstairs, had lunch with my sisters who were there and said: 'I can't marry him, I can't do this, this is absolutely unbelievable.' They were wonderful and said: 'Well bad luck, Duch [her nickname, short for Duchess], your face is on the tea towels so you're too late to chicken out.'"[11] She had no idea her bridegroom also had to be coaxed to the altar.

So Charles and Diana took their vows, had their sons, made a stab at building a marriage and a much better job of destroying it. Defined not only by this period, but so often defined against Diana, the Prince is most frequently mistaken for a person lacking in feelings. A man who did not already know what love means might have developed a deeper affection for his fragile partner. Guilt often pushes people into behaving worse, not better. Damaged by formative years of being told to deal with his feelings by burying them, criticized for his failure to do so, the Prince sometimes meted out similar treatment to his wife, like the syndrome of an abused child who grows up to abuse.

The question of whether he ever loved her is problematic, like everything about the relationship. At the beginning of the marriage he imagined he could love her. He loved the idea of enveloping domesticity and children. He always loved the boys. Yet he was at sea when it came to dealing with his wife. When trying his hardest to respond to her obvious turmoil, he turned to the wrong people for the support he could not provide: not only to Laurens van der Post, but most startlingly to the show-business personality Jimmy Savile. But better advice—the best—could never have reconciled the Waleses. Their brief period of amity was based on the sense of a joint project done well: they reveled in the experience of pleasing Queen and country. Greater forces pulled them apart. This wasn't just the clash of two ill-suited people, beauty versus beast, or of their courts and champions, though it became all of those things. It wasn't simply that Diana discovered that her star power had grown independent of the institution that granted it. It wasn't just about a lack of common ground. Camilla shares only some of Charles's interests. In many ways—in the intensity of their emotions, their febrile passions, their desire to make an impact—Diana and Charles more closely resembled each other. Both grew up starved of affection. Both sometimes channeled their neediness into acts of great kindness, at other times gave in to self-absorption. The unbridgeable conflict was generational.

"[Diana] was the expression of a huge change in our way of relating to each other, that has happened in the last 40 years, where emotion has completely taken over reason," says Lucia Santa Cruz. "The previous generation were taught that emotions were a bad advisor, that they had to be subordinated because emotions include fear, hatred, resentment, anxiety and so forth and therefore they must be controlled. He was very much an expression of that old upbringing."[12]

There is an irony here. Much of the philosophy the Prince now advocates, explained in later chapters of this book, revolves around the conviction that too rational an approach is reductive; the spirit—and the emotions—must be equally engaged for a holistic, harmonious relationship with the world and, presumably, your spouse. "He's completely intuitive," says Tim Knatchbull. "I know very few people who are as emotionally intelligent as Prince Charles because that's all part and parcel of the spiritual intelligence of the man as well. It's not just about doing, it's about feeling. It's about intuition and it's about faith. It's about the metaphysical. It's about love. And therefore if you're in that territory it's second nature that it's about emotion as well. He's a very emotional man. And many of the most emotional people I know, if they don't choose to wear it on their sleeve all the time, they carry it around with them and it will come pouring out in other ways, in their appreciation of great art or music or ballet or whatever their outlet is."[13]

Watching Charles now, it is easy to see how close to the surface his emotions always are. He has a thin-skinned quality—veins that pulse when he's displeased, a childlike delight that sometimes breaks through. But as a young man raised in the postwar era by the most austere of parents, the Prince not only lacked the equipment to understand his young bride, he recoiled from the messiness of the emotions she so liberally splattered. She brought to their combustible pairing an upbringing at least as dysfunctional as his own, but with radically different results. His background endowed him with a homeopathic reflex, to treat like with like. If the burden of royal life is making you sick, the answer must be to take on more of the burden.

Archbishop Runcie remembered having tea with Sarah, Duchess of York, "in a very lofty corner of Buckingham Palace" during her breakup with Prince Andrew. "She'd just come back from some public engagement, and was trying to live in that echoing place, and I felt sympathy for her. . . . And she said, 'I just can't take the stiff upper lip syndrome. And the you-are-never-ill syndrome. And that's what got Diana."[14]

IF THE PRINCESS HAD SWERVED AT THE ALTAR OR IF HER FIANCÉ'S fevered eve-of-marriage misgivings had led him to break off the engagement, the monarchy would doubtless have faced an immediate backlash. Instead, it would be the disintegration of the ill-matched, ill-considered union that posed the most serious threat to the monarchy since the abdication. The annus horribilis, 1992, saw Princess Anne divorce her first husband, Captain Mark Phillips, and Prince Andrew separate from the ebullient Sarah. The siblings' failed marriages, though far from demographically unusual as UK divorce rates spiraled, undermined one of the key symbolic functions of monarchy: to present to its subjects an idealized view of themselves, happy and glorious.

Diana understood that transaction as she understood the implications of destroying the illusion. She was many things, but she was never, ever dumb, though she at least once described herself as "thick as a plank."[15] She could read people including her husband as he could not read her, and she could seduce almost anyone if she set her mind to it, male or female. Charles never entirely succumbed. The legacy of that rare failure and the ensuing battle for public sympathy endures in a global fan base that stoutly leaps to Diana's defense and a global media that still sometimes fights her corner, even if an increasing proportion of her army barely remembers her.

During the last decade of the twentieth century, the Waleses' conflict polarized Fleet Street and spilled across TV screens and bookshelves. That there was public appetite for royal gossip had been clear since the publication in 1950 of *The Little Princesses*, an account by a former governess to the Queen and her sister, Margaret, of their childhood. It became a bestseller, earning its author, Marion "Crawfie" Crawford, a fair whack of money and a painful estrangement from her erstwhile charges. Her revelations, by today's standards, were a tame brew. The thirteen-year-old Princess Elizabeth seems much taken on a visit to the Royal Naval College in Dartmouth by an eighteen-year-old cadet, Prince Philip of Greece, a "fair-haired boy, rather like a Viking, with a sharp face and piercing blue eyes . . . good-looking though rather offhand in his manner." At the tennis courts, the boy "showed off a good deal, but the little girls were much impressed," recounted Crawfie. "Lilibet said, 'How good he is, Crawfie. How high he can jump.' "[16]

This sort of stuff was grist for satirists who continued chipping away at the edges of monarchical reverence and never succumbed to the self-censorship that gripped newsrooms for the first half of Elizabeth II's reign. In 1963 the comedy series *That Was The Week That Was* ran a sketch sending up the commentaries of Richard Dimbleby, father of Jonathan. He was the BBC's first war correspondent and went on to front coverage of the Queen's coronation and other big moments in royal life. In the sketch, the royal barge sinks, pitching the Queen into the water. "The Queen, smiling radiantly, is swimming for dear life," says a Dimbleby soundalike. "Her Majesty is wearing a silk ensemble in canary yellow."

The latex Windsors created by the television show *Spitting Image* in 1984 depicted the royals as both stupid and venal, abusing commoners, each other, and every vowel. "Charles" is distinguished by hydraulically controlled ears and a compulsion to cavil about "monstrous carbuncles," the term his real-life original used to torpedo a planned extension to the National Gallery. *Spitting Image* also conceived its own version of the Changing of the Guard ceremony, "that most glorious of royal traditions, steeped in history, the Changing of the Wives." "Of course it looks so easy but to make it all possible, there's actually been a lot of hard work and precision planning," the announcer intones. "By Camilla." Diana might well have chortled at that scene. According to the actor and writer Stephen Fry, who knew her and remains close to Charles, the Princess confided that she was a regular viewer of *Spitting Image*. Her in-laws hated it, she told Fry. "I absolutely adore it."[17]

Before Morton, newspapers assumed, probably correctly, that their readers would not thank them for this sort of lèse-majesté. Columnists might sometimes question the cost of the monarchy and turn a skeptical eye on the Prince's advocacy for the environment or against carbuncles, but many editors chose to downplay the gathering omens of the Waleses' marital implosion. Executives at Rupert Murdoch's News International group decided to mothball one of the biggest potential scoops they had ever received. A retired bank manager called Cyril Reenan, whose hobby involved using a scanner to listen in on radio communications, approached the *Sun* newspaper in 1990, with a tape of a telephone conversation he had tuned into the previous New Year's Eve. The woman on the tape sounded just like Diana, and *Sun* reporters would identify the man who crooned "I love you, love you, love you" and called her "Squidgy" as an upper-crust businessman named James Gilbey. After discussions at News International, the tape—which would later become known as "Squidgygate"—was locked in a safe.

"It just didn't seem right or proper to carry it," recalled Andrew Knight, at the time Chairman of the company. "The feeling of myself, and I'd always been a royalist and remain one, and also of Rupert Murdoch, was simply that these stories were too explosive to carry. The irony is that by the time these events started coming out, Mr. Murdoch had come to the belief that the royal family, although it was the pinnacle of a system of snobbery that he didn't relish, nevertheless on balance was a good thing and he was reluctant to see it undermined. . . . He knew that Middle Britain, the sort of stalwart core of Britain, is pro-royalist and it wasn't his job to undermine it."[18]

It took another two years until Murdoch changed his mind and greenlit the Morton serialization. In the meanwhile, Reenan's wasn't the only tape in circulation. Two or three more copies of the same conversation did the rounds while the *Daily Mirror* laid hands on a counterpart recording, inevitably dubbed "Camillagate." This was the late-night conversation in which Charles and Camilla planned their next assignation and chatted with an intimacy that was not only sexual but emotional.

The War of the Waleses blurred the definition of public interest journalism. Nobody would doubt the prurient fascination of hearing the Princess comparing herself to a soap opera character who gets pregnant by a man who is not her husband[19] or the Prince, combining his trademarks of humor and self-pity into one unfortunate, unforgettable image, that sees him transformed into a tampon in his attempt to maintain sexual contact with his mistress. "My luck to be chucked down the lavatory and go on and on, forever swirling round on the top, never going down," he said.[20] This was certainly stuff that interested the public, but didn't necessarily qualify as public-interest journalism. Public figures are entitled to private lives, however messy. After Morton's book destroyed the compact between the British press and the palace, editors would argue that publication of Squidgygate and Camillagate served the public interest in a more profound way, as defined by their recently established regulatory body, the Press Complaints Commission (PCC): "Preventing the public from being misled by an action or statement of an individual or organization." The establishment had tried to cover up the sham at its heart. The 1993 Calcutt report, a review into the effectiveness of the PCC, unwittingly upheld a lie—"that rumors linking the Princess and her friends with involvement in leaking information to the press were baseless."[21]

The palace hadn't told journalists the truth about the Waleses, and not just because the truth represented a danger to the monarchy. Officials didn't always know what the Waleses were up to and when they did, they sought to draw the line at commenting on matters that crossed the line into the private domain. They were used to being helped in this endeavor by their charges, who had historically approached most interactions with the media with all the enthusiasm of vampires invited to dip carrot batons in aioli.

The Princess was a different proposition, an instinctive media player who could "sense a camera at a thousand yards," as Gilbey said admiringly.[22] About a year after the publication of Morton's book, Charles's biographer Anthony Holden received a mysterious phone call. It came, he says, "from a mutual friend who told me to be at the restaurant San Lorenzo at Knightsbridge circa 12:40 p.m." Holden had written a cover story on Diana for *Vanity Fair* and she had decided to show her appreciation. She "swept in" with her sons, pretended surprise, and then invited Holden to join them. Holden remembers, "I thought A) this is wonderful and B) Prince Charles has never thanked me for anything." Several more lunches followed and then a one-on-one interview "once the divorce and the [settlement of] £17 million was safely in the bank."[23]

She played innocent when the Morton biography first appeared. Dickie Arbiter, Royal Press Secretary at the time, at first accepted Diana's assurances that she had no involvement with the tell-all. "I said to Diana, 'I want you to look me straight in the eye. What do you know about Andrew Morton's book?' And she did look me straight in the eye and she said 'I don't know anything,'" he remembered.[24] Patrick Jephson, the Princess's Private Secretary, resigned after she bypassed him to secretly film her *Panorama* interview, later remarking, "I always thought that Diana did her best talking when she kept her mouth shut."[25] Many in the royal households, including the Queen herself, harbor similar sentiments about the Prince and despaired as he let himself be drawn into fighting the Princess on her terms.

Two years before the Morton bombshell, the Prince invited Jonathan Dimbleby to Highgrove. Dimbleby had established a reputation for hard-hitting foreign affairs journalism. He found the Prince "just outside in the garden on the patio. He was wearing a white suit and looking fresh and crisp and he was alone and we shook hands in the slightly limp way that royals shake hands and he said 'I hope you don't mind being out here' and I was looking at this beautiful environment and I said 'Well I think I can bear it.' He laughed and that broke the ice and of course I'd taken an interest in what he'd done already and I was attuned and sympathetic to quite a lot of it so we sat down," says Dimbleby. "He said 'What's this idea to make a film?' He affected that it was something that was going to come from me as opposed to coming obviously . . . [from the Prince's aides]. In reality they had said to themselves 'We need to do something' I presume."[26]

The ostensible peg for the film would be the twenty-fifth anniversary in 1994 of Charles's investiture as Prince of Wales; the real spur was the Prince's PR problem. He could certainly draw attention to issues, but not, as his wife did, primarily by letting images speak. Charles's loud forays into issues such as architecture and the environment galvanized debate but also drew scathing commentary and fed ready-made material to stand-ups. The Prince hoped Dimbleby would set out his stall as a serious public figure, counter some of the negative publicity he reaped, and perhaps wrest some of the limelight back from his wife. As the conversation with Dimbleby continued, the Prince said, "I suppose you'll want to write a book as well, will you?"[27]

The Prince granted access to his private correspondence and diaries, facilitated meetings with his friends and family, and eventually read and annotated Dimbleby's manuscript. He provided lengthy interviews and allowed Dimbleby to observe him at close quarters.

The twin-track studies provided the clearest picture yet of Dimbleby's conflicted protagonist. Yet appearing after Morton's *Diana: Her True Story* had painted the Prince as a cold fish whose cheating drove the Princess to an eating disorder and suicide attempts, Dimbleby's project inevitably became the vehicle for the Prince's riposte. "I was very anxious for it not to be a sort of arms race, because the other book was actually such a real frustration to me. . . . I knew there were issues about 'was he faithful, wasn't he unfaithful?' and I had to deal with that," says Dimbleby. He felt he must probe the marriage or see "the whole rest of the film overwhelmed by the fact that I hadn't," but he started gently.[28] "Were you, did you try to be faithful and honorable to your wife when you took on the vow of marriage?"

"Yes, absolutely," said the Prince. "And were you?" Dimbleby persisted. "Yes," the Prince repeated, "until it became irretrievably broken down, us both having tried."[29] The exchange confirmed there had indeed been three people in the Waleses' marriage and raised questions that still rumble about the Prince's fitness to be a figurehead for the Church of England.

Dimbleby had begun to wonder if Diana might suffer from an underlying psychological condition because of problems she had acknowledged and the testimony of people who knew her (but not, he insists, of Charles himself), but in the end the biographer chose not to speculate. "I was curious enough to test the proposition that she might have been suffering from one or another form of personality disorder," he explains. "However, I came to the conclusion that it would be wrong to publish such a sensational conclusion: too speculative and certain to cause distress to all closely involved, not least to my subject."[30]

Another author, Penny Junor, was one of the first journalists to go into print with the speculative diagnosis that Diana suffered from Borderline Personality Disorder. Junor also published the first detailed response to the Morton revelations, in *Today* newspaper, entitled "CHARLES: HIS TRUE STORY."

The newspaper attributed the rebuttal to friends of the Prince. "All sorts of people, self-appointed members of his party, attempted to hit back," recalls Richard Chartres. "But I don't think he inspired all that."[31] Other members of Charles's inner circle say that he explicitly asked that they not get embroiled in a briefing war. Hostilities ensued on both sides anyway. Nicholas Soames, by this stage Minister for the Armed Forces, gave an interview on the BBC after the broadcaster had screened Diana's *Panorama* confessional, suggesting that the Princess was in the "advanced stages of paranoia." She had certainly been right about the Prince's undimmed love for Camilla. "Well, there were three of us in this marriage, so it was a bit crowded," she told Martin Bashir.[32]

These days the irrepressible Soames proves circumspect about the Princess and her state of mind. He says only that the failure of the marriage was "one of nature's great tragedies," adding, "Of course the press loved the fairy tale going wrong, the wicked man and another woman."[33]

As THE MARRIAGE DISINTEGRATED, PALACE AIDES AND THE PRINCE himself began to realize the dangers of Diana unleashed, to the monarchy but especially to the Prince's brand and the charitable empire he had painstakingly built. Diana did the traditional royal thing—the wordless symbolism—better than her husband ever could, and with a dimension the otherwise spotless Queen certainly never brought to the job. The Princess radiated empathy, or at least appeared to, and the sense that she was herself a victim deepened this aura. The Prince, for all he has endured hardships, is least attractive when he lets his own victimhood show, nor is he a type that photographs well sitting at a hospital bedside or stroking a hand.

The Princess won every test of strength too. When the Prince sent Mother Teresa flowers for her birthday, Diana caught a flight to Rome to visit her in person. Diana responded to rumors of her instability with displays of defiance. "Ladies and gentlemen, you are very lucky to have your patron here today," she told an audience at an event for the charity Well-being of Women. "I am supposed to have my head down the loo for most of the day. I am supposed to be dragged off the minute I leave here by men in white coats. If it is all right with you, I thought I would postpone my nervous breakdown to a more appropriate moment."[34] She warned the royals via *Panorama* that they shouldn't underestimate her. "She won't go quietly, that's the problem."[35]

As she grew stronger, Charles declined. Those close to the Prince were alarmed. His emotions cycled rapidly; his mistrust and isolation increased, "the slough of despond somehow mixed up with the 'people are out to get me' bug," says an insider. "I've seen him kicking paving stones in the belief that they jumped up and hit him." The Prince felt under pressure from all directions—Diana, his parents, the press. Some in his retinue, far from helping him to regain perspective, played politics for their own advantage, says the source.

His friends did their best to buoy him. Emma Thompson wasn't yet a household name when she got to know the Prince—they met through her then husband Kenneth Branagh when the Prince became a patron of Branagh's Renaissance Theatre Company. She would send Charles entertaining bulletins about the "theatrical adventures [of the Renaissance Theatre Company]. I thought he's patron of so many things, I wonder what kind of feedback he gets," says Thompson. She became aware of his misery and isolation as the marriage disintegrated. "The Diana business was so difficult for both of them, so much expected and sort of arranged, so tremendously difficult," she says. The Prince would be so downcast that "I would get periodic messages from the boys that look after him at Highgrove saying 'You couldn't drop him a note because he's a bit low in the water' so I'd pick up my pen and write as funny a letter as I could think of."[36]

He came away from the marriage with his reputation disfigured, his girlfriend vilified, his relationship with his sons bruised, his claim to the throne apparently weakened. Diana emerged a global icon in her glowing prime. To those who didn't know the realities of her difficult existence—the constant press attention, the anguish at frequent separations from her sons, the obstacles to finding a new partner, and her own unresolved turbulences—her future looked bright. Financially she was sitting pretty too, entitled to the use of Kensington Palace and given a reported settlement of £17 million ($27.3 million).

The divorce provided a tantalizing peek into the Prince's finances. Geoffrey Bignell, an adviser to the Prince, claimed Diana's lump sum required the liquidation of "everything, all his investments, so that [the Prince] could give her the cash. He was very unhappy about that. . . . She took him to the cleaners."[37] Palace sources dispute the idea that the settlement left the Prince strapped and say that he would never have been in danger of real penury anyway, thanks to his mother's considerable wealth and his income from the Duchy of Cornwall.

The balance of public opinion at the time of the divorce, and most likely now, was that Diana deserved every penny she got. If the Prince hoped the split represented the possibility of a fresh start—and an end to the war of the Waleses—he was quickly disappointed. Editorials attacked him and his mother for their supposedly mean-spirited decision to "strip" Diana of the style "Her Royal Highness," though the proposal emanated from Diana herself. As a plain Princess, the newly single Diana immediately cut back her charitable patronages from over one hundred to six and adopted a new cause, lobbying on behalf of the Red Cross for a global land-mine treaty. In so doing, she strayed beyond the skull-and-crossbones signs demarcating territory the Prince believed he had claimed for himself. Suddenly she appeared to be repositioning herself as an activist, and one at least as effective as the Prince, possibly more so.

Her January 1997 trip to Angola attracted the sort of criticism that until then had also been his sole privilege. A junior British defense minister, Earl Howe, described her trip as "ill advised . . . not helpful or realistic." "We do not need a loose cannon like her," he said.[38] She had landed in Luanda accompanied by a disoriented pack of royal reporters used to the sort of trips the Windsors usually take, preplanned to the finest detail, recce'd to the max. Instead they found themselves trailing the Princess to the desolation of Huambo, a town ripped apart by conflict, and thence to the yet riskier Cuito Cuanavale, where, in body armor and a visor—photogenic, but little protection against a blast—she twice picked her way through a minefield, in an area that had been at the center of a six-month battle during the country's civil war. At the battle's conclusion, both sides claimed victory. In the ongoing war of the Waleses, she seemed to have gained the upper hand.

In December of the same year, the United Nations General Assembly adopted the Ottawa Treaty, banning the use, production, stockpiling, and transfer of antipersonnel mines. Diana did not live to witness a triumph that she had helped to secure. Her death in the Paris car crash, and the Queen's muted reaction, deepened the crisis around the throne. Some conspiracy theorists blamed land-mine manufacturers or the Windsors—or an unholy alliance of the two. Others preferred to blame secret cults or giant lizards. The Prince, seized not only by grief but guilt about his failure as a husband, blamed himself. He focused on his sons' obvious needs, worrying about their loss and never acknowledging his own.

That the accident freed the Prince from daily competition and conflict and removed the most obvious obstacle to his eventual marriage to Camilla intensified his discomfort. He appears to be sensitive to accusations that he benefitted from Diana's death, perhaps not least because on some level he may fear that they are true. After the convulsive sorrow of her funeral and the scrappy years that followed, the royal scandals and inquests, the Prince has arrived on what Nicholas Soames calls "the broad sunlit uplands. . . . He's a happy man now, Prince Charles. He's got a rhythm to his life. He's content."[39]

Would the Prince have reached this equilibrium if Diana still lived? The question is unanswerable, but there's one factor that would certainly have played into any alternative outcome. The media rarely treats older women kindly and would likely have shredded a Princess past her tabloid prime. Instead Diana remains a presence, a threat too diffuse and gauzy to combat easily. She has come to represent the limitations of an old, crusty institution that seemingly couldn't cope with her modernity, an unlikely champion for the republican cause. She has mutated into a symbol of female empowerment, the docile child bride transformed into a broad-shouldered amazon eternally striding through minefields. Another incarnation conflates her with Mother Teresa, who died just five days after the Princess, on September 5, 1997, and was beatified in 2003.

Dealing with his ex-wife would never have been easy for the Prince; combating an immaculate wraith is impossible. This Diana will never fade, never go quietly.

CHAPTER 5

Wolf Hall

//

THE COURT OF THE HEIR TO THE THRONE CRACKLES WITH TENSION. His strengths and fallibilities result in creative but combustible constellations. Avid for knowledge and always insecure about how much he already knows, the Prince is strangely unguarded as he hoovers up ideas, from books and articles and programs he hears on the radio and most often from the people he meets. In a room heaving with guests, he'll suddenly freeze like a truffle hound scenting a delicious possibility. He co-opts new advisers on slight acquaintance because they talk a good talk or come recommended by one of his established sages. (Others might term members of his kitchen cabinet "gurus," but this word has uncomfortable resonances for someone so often mocked as a hippy.)

Charles hasn't always chosen his sages wisely. Fame, and especially his brand of relentless, lifelong fame, muddies signals. It's hard to know whom to trust; soft soap is always in greater abundance than gritty truth telling. That factor, combined with his native insecurity, means he doesn't always believe he's earned the praise that comes his way, while criticism has the power to cast him into despair. Like many in the public eye, he is shaped by celebrity, resentful of press intrusion yet also dependent on the external validation it provides. Diana suffered from this syndrome more acutely than he; Camilla appears unusually resistant to it.

Some advisers arrive at his court already household names or prominent in their fields. Elites gravitate toward each other because they imagine they have less to fear from each other. Ad hoc consultants cohabit uneasily with Charles's paid employees. Turf battles between these classes and especially within the ranks of those who call him "the Boss" are common and bloody. Life at court and its offshoots can be every bit as brutal as in the days when a twitching arras might signal a hidden assassin. One former householder refers to Clarence House as "Wolf Hall," in reference to the treacherous and opportunistic world depicted by Hilary Mantel in her fictionalized account of the rise of Thomas Cromwell under Henry VIII.

Such impulses are intensified by the Prince's habit of expanding his aides' jurisdictions. Apart from his time in the Navy, he has never held a paying job and doesn't understand the anxiety such moves can create; no student of management theory, he believes rivalries promote better performance, rather than recognizing the glitches and strains that territorial disputes can cause.

His mother's courtiers tried to rein Charles in during his youth as he struggled to build the Prince's Trust. He won't let that happen now. "What he really doesn't like people doing is fobbing him off. He'll just ask five other people," says Andrew Wright. He adds: "The Prince likes getting three or four opinions on a subject, so you know he isn't just going to come to you and say 'What about this?' so that's reality and you may as well enjoy it. Which most people do. It's an extraordinary but stimulating environment."[1]

Wright appears to relish his job in its infinite variety. Appointed as Treasurer to the Prince and director of his charitable foundation, the chartered accountant and former senior banker unexpectedly found himself also immersed in the Prince's Romanian interests. But some others within Charles's court feel oppressed by their changing job descriptions or threatened as colleagues are instructed to undertake work on turf they consider their own. Moreover, efforts to rationalize and restructure the Prince's charities, to future-proof them against a time when Charles can no longer do as much to sustain them because he has ascended to the throne or some other place, have been triggering bouts of infighting for years. One casualty was a plan to bring all the charities and initiatives under one roof in London's King's Cross redevelopment area, creating cost efficiencies and also higher awareness and better branding. Sources say internal conflicts scuppered the scheme after tens of millions of pounds had been spent, wasting money instead of saving it.

Changes to the charities and Clarence House reporting lines have been running in tandem—and not infrequently at cross-purposes—with Buckingham Palace's drive to accommodate the Queen's slowing pace and the eventual transition to a new head of state. When the "big house," as Clarence House insiders call Buckingham Palace, embarked on reintegrating the devolved royal press operations under Sally Osman, originally hired in April 2013 to head up the Prince's communications team, their efforts encountered unexpected resistance. Charles is increasingly looking for ways to build his activities into the head of state role rather than tapering them off as the big house envisages. His independence, asserted over many years, is also not something he will readily cede, a sentiment echoed at Kensington Palace, where the young Princes are unfurling their wings.

The culture of each court reflects its principals: Buckingham Palace is measured and stately; Kensington Palace is more relaxed in outlook, a little hipper but also inclined to make beginner's errors. The Clarence House and St. James's Palace complex is passionate, stocked with aides who, like the Boss, are more likely to attract censure for caring too much than caring too little. "New people would come into the office and I would say to them: 'Number one, you're going to work harder than you've ever worked in your life.' They'll say 'I've always worked hard' and I'd say 'No you haven't. You absolutely haven't.' Three weeks later they turn up—'I'm so exhausted'—and I'll say 'I did tell you,'" says Elizabeth Buchanan, the Prince's former Private Secretary. "In the ten years I worked for him, I would probably count ten weekends when I didn't have conversations with him on the weekend. . . . He's trying to save the world, dammit! If you can't stand the heat, get out of the kitchen."[2]

Organizational weaknesses in that kitchen sometimes impel Charles's charities and initiatives to retrench or embark on more thoroughgoing reinventions including name changes and mergers. So prolific is his brand of philanthropy that nobody at Clarence House can say how many charities he has founded over the years, though the count certainly stands at well over twenty-five.

*   *   *

CHARLES'S IDEAS-FIRST, FEASIBILITY-SECOND APPROACH HAS NEVER been checked by the realities that impact ordinary start-ups. As soon as he is seized by a notion, he asks several different people to begin work on realizing his vision. His position and resources mean that his brainchildren have a better chance of entering the world than if they were conceived by a commoner, and have sometimes been kept alive when other operations would falter and die.

Yet the glaring systemic weaknesses of the court also make the achievements of the Prince and his courtiers all the more astonishing. The court has become the headquarters of an umbrella organization fostering established charities and start-ups, initiatives and events, and that's in addition to the daily grind of more traditional royal work. One reason it is able to do this is because its de facto chief executive is passionate and driven and instills these impulses in his staff. Courtiers may not always wish the best for each other, but they are dedicated to the Prince.

He is largely unaware of the machinations of internal politics and when complaints are brought to his attention, he is sometimes apt to penalize the complainant. Suspicious of the world at large, he values individuals who seem to him to have proved their loyalty and takes criticism of those individuals not as a sign that he should reassess that faith but as a reason to redouble it.

Michael Fawcett is a conspicuous beneficiary of this tendency. He ascended through the ranks from being a Buckingham Palace footman to serve as the Prince's valet. He resigned amid allegations of bullying, only to be reinstated and named the Prince's Personal Consultant in recognition of his trusted position. In November 2002, Fawcett came under a different kind of pressure in the wake of an aborted trial. Diana's former butler Paul Burrell had been charged with stealing items of her property. Burrell pleaded not guilty, forcing the courts of Charles and his mother to divulge at least some of their secrets to a court of law, which they did, with great reluctance, until *Regina v. Burrell* came to a skidding halt. Regina—the Queen—recalled that Burrell told her he had taken some of Diana's papers into safekeeping. Less than five weeks later, the Crown abandoned a parallel trial against another former royal butler, Harold Brown, accused of

Uneasy lies the head: Charles glimpses the future at the Queen's coronation, 1953.

The Beatles era, Windsor-style, 1968. Left to right: Philip, Andrew, Charles, Elizabeth, Edward, Anne, and a corgi.

In command but not master of his fate: Charles on the bridge of the minesweeper HMS *Bronington* in 1976.

No longer in play: Charles talks to Camilla at a 1975 polo match. She had married Andrew Parker Bowles two years earlier.

A fairytale unfolds: Charles and Diana kiss for a rapt public on their wedding day, July 29, 1981. Both suspected their relationship might not endure.

Unhappier family: The couple doted on their children, but by 1986 the union was failing.

Not single spies but in battalions: the Waleses in March 1992 after news that Diana's father had died. The annus horribilis would end with the announcement of their separation.

Happier family: The Queen follows newly married Charles and Camilla after their blessing at St. George's Chapel, Windsor Castle. The logistics of the 2005 wedding proved tricky.

Peace and reconciliation: An unofficial theme of Charles and Camilla's life together, it was also the official theme of their 2014 visit to Colombia.

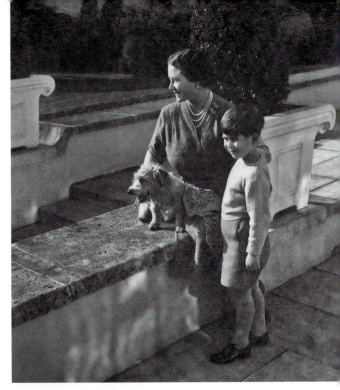

Enduring influence: Prince Charles with the Queen Mother at the Royal Lodge, Windsor, in 1954.

Father figure: His great-uncle Louis Mountbatten, here with Charles in 1970, gave copious advice, good and bad.

Altar ego: Nicholas Soames, friend of Charles since boyhood, serves as his Equerry in Bermuda in 1970. Soames later raised concerns about the marriage to Diana.

Close friend, not girlfriend: Lucia Santa Cruz leaves a London theater with Charles in 1970.

His not-so-humble servant: Michael Fawcett, then Charles's valet, keeps the dogs on the leash during a 1990 shoot on the Sandringham estate.

"Better than sex": Emma Thompson's joke to *Time* magazine about the pleasure of dancing with her longtime friend Charles made global headlines in 2013.

Soundings: In 1985 Charles speaks with Michael Elliott, left, and Mark Malloch Brown, both from less rarified backgrounds than some of their colleagues at *The Economist*.

A different kind of estate: touring an inner-London housing project in 2001.

Three in the marriage: In 2012 Charles and Camilla play host to the Dalai Lama.

Blood on the dance floor: Charles's participation in a sword dance in Saudi Arabia in 2014 provoked cutting criticism.

Fleet of foot: Charles showcases British talent during his 2014 trip to Mexico.

The heart is wherever the home is: Charles and Camilla at Llwynywermod in 2009.

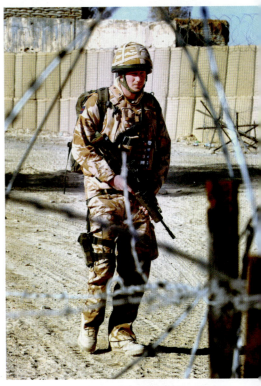

The heir: William at the controls of a
Sea King helicopter, 2011.

The spare: Harry serving in
Afghanistan in 2008.

Two families, four generations: Kate holds George at his 2013 christening, surrounded,
clockwise, by the Queen, Philip, Charles, Camilla, Harry, Pippa Middleton, James
Middleton, Carole and Michael Middleton, and William.

selling official gifts. (Like official residences, such gifts belong to the state, not to the royals.) Brown, too, rejected the charges.

The police investigations had taken evidence from Diana's eldest sister, Lady Sarah McCorquodale, about a missing microtape, allegedly recorded by Diana and containing a rape claim by a valet called George Smith against another member of Charles's household. Smith—a Falklands veteran who suffered from post-traumatic stress syndrome—had left the Prince's employ with a $48,000 settlement and assistance with medical bills including residential treatment for alcoholism. He would die, aged just forty-four, in 2005. Journalists looking for further signs of dysfunction in Charles's court focused on the disposal of his gifts, quickly discovering that the aide they dubbed "Fawcett the Fence" oversaw much of the process.

At the request of the Prince, his then Principal Private Secretary, Michael Peat, and Edmund Lawson, a Queen's Counsel, launched an internal inquiry into these reports. The inquiry did not weigh the rape claim. They found that Fawcett and other staff had sold official gifts in the absence of explicit guidance not to do so, and that Fawcett had "infringed internal rules relating to gifts from suppliers," accepting "as a mark of gratitude" from "professional friends" both low- and high-value gifts, from Champagne and chocolates to a Tiffany watch, a Cartier alarm clock, and a Pasha pen.

But, they added, "opprobrium cannot attach to this [the selling of items or accepting of gifts] because the rules were not enforced and he [Fawcett] made no secret of such gifts. Press suspicions were understandably aroused by his involvement in the sale of gifts (which, unknown to the media, were all authorized by the Prince of Wales) and by it being widely known that he received valuable benefits from third parties." They went on to identify at least some of the reasons that resentment against Fawcett had bubbled. "His robust approach to dealing with some people combined, perhaps, with his having been promoted from a relatively junior position within the household, undoubtedly caused jealously and friction in some quarters."[3]

Though cleared and backed by the Prince, Fawcett resigned again, only to reappear in a new guise, as an independent events organizer. His first client was Charles, who promptly hired his erstwhile aide to oversee Prince William's twenty-first-birthday celebrations in June 2003. By that November, Fawcett featured at the center of less festive coverage after the

Guardian successfully appealed an injunction originally lodged to stop the *Mail on Sunday* from running a story naming him as the royal servant about whom another royal servant—presumed to be George Smith—had made unspecified allegations (unrelated to the rape allegations) concerning an anonymous senior royal.

The *Guardian* did not identify the senior royal as Charles; Peat did that, in an interview that raised more questions than it answered. "I just want to make it entirely clear," Peat said, "even though I can't refer to the specifics of the allegation, that it is totally untrue and without a shred of substance. . . . Firstly, the Prince of Wales has told me it is untrue and I believe him implicitly. Secondly, anyone who knows the Prince of Wales at all would appreciate that the allegation is totally ludicrous and, indeed, risible. And thirdly, the person who has made the allegation unfortunately has suffered from health problems and has made other, unrelated allegations which have been investigated by the police and found to be unsubstantiated."[4]

Someone of a different temperament than the Prince might have cut Fawcett adrift at this point. His refusal to do so did little to quash the fanciful speculation about the nature of the bond between the married Fawcett and the uxorious Prince. A front-page story in the *News of the World* claimed that Peat had asked Mark Bolland, the Prince's former Deputy Private Secretary, whether Charles might be bisexual. Bolland, by this stage writing a gossip column for the *News of the World*, reported that he told Peat "emphatically that the Prince was not gay or bisexual."[5] In such a context, any denials are as likely to stoke skepticism as to quell rumors, though Bolland, himself gay, later made clear that he had meant what he said. The Prince "pays a lot of attention to his appearance, but a lot of straight men are like that," Bolland told the *British Journalism Review* in 2004. "I always remember him leaving a Versace show and talking to his bodyguard about the models, and Naomi Campbell in particular. It was very much a boys' conversation. I said I felt excluded, and he said, 'but Mark, there was plenty for you to look at as well.' He's very liberal, and there isn't an ounce of homophobia in him, but there's no way he's got any tendencies in that direction."[6]

THERE HAS LONG BEEN SMOKE WITHOUT FIRE BILLOWING AROUND the Prince's sexuality. There is also a thriving gay subculture at the Windsor courts that fuels gossip and trades in it. The Queen Mother is reputed to have reprimanded two retainers holding forth outside her door: "When you two old queens have stopped nattering, this old Queen is dying for a gin." The high camp of royal life holds an allure that attracts gay men to all the royal households and in the Prince has also found an employer who identifies with people who feel themselves to be outsiders. That's not much use to anyone who is made to feel an outsider once in his employ.

In 2004, Elaine Day, a former personal assistant to Mark Bolland, alleged sex discrimination and unfair dismissal from her St. James's Palace job, producing an annotated memo to support the allegations which the tribunal later rejected. "What is wrong with everyone nowadays?" the Prince had scrawled on the margin. "Why do they all seem to think they are qualified to do things far beyond their technical capabilities? People think they can all be pop stars, high court judges, brilliant TV personalities or infinitely more competent heads of state without ever putting in the necessary work or having natural ability." He questioned "the learning culture in schools" and a "child-centered system which admits no failure."[7]

His rant drew wide coverage, not least because it mirrored charges frequently leveled at the Prince himself: that he imagines himself qualified to pronounce on issues that should properly be left to experts or elected government. His critics challenge his right to intervene and his abilities to do so meaningfully. The invective also seemed to confirm that Charles believed, as Day told the tribunal, that "people can't rise above their station." The reality is more complex. A closer examination of his book *Harmony* and Charles's philosophical underpinnings reveals a belief in a natural order that is inherently conservative, but as he pointed out in a blast against Day's charge at a private Lambeth Palace seminar, he created the Prince's Trust to promote social mobility. "The idea that I think that people should not try to rise above their station is a travesty of the truth, nor indeed have I ever used any such words or anything like them," he told an audience of bishops. "For the last thirty years, I have done all I can to give young people who have limited opportunities, usually through no fault of their own, a chance to succeed."[8]

Fawcett's rise stands in mute support of this point, but his history also demonstrates the lack of the sort of formal human resources procedures in the Prince's household that might have smoothed the edges off his management style and shielded him from resentment.

More than a few people privately blame bruising experiences working for Charles—or unceremonious departures from his side—on Fawcett and others who gain the princely ear. A prominent businessman, coaxed by the Prince on the basis of a few meetings to help set up an event with his household, speaks with amazement about the glaring flaws in its organizational structure. "No company would be expected to run along these lines," he says. His impression was that aides obstructed planning in order to be able to tell the Boss of problems that they then would solve. "There was a lot of back-stabbing," says the businessman. "There are certain people who because they're pretty cunning in the dark arts but loyal and able and they're good at their timing also involve themselves in the dark arts of undermining other people," says an insider. "I think [the Prince] hasn't always been best served by this."

While Charles may not run a cohesive ship, many of the individuals aboard are properly talented. One of these, for all the criticisms lobbed against him, is Fawcett. The Prince, always liable to empathize with victims, may therefore have been more determined to protect his aide than to discipline him, but he also recognized in Fawcett a rare skill set. In 2011 the Prince made Fawcett Chief Executive of a project close to his heart, Dumfries House, "not the wisest deal that's ever been done," says an insider, who then admits, with surprise, that Fawcett seems to be doing a good job.

The former aide has a gimlet eye for detail that he brings to bear in planning functions and latterly also in overseeing the restoration of the house and grounds and working to put the estate's finances on a sustainable basis. He mixes easily with the Bond villains at fund-raising dinners but never imagines himself to be a guest. He is always watchful, always alert to potential disruptions in plans and schedules. He gets on with Camilla and she with him; she appreciates the people who help to keep her husband on an even keel. The Prince can relax around Fawcett because he trusts him completely. Slimmer and sleeker than in the days of his tabloid infamy, Fawcett has grown a beard that would sit nicely above a ruff and doublet. His power at court is undimmed.

MARK BOLLAND DIDN'T FARE QUITE SO WELL. HE HAD JOINED THE Prince's staff in 1996 and the following year earned promotion to the rank of Deputy Private Secretary. His greatest achievement in the turbulent years that followed was to start easing public acceptance of Camilla's relationship with Charles. But complaints about Bolland flowed from Buckingham Palace and in particular from aides to Princes Andrew and Edward who accused Bolland of promoting his charges at the expense of members of their household. "In the minutely-plotted world of spin and manipulation, it seems that if the Prince's stock is to rise, another's must fall," reported journalist Peter Foster in a long *Daily Telegraph* profile of Bolland that appeared to have been briefed by Bolland's enemies within the palaces. "The Earl and Countess of Wessex are not alone in believing that they have been the victim of an aggressive campaign to blacken their names."[9] The piece revealed Prince William's nickname for Bolland—Blackadder, after the Machiavellian Lord played by Rowan Atkinson in the eponymous TV comedy and later the name Bolland adopted to write his column for the *News of the World*.

When Bolland left in 2002, he did so with a freelance contract to advise the Prince, though without the honor that routinely rewards former aides for their services. This looser relationship ended, said Bolland, after Charles found he could not get hold of him to discuss a story that had blown up. "That went down very badly with him and made him think: 'Well, is Mark really there for me any more?' One had a sense that he felt a great unhappiness. I did have a peculiarly clear understanding of him at a particular moment in his life, simply because I knew Camilla so well, and I had grown to understand him through her eyes. Sometimes you end up knowing too much about people and their characters, and you lose a sense of detachment. I was starting to be used by him directly, and by him through her, as a way of second-guessing other people who worked for him. While I was there, people coped with that. When I was merely a consultant, I think it irritated them. It wasn't fair on them, and it was proving very distracting for me."[10] Insiders suggest Bolland may well have eventually returned to the inner orbits if he had not backed the *Mail on Sunday* in its decision to publish the Prince's China diaries. The Prince had always liked him.

Bolland burned bridges, but those who make it into Charles's circle of trust rarely find themselves fully exiled. More often working for the Prince is like a stay at the Hotel California: you can check out any time you like, but you can never quite leave. Elizabeth Buchanan resigned as the Prince's Private Secretary in 2008. The *Daily Mail* marked her departure with an article headlined "CAMILLA AND THE BLONDE PRIVATE SECRE-TARY WHO'S PAID THE PRICE FOR BEING TOO CLOSE TO PRINCE CHARLES." "Those who observed the icy atmosphere between the tall and imperious 'Miss Nannypenny'—as the unmarried Ms. Buchanan was known around the Prince's office—and the Duchess, always believed the private secretary would go sooner, rather than later," reported the *Mail*'s Richard Kay and Geoffrey Levy.[11] But Buchanan had not been banished. After the death of her father she faced either selling her family farm or running it herself. She chose the second option. The Prince had asked her to stay but accepted her decision and called her on the first day of her new life to check that she was in good spirits.

"I'm covered in cow dung normally," she says, sitting in the lounge of a plush London hotel near the Clarence House and St. James's Palace complex, her hair—blond as advertised—well brushed and not a trace of the farmyard about her person, her manner far from imperious. She remains deeply engaged in the Prince's work, advising on his many schemes and initiatives aimed at rural communities.[12]

He has always opened up in the company of vibrant women who refuse to recognize the cold boundaries of royal formality, even if they all duti-fully call him "Sir." Kristina Kyriacou, the Prince's communications sec-retary and one of his closest confidants, built a successful career in music management and working for Comic Relief before joining the Prince's staff. Charles recruited Kyriacou personally, politely asking her then client Gary Barlow if he would mind sharing her time.

The effervescent Julia Cleverdon held key positions in the Prince's household across three decades. For seventeen years she built up Busi-ness in the Community (BITC) as its Chief Executive, working to instill a commitment to corporate social responsibility in British companies and turning the Prince's ideas into workable programs. Cleverdon was most recently employed as the Prince's chief adviser coordinating his charities in Clarence House. That post disappeared in the restructuring, and sources suggested she had fumbled the launch of a campaign called Step Up to Serve, but she retains a role at court, still billed as Vice Presi-dent of BITC and Special Adviser to the Prince's Charities on responsible business practice. The Prince doesn't like to let anyone go if he can help it.

At the beginning of his married life, even as he began to perceive the obstacles to building any kind of stability with Diana, Charles tried not to let her go. He was hampered in his efforts by his inadequate understanding of her distress or her difficulties in adjusting to life at court. It is all he has ever known, whereas immigrants to the planet are rarely prepared for the lack of privacy or by the chill of its climate. The palaces are literally cold, and then there's the bracing culture that expects inhabitants to grit their teeth and do their duty.

In the depths of misery, the Prince could tap reservoirs of Windsor spirit in his public work. "From when he was little, he's always looked anguished, as if the weight of the world was on his shoulders," observes Emma Thompson. "He's the eldest son of the queen. It's a heavy burden and there's no question about the fact that it's deeply isolating and can be very lonely. . . . Like stardom of any kind, you are required—he is required on a daily basis and at all times—to be incredibly nice and open and warm to lots and lots of people who cannot feel themselves to be on a level with him, so he has to be even nicer so that they don't feel he's being superior. Compensating for the position is terrifically hard."[13]

In private, as his marriage festered, he could be querulous or almost catatonic with gloom. Equipped with only two entwined responses to problems—the Windsor way and the Gordonstoun way—and realizing that neither of these worked for Diana, he let himself be persuaded to seek sustenance in equally unpromising places. His mentor Laurens van der Post recommended the services of his own wife, Ingaret, "a gifted interpreter of dreams," though not a trained analyst.[14] Charles consulted her. For Diana, van der Post recommended the services of Dr. Alan McGlashan, an aged Jungian psychiatrist. After several sessions with the Princess, McGlashan concluded that she was unhappy but not unstable.

After a journalist spotted the Prince emerging from McGlashan's consulting rooms in 1995, Charles was widely reported to be in analysis. In an interview after McGlashan's death, his widow, Sasha, denied that his relationship with the Prince was professional. It had been, she said, "a supportive friendship."[15] Whatever its basis, the relationship mattered enough to Charles that he visited McGlashan regularly, and later added a bronze bust of the psychiatrist to a kind of informal shrine he has erected in the gardens at Highgrove to people he admires. (His friend Patrick Holden is also represented in the lineup; so is environmental activist Vandana Shiva.)

The Princess had long stopped seeing McGlashan but continued with therapy, formal and informal, seeking out mainstream practitioners and a fringe of alternative and complementary options, from clairvoyants to colonic irrigation. Unconvincing as some of these choices appear, none now seems so jaw-dropping as the guidance provided by Jimmy Savile, DJ, broadcaster, and now known sex offender.

Charles and Diana were by no means the only people Savile duped. He met royalty through charity work for the Royal Marines, which brought him into contact with Mountbatten. Mountbatten introduced Savile to Prince Philip and other royals. Savile described himself to his biographer, Dan Davies, as a kind of "court jester." "Royalty are surrounded by people who don't know how to deal with it. . . . I have a freshness of approach which they obviously find to their liking."[16]

Janet Cope, Savile's personal assistant for three decades, told Davies of a thick file of correspondence between Diana and Savile. That accords with Diana's casual mention of a conversation with Savile in the Squidgygate tape. "Jimmy Savile rang me up yesterday, and he said: 'I'm just ringing up, my girl, to tell you that His Nibs [Charles] has asked me to come and help out the redhead [the Duchess of York], and I'm just letting you know, so that you don't find out through her or him; and I hope it's all right by you.' "[17]

Savile's behavior during his visits to St. James's Palace had rung alarms, but nobody seems to have told Charles. In her account of palace life, Sarah Goodall, a former Lady Clerk to the Prince, describes him licking her hand. She also claims Savile provided marital advice to the Waleses. That claim was repeated in a 2014 edition of *Panorama*, the investigative TV series that had given Diana a platform for her bombshell interview nineteen years earlier. "It is ridiculous to suggest that His Royal Highness sought marital advice from Jimmy Savile," said a Clarence House statement, broadcast as part of the film. "On the few occasions Jimmy Savile visited St. James's Palace, it was as a guest of a member of the household and as such he would have been accompanied."

The statement also responded to a claim in the film that health officials were "gobsmacked" to find Savile at a Highgrove meeting convened by the Prince to protest the threatened closure of emergency services at a nearby hospital. After the meeting finished and the Prince departed, Savile allegedly warned one of the officials present that making the Prince unhappy could cost the official a knighthood. "It is possible that such a meeting took place," the Clarence House statement continued. "However, we cannot comment on any alleged threats after the Prince left the room. It is certainly not the case that he knew, sanctioned or encouraged this form of behavior by anyone."[18]

That sounds all too likely. Courtiers and advisers not infrequently do things in Charles's name that he would be unlikely to sanction or encourage. Yet the detail of the meeting also rings true. People working for the Prince are used to finding their projects disrupted by unwanted input from unlikely quarters. The Prince "is basically as distrustful as ministers are of advice from one source," says an insider. "So you have a tendency to get some pretty surprising people reading things, checking things, coming up with an alternative view, some of whom are really quite difficult."

Savile had persuaded top politicians to give him the run of several hospitals, trusting him to make policy and personnel decisions and move unchaperoned among patients. To the Prince this made Savile an obvious person to tap for advice on navigating Britain's health authorities.

But Charles also consulted Savile on other matters. One source tells of an occasion when the Prince asked his famous occasional adviser to read over a speech he was due to give on a topic unrelated to health care or any field in which Savile had expertise. Savile made no amendments on that occasion.

NOBODY—AND CERTAINLY NOT SAVILE—WOULD HAVE BEEN ABLE TO fix the Waleses' relationship. As their camps washed dirty linen in public, the House of Windsor faced its toughest test since the abdication. Only the occasional beam of daylight had caught the sovereign and her children behind the scenes. The documentary *Royal Family*, based on footage of its titular subjects shot over an entire year as Charles prepared for his investiture as Prince of Wales, enjoyed just one outing only, in 1969, attracting audiences of 23 million in Britain and a further 350 million worldwide, before the Queen demanded the film be withdrawn. The royals are seen struggling to barbecue sausages; in another scene the Queen makes awkward small talk with President Richard Nixon, who would resign in 1974, a move precipitated by revelations of conversations he assumed would stay private. Anne, the Princess Royal, summed up the family's distaste for their telly adventure: "I always thought it was a rotten idea. The attention that had been brought on one ever since one was a child, you just didn't want any more. The last thing you needed was greater access."[19]

She was right, but only up to a point. The reason that the monarchy continues to flourish while other pillars of the establishment totter is because it is rarely seen to chase popularity by yielding to popular opinion. Its unique selling point is consistency. Yet its success is also based on managing change, rather than standing against change. The institution develops in parallel with the people it claims to represent. As televisions took pride of place in British living rooms, the Windsors had to let cameras into their living rooms. The family learned from the mistake of the first documentary, quickly figuring out how to hide in plain sight, carefully controlling subsequent access and output. But the nature of that output had to change too. The greatest stumble of the Queen's reign came after Diana's death when the sovereign didn't realize her subjects had come to believe only in emotions they could see. Old-school Windsor restraint sits uneasily with the touchier-feelier, therapized, confessional spirit that found its zenith in Diana.

Charles himself remains caught uneasily between those two impulses, schooled to royal *omertà* and the product of a culture that tells him that to express emotion is to cheapen it, yet also brimming with emotions. To Nicholas Soames, this struggle appears heroic. "The other day someone was on a television show and apparently they didn't show enough emotion so there was a terrible row in the *Daily Mail*, 'They haven't shown enough empathy,' whatever the bloody hell it is, they haven't cried when they've won a competition," he says. "Well there is no point looking to the Prince of Wales to do that. He will not play that game, because he is in my view morally honest and intellectually honest."[20]

The problem for the Prince is that he did, for a while, play the game, just not enthusiastically or well. The Waleses' conflict damaged the control mechanisms and opened Walter Bagehot's dictum about preserving the mystery of monarchy to ridicule. Revelations continued to flow after Diana's death thanks to a tidal wave of official reports, inquiries, acrimonious court cases, and a roaring trade in gossip and harder-edged information.

The paradox of palaces is that they are at once thoroughfares, their carpets worn thin by visitors and retinues, and nests of secrecy and intrigue. They are the least private of homes and the most resistant to oversight. They breed plots and foment mysteries.

Neither journalistic investigations nor legal inquiries have ever finally pinpointed the source of the Squidgygate and Camillagate recordings. The tabloids' initial reticence to publish the transcripts would seem to exonerate them from involvement. The quality of the recordings, and the odds against one or more radio ham staying locked onto the signals for the duration of the calls, raised doubts that such amateurs could have picked up the transmissions unaided. Audio analysis commissioned by the *Sunday Times* found anomalies suggesting that the conversations may have been recorded and rebroadcast for Cyril Reenan and other radio enthusiasts to discover.

Meaningful motives are just as difficult to establish. Both sides in the War of the Waleses sustained damage from the release of the tapes. As for potential perpetrators, GCHQ had the capacity to tap into conversations but joined with the other intelligence services in a statement in 1993 giving "categorical assurances denying any involvement in intercepting, recording or disclosing telephone calls involving members of the Royal Family." GCHQ's former chief, Sir John Ayde, and Sir Richard Dearlove, head of MI6 until 2004, repeated these denials in person at the inquest into the deaths of Diana, her boyfriend, Dodi Fayed, and their driver, Henri Paul. Lord Fellowes, Diana's brother-in-law through marriage to her sister Jane and, at the time the recordings emerged, the Queen's Private Secretary, also testified that spies' involvement seemed "unlikely . . . they have better things to do."[21]

But Fellowes told the inquest—which ran from October 2007 to April 2008 at London's Royal Courts of Justice, at a cost to the taxpayer of $4.5

million—that the Queen routinely ordered Buckingham Palace to be swept for bugs and revealed that the tapes had triggered "discussions" with the security services. The aim, he said, was "obviously if there had been anything nefarious done, that it should be discovered and punished. But the main strand of thinking in Buckingham Palace, if I can put it broadly, was that this had happened and what action should be taken to ensure that it did not happen again."[22]

Fellowes's dry confirmation of palace fears of bugging, sensational in another context, sank in a welter of wilder claims and intimate details as 268 witnesses gave statements or took the stand. They ranged from people who happened to be on the scene of Diana's death to key figures from her life. Paul Burrell told the court on the first day of his three-day testimony that he knew his employer's "every waking thought." By day three, he rowed back. "I'm not sure I knew her better than most, but I knew her very well." Hasnat Khan, Diana's lover from 1995 until she met Dodi, provided a statement full of pathos. The Princess, like her ex-husband, observed normal life from an enforced distance. "Diana was also not used to doing everyday things that the rest of us take for granted," Khan's statement revealed. "For example, we once went to the pub together and Diana asked if she could order the drinks because she had never done so before. She really enjoyed the experience and chatted away happily to the barman."

Some familiar faces stayed absent from this parade. Neither Charles nor any blood members of his family were called to give evidence, sparing short-term embarrassment but reinforcing the sense of royal exceptionalism and an establishment quick to close the shutters. To conspiracy theorists, this appeared more significant, a sign of guilt. When Dodi Fayed died alongside the Princess, his father, Mohamed Fayed, the owner of the department store Harrods, expected to be embraced by the Windsors in shared grief. The embrace never came. The royals recoiled from Fayed, believing he had flaunted his links with Diana in life and now would turn her death into a promotional opportunity. As she traveled to Paris with the Prince to retrieve the Princess's body, Diana's sister Sarah McCorquodale asked Charles about the arrangements for transporting the coffin on arrival back in the UK. "One thing's for sure," he replied. "She's not going into London in a green carriage drawn by horses."[23] The Harrods carriage, painted in the store's green and gold livery, was often deployed to ferry celebrities to the launch of its seasonal sales.

Fayed at first blamed the paparazzi pursuing Diana and Dodi for provoking the fatal collision in the Pont de l'Alma tunnel. He came instead to imagine "that Dracula family," as he called the Windsors, had orchestrated the crash to prevent the Princess from marrying his Muslim son. At the inquest, he anatomized an elaborate plot, alleging the knowledge or active participation of the senior royals, Tony Blair, the security services, Fellowes, some of Diana's friends, former London police chiefs, the British ambassador to France, French toxicologists and medics, three of his former employees, and Henri Paul, who lost his own life in the crash.[24]

Conspiracy theories are hardy plants that flourish in the most arid of soils. The rich compost of this tragedy continues to nourish all sorts of exotic blooms. The inquest reached the same central conclusion as earlier investigations in France and Britain: that the car hit the wall of the tunnel not by design but accident, caused by Paul, driving at excessive speeds after drinking, with paparazzi in pursuit. Yet anyone entering "Diana death" in online search engines falls down a rabbit hole into a universe in which Fayed's version of events seems positively tame. In some tales the murderers hijack the Princess, forcing her into a vehicle concealed as an ambulance before doing the deed; another hypothesis sees the Mercedes, and its occupants, compacted in a crusher. A persistent meme depicts the Windsors as giant shape-shifting extraterrestrial lizards who snuffed out the Princess and continue to pose an existential threat to all surviving humanity.

Such views remain on the fringes but cloud wider opinions of Charles. There isn't an obvious way to confront this problem other than to find ways to let the public get better acquainted with the real Prince. The press operations at Buckingham Palace and Clarence House have expanded and professionalized, and stocked their ranks with talented people who have worked in mainstream news organizations, wrangled celebrity clients, or survived the white heat of government media management. There are dedicated teams assigned to the main royal brands; the Queen personally approved a slick royal website and separate feeds on social media such as Facebook, Twitter, and Flickr that seem to dovetail nicely with her mantra of being seen to be believed. Her children and their children may appear more open than she is, but apart from her eldest, they rarely talk about anything of substance. Their private lives, for the most part, remain private. Camilla, styled HRH Duchess of Cornwall on marriage to Charles, has made a smooth transition from public enemy to royal asset. Everything appears calm. Yet the royals are no closer to solving the old dilemma of how much daylight to let in or confronting the new reality: that they may not have a choice in the matter.

It's not just that confidentiality agreements have failed to deter serial former employees from "doing a Crawfie," publishing memoirs of royal service that tend to be far less gentle than Marion Crawford's sunshine-infused original. During the War of the Waleses, media organizations that played by the existing book floundered in a brash new free-for-all, read-all-about-it scrum in which not only Murdoch's *Sunday Times* but its red-top stablemates the *Sun* and the *News of the World* turned out to be the newspapers of record. Now all mainstream news organizations are trying to navigate still bigger changes. Their representatives know the rules, even if they sometimes transgress them. New media and citizen journalists—and that's everyone on Twitter—may not know that there are any rules and are as likely to take cues from Edward Snowden and Julian Assange as from dusty jurisdictions mumbling about privileged communications and the right to privacy.

Outside the palace gates, the pressure for transparency is growing. Within palace walls sits a future king whose irrepressible desire to communicate should logically herald fresh moves toward greater openness. That isn't happening. His court has grown more clenched. Yet Charles has many things to be proud of, not least his first and biggest charity.

CHAPTER 6

Helping and Hindering

//

YOU NEED TO LISTEN TO EACH OTHER. IT'S RESPECT," SAYS TEAM leader David Tovey. A girl raises her head from the table and stares at him with kohl-rimmed eyes. "I wasn't talking," she says. "I was sleeping. You lot are waking me up."

That's the central purpose of the twelve-week Team Program, the seventy-fourth run at this location, in Merton, South London, and of every program and project run by the Prince's Trust: to wake people up, then to provide them with the tools to realize their potential. Seventeen-year-old Tanya Djemal knows that, even as she puts on her small show of defiance. She is beginning to think she might harbor ambitions in the longer term to go to college, she says in a voice so small that the whirr of an overheated computer threatens to drown her out. Her acting up in front of the group masks a crippling timidity that complicates one of the tasks the Trust has set participants: to secure a three-week work placement. The Team Program is aimed at sixteen- to twenty-five-year-old NEETs—the reductive acronym denotes young people Not in Education, Employment or Training; by the end of the course, they will hopefully be moving toward college, apprenticeship, or a job. Djemal recoils from the idea of interaction with children. Her work experience must involve "food or animals," she says.

For her and the thousands of others who pass through the Prince's Trust programs in Britain every year—58,804 in 2013–2014—the placement will provide a glimpse into a world that seemed beyond reach, in which life isn't just about survival but holds the possibility of love and friendship and personal development and professional achievement. "I came to the Prince's Trust to get a brighter future and to change my past," says twenty-year-old Matt Jelinek, who spent the first half of his life in Poland and the second being bounced around the English education system and excluded from three schools. Everyone has different stories about how he or she arrived at the Prince's Trust, but all the narratives describe alienation and exclusion.

Jelinek and Djemal and their fellow participants, encouraged by Tovey to function not as competing individuals but a cooperative unit, are beginning to taste the unfamiliar sweetness of belonging. Tovey has already helped them to bond during a week at an adventure center in the Peak District. For several of their number, it was the first time they ever ventured beyond city limits. Tovey, a former advertising executive who retrained as a teacher and Prince's Trust Team Leader, laughs remembering the fascination sheep held for these children of grubby suburbia, then grows serious as he talks about a hike up the famous moorland plateau Kinder Scout and a tranquil moment with Jelinek as they stopped to admire the view. "Matt was telling me how amazing it was to get away from everything to center himself. If he gets nothing else from these 12 weeks, he's got that."

Not one among this recent intake to the Prince's Trust has linked the organization to a real live Prince. Some charities with charismatic founders resemble reverent cults, in which the founder serves as a demigod and personification of values. The Prince's Trust, by contrast, aims to imbue its alumni with a sense of their own potency—*plus est en vous*.

If clients do encounter the Prince when he visits Trust projects or holds fund-raisers or events to honor the achievements of Trust participants, they see an older man in a double-breasted suit, surprisingly easy to talk to, ready with a joke, but apparently light-years away from their own experience. They are right, of course. Yet Charles too was young once, isolated, vulnerable, and directionless. In learning to give to others, he found his direction.

* * *

LIKE MOST ORGANIZATIONS SET UP BY THE PRINCE, HIS LARGEST AND most successful charity sprang into life without a detailed plan or defined target, but from a single idea that gripped its creator. In 1972, George Pratt, the Deputy Chief Probation Officer for Inner London, defended a pilot scheme he had helped to devise under which some offenders guilty of minor crimes undertook community work instead of serving custodial sentences. The scheme proved so effective that within three years it had become a nationwide standard, but its debut attracted hostile headlines about soft options and pampered criminals.

After Charles heard Pratt interviewed on the BBC Home Service radio, he invited the probation officer to Buckingham Palace to discuss whether young people might be coaxed away from potential criminality by getting them involved in Gordonstoun-style volunteering. The Prince proposed setting up a network of community fire brigades on inner-city estates. Pratt warned him that putting fire-fighting equipment in the hands of vandals might not produce the anticipated effect. Undeterred, Charles convened a series of meetings with Pratt—who would become the Trust's first Chairman—and with social workers and a range of experts he thought might be able to refine his idea into something practicable and constructive.

Charles left active service in the Navy in 1976—the same year the Prince's Trust came into formal existence. He had commanded a ship, but back in the Palace he was expected not only to bow to the Queen—whom he has always revered—but accept directions from courtiers who treated him with condescension. He came close to giving up, but instead learned to push back. He sometimes did so with the combustive anger of a person unused to asserting himself, and sometimes still does, or more often slides into bleak moods that those close to him learn to negotiate. "He always reminds me of a day in April," says an insider. "It can be bright sunshine and then the clouds suddenly appear from nowhere and then they clear and it's bright sunshine. He's got a million things on his mind all of the time, but when the sun comes out he can have you crying laughing with him within seconds."

When officials cited security risks and canceled Charles's excursions to see at first hand inner-city hardships, he insisted that alternative visits be organized. When Buckingham Palace tried to put the brakes on his activities, the Prince forged on regardless. "I just felt what we need at that young age is somebody to take an interest and to show concern but also to give you that self-confidence and self-esteem which I do believe is absolutely critical if you're going to be able to achieve anything later," he says.[1]

Skepticism about the Trust wasn't entirely unfounded. Its first programs—including a Gordonstounian notion of training young offenders as lifeguards—were small-scale and experimental. The charity had scant resources and the Prince had not yet learned, in the words of Sir William Castell, Chairman of the Wellcome Trust since 2006 and from 1998 to 2003 of the Prince's Trust, to "pick pockets."[2] The organization's start-up funds were far from princely: its founder's Navy severance pay of $11,925, his fee of $6,500 for an interview about George III given to a US television company (the first time but not the last the Prince would argue that Mad King George was cruelly underrated), and a $3,225 donation from Harry Secombe, one of a trio of performers who starred in Charles's favorite radio comedy series, the *Goon Show*.

These days the Trust needs to raise about $1.6 million per week just to break even. About a third of its income comes from private donations, mostly at the corporate level and wealthy individual donors, many of them personally persuaded to their generosity by the Prince. As the Prince takes on additional head of state duties, the pressure on his time is increasing, and the Trust is adjusting accordingly. "It's about using his time much more effectively and more cleverly," says Martina Milburn, Chief Executive of the Trust since 2004.[3]

It will never be as easy to raise money for the benefit of the Trust's spiky clientele as for children or, in the UK, animals. Nevertheless, potential donors have become more alert to the problems of social exclusion and youth unemployment, not least since these blights manifested in noisy movements such as Occupy, pitching tents in Zuccotti Park on Wall Street or by the steps of St. Paul's Cathedral, and in less choate protests such as the riots that ignited in Tottenham, North London, in 2011. Thirty years earlier, similar alarm calls sounded among the comfortable classes as violence spread from one English inner city to another. Then, as with the more recent riots, politicians disagreed over the causes of the unrest, but nobody could assume the problem would go away of its own accord or keep to itself in the rougher parts of town, visiting misery only on those who already had little to lose.

For the nascent Trust, the trouble carried a silver lining: easier access to funds, not only from private donors but the state sector, which now accounts for about a third of the Prince's Trust income. Margaret Thatcher's Secretary of State for Employment, Lord Young, agreed to match any funding the Trust raised for its newest program, providing seed funding to young entrepreneurs. In 1988 Young's pledge delivered a delicious windfall to the Trust, when a fund-raising drive to mark the Prince's fortieth birthday succeeded in hitting its $64.5 million target and the government had to match that figure.

As the Trust grew, Charles dedicated ballooning hours to helping the charity grow further still and to building additional charities and initiatives, some conceptually related, such as the Prince's Youth Business Trust (later folded back into the Prince's Trust) and Business in the Community; others representing different strands of interest, such as the Prince of Wales's Institute of Architecture, which then went through several name changes to become his Foundation for Building Community. His Gordonstounian impulses also kept trying to find expression in programs designed to reintroduce to Britain a form of national service that would inculcate in the young the sense that by helping their communities they could also help themselves. The Prince of Wales Community Venture, tested in Sunderland, Llanelli, and Birmingham from 1986 to 1989, was its first incarnation. The Prince's Trust Volunteers, launched in 1990, eventually developed into the Team Program. Another version of this vision emerged in 2013 with the launch of the Prince's Step Up to Serve campaign to bolster youth volunteering, backed by all three of Britain's main political parties.

Always on the move, a habit he has never since broken, Charles shuttled from one meeting to another, schmoozing donations, discussing strategies, ever more focused in his desire to make a difference. His increased activity reflected a growing sense of purpose and his own power to make things happen, but also coincided with the final disintegration of a home life that had never been homely. This was no coincidence, says Julia Cleverdon. "As the marriage became more separate—like many in that situation—he became more and more of an entrepreneurial workaholic and the charitable initiatives began to multiply."[4]

Money enables, but without conviction and credibility the Trust would not have survived. The best advertisements for the Trust are its alumni. Idris Elba, who at sixteen joined the National Youth Music Theatre with a grant from the Trust, went on to star in TV shows such as *The Wire* and *Luther* and as the hero of *Mandela: Long Walk to Freedom*. Steven Frayne, better known as the magician Dynamo, got money for the laptop and video equipment that he needed to make a DVD of his stunts, *Underground Magic*, which launched his career. He has his own television series and, as he revealed to an interviewer, "I've peed in the same toilet as the Queen." A regular at the Prince's receptions at St. James's Palace on behalf of the Trust, he baffles fellow guests with sleight-of-hand illusions. "P. Diddy ain't got nothing on Prince Charles when it comes to putting on a party," he once enthused. "Charles throws the best parties."[5]

James Sommerville, since 2013 Vice President, Global Design at Coca-Cola, is another Trust success story. He cofounded the design company Attik in 1986 with a $3,200 loan, eventually selling the business to advertising giant Dentsu. "If [the Prince] was in industry he would be a [Richard] Branson or the late Steve Jobs; he'd be one of those entrepreneurs of the world who've got that great vision," says Sommerville.

The comparisons are apt. Apple's Jobs accumulated a track record as a brilliant innovator but sometimes teetered on the edge of failure when his ambitions outstripped his abilities to deliver. A similar pattern defines Virgin Group founder Branson's long career of serial entrepreneurship.

Quite a few of the people working for the Prince "can't add up," says one insider. The Prince's Trust for a long time lacked rigor. The statistics produced didn't always stand up to scrutiny; the effectiveness of programs wasn't always closely enough monitored. Tom Shebbeare was the Trust's first full-time director. Until then, the organization had been stocked by people on secondment and enthusiastic co-optees and volunteers. "He's a fantastic bloke, the Prince, absolutely fantastic bloke in a most impossible position and for me—not a mad monarchist—I found him absolutely fantastic to work for," says Tom Shebbeare, who now works for Branson, as the Chairman of Virgin Money Giving and Virgin StartUp, the Virgin Group's two nonprofit arms. "He's sometimes tremendously inspiring and lateral thinking and says 'yes' to things most people would say 'no' to. He was a great boss, great company. But," says Shebbeare, "possibly too nice."[6]

* * *

WHEN THE TEAM PROGRAM IN MERTON COMES TO AN END, PARTICI-
pants who have completed the course take part in a final ceremony, witnessed by friends and family. One by one they describe to the audience
what they've got out of their experiences and what they plan to do in the
future. That may not sound like a big deal, but two months earlier not one
of them had much of a life plan beyond getting through another day.

Matt Jelinek, who put on a boisterous front from the early days, now
seems more quietly assured, less the class clown. "Something you learn on
the course is you get back what you give," he says. "The entire program was
amazing."

Everybody looks different, calmer, confident, more upright, more open.
Tanya Djemal has undergone what may be the greatest transformation. She
has found her voice. As her mother and grandmother watch with pride and
astonishment, she stands up in front of a room full of people and begins to
speak, fluently and clearly. She got a work placement in a hair salon, and
thrived. She's heading back to college to retake her English and Math exams
and she thinks she knows what she might want to do further down the road.
She's fascinated by bats and would like to join an organization dedicated to
protecting creatures that are often misrepresented and misunderstood. It's
an ambition the founder of the Prince's Trust would surely applaud.

The model and methods that proved so effective for her and Jelinek and
thousands of other Trust alumni in Britain are being exported to other
countries and cultures. As youth unemployment has risen since the global
financial crisis, twenty governments or government-affiliated organizations
outside the UK have contacted the Trust for advice and with a view to
launching Trust programs or their own schemes. Despite the burgeoning
calls on his time, Charles insists on retaining his role in the overarching
strategy of the Trust as well as its fund-raising side. Martina Milburn—
approachable, unforced, and un-posh, like many of the Prince's preferred
people—says she's used to him "holding my feet to the fire. He will regularly say he doesn't mind how many people we help as long as the help we
give those young people is the best it can be."[7]

She has noticed—it is impossible not to—that Charles is most at ease
where he should be least at home, far from Planet Windsor and surrounded

not by courtiers or sycophants but young people, finding a welcome and a sense of kinship that eluded him in his own youth. "He has an amazing ability to talk to teenagers," says Milburn. "I've sat with him in colleges, in classrooms, in prisons, sink estates, youth clubs, you name it, he just has a connection. . . . He is genuinely interested in their lives and somehow they sense that, with that human connection. I've seen other people do it, notably politicians, and get it badly wrong because they're not really that interested, and they come to tell young people their view or the latest government policy change. The Prince does it completely the opposite way round. The Prince always asks them first. Somehow they sense he's genuine."[8]

It is more than that. The Prince sees himself in every Prince's Trust client. "My great problem in life is that I do not really know what my role in life is," he told an audience at Cambridge University when he was twenty-nine. "At the moment I do not have one, but somehow I must find one."[9] The Prince's Trust helped him, as it has continued to assist many others, to find a purpose in life.

THE RAIN STARTED OVER THE UNITED KINGDOM IN DECEMBER 2013 and for two months rarely let up. By this drear beginning of February, roads had turned into rivers, fields were lakes. Island villages, ringed by citadels of sandbags, wondered when outside help might come. Politicians, safe and warm in Westminster, appeared not to notice or care. More than five hundred miles to the north, at Birkhall, Charles watched the news reports, as he often does, and worried, as he always does, how he might help. That same evening he wrote letters to key parties and spoke to aides. On February 4, clad like the countryman he is in hunting jacket and Wellington boots, he arrived in Somerset and waded into the muddy waters of political controversy.

The Prince gave generously of his time to hear the stories of people directly impacted by the flooding. "One of the most important things is listening," he says. "You don't just have to bang on at people."[10] He brought comfort, not only of a pastoral nature but a chunk of aid, $80,500, from the Prince's Countryside Fund matched by a donation from the Duke of Westminster, one of Britain's largest landowners. So far, so stately: but then a microphone picked up a comment to a local farmer during the sort of conversation that by palace convention is deemed private. "There's nothing like a jolly good disaster to get people to start doing something," said the Prince. "The tragedy is that nothing happened for so long."[11]

A Downing Street spokesman responded swiftly: "The Prime Minister has repeatedly said that the situation that a number of communities in the Somerset area find themselves in is unacceptable." By February 7, David Cameron had pulled on his own Wellingtons to survey the "heartbreaking" damage, promising the government would "do everything that can be done" and attributing the disaster to cuts made during an earlier administration. By February 11, so many politicians had togged up in waterproofs to tour scenes of devastation that the appropriately named Jim Waterson of the website BuzzFeedUK was able to compile a photo feature entitled "21 Pictures of Politicians in Wellies Staring at Floods."[12] Along with the deluge of fresh publicity, benefits to flood victims flowed, not only an extra $226 million for flood defenses allocated in the government's March budget, but immediate help from major banks in the form of repayment holidays, extensions to loans, and reductions or waivers of fees, a commitment that totted up to $1.2 billion.

The day after his Somerset trip, suited and de-booted, the Prince returned to the ground zero of another political debate. He originally came to Tottenham in North London in August 2011 as glass still crunched underfoot and buildings still smoldered. Five people died over six nights in the riots that enveloped the borough after police shot and killed a Tottenham resident called Mark Duggan spread across the capital and to other English cities; businesses, homes, and cars were torched. In the aftermath, policy makers tussled over possible reasons for the unrest with all the determination of looters competing for a crate of designer trainers. Charles believed that the riots were a cry for help from people without hope or opportunity. He set six of his charities to work in Tottenham and continues to return to assess progress. This was his fourth visit. "He has come back," says David Lammy, the local Member of Parliament. "No other major national figure has been back as often as he has, and bringing all of his charities. That is commitment and it's an unsung commitment because it's not done with fanfare."

Lammy describes himself as a "big, big fan" of the Prince but among Westminster politicians, opinions of Charles, like attitudes to the monarchy, are divided and often deliberately obscure. There are almost certainly more republican MPs than the 15 of the Commons' 650 members who are openly signed up to the campaign group Republic, but even before approval ratings rose for the Windsors and plummeted for the political classes, republicanism looked like a potential vote loser.

The assumption among Westminster republicans echoes the wider view: the Queen is inviolable; her son and heir is not. "Some of [the Prince's] ideas are fine, some foolish, and some eccentric. But he cannot keep a lid on them. He suffers from a compulsive urge to influence government," complained Paul Flynn, one of the avowed republicans in the House of Commons.[13] John Major demurs. "He [the Prince] never in my experience overstepped the marks of propriety at all."[14] Ministers and former ministers from various eras, the recipients of the Prince's famous black spider memos, paint a more complicated picture. Charles has supporters and critics on the right and the left. In their descriptions he often emerges as political, but rarely party-political. The Prince "avoids a simplistic left-or-right characterization. He doesn't go venturing views about tax rates," says a former Cabinet minister. "The issues he's chosen—environment, conservation, inner-city renewal, youth—they're not left or right issues."

Nicholas Soames issues a stout defense of his friend's dealings with the body politic. "When I became a minister, Prince Charles did get in touch with me on official matters. He came back through Hong Kong when we still had a big military presence there and he said 'I think you ought to know . . .' and told me something and I was very, very, very grateful to be told." Soames leans back in his chair and the skulls on his braces grin a little more widely. "It's easier to see from his point of view almost than anyone else's. Because people have absolute trust and confidence in him and they talk to him. And from time to time he thinks ministers ought to know about it. Well good for him, I say. I don't know a single minister who minded."[15]

The Prince, says Emma Thompson drily, "has friends from all political persuasions." She recalls an evening spent with the Prince and Duchess during Augusto Pinochet's involuntarily extended London sojourn. (The former Chilean head of state had been arrested on an indictment issued in Spain citing multiple human rights violations under his military dictatorship.) "We were sitting at dinner, just [Charles] and Camilla and [Thompson's actor husband] Greg [Wise] and me and she was saying 'I do think you ought to lend Pinochet your plane' and there was a loud snort from HRH who looked over at me and said 'I don't think Em would approve,' knowing me to be a raving lefty."[16]

"There are two very different issues," says the former Cabinet minister, mulling the question of princely interventions. "One is a constitutional propriety issue and another is the content of his views. What I think is happening is that those who don't like the contents of his views are alleging constitutional impropriety as a way of undermining the views he holds. Secondly, those who don't like his views present them as wacky. Both the charge of impropriety and the charge of wackiness seem to me to be completely unfounded. I took him seriously and he took me seriously." The speaker rejects an idea that is central to concerns about the Prince: that he wields disproportionate behind-the-scenes influence because of his royal status. "There's the issue: does his passion overreach the boundaries of his constitutionally limited role? Well not if you're a serious minister because if you're a serious minister you decide whether you agree with him or not. There's no injunction to agree with him."

Tony Blair frequently disagreed with Charles. Over two volumes of edited diary extracts, Blair's former communications chief Alastair Campbell detailed the tensions that flared between Prime Minister and Prince over a range of issues. The Prince opposed Labour's proposed ban on fox-hunting and gave Blair "a long paper on hunting and why it was good for the environment." The Prince's fears that the creation of a European defense force, backed by Blair, would undermine NATO and Britain's special relationship with the United States leaked to the *Daily Mail*. The Prince expressed reservations to Blair about Britain's rapprochement with China, saying he felt "very strongly" about China's actions in Tibet; he failed to attend a state banquet for Jiang Zemin. The Prince's aides publicly denied an intended snub toward the Chinese leader but Campbell claims they surreptitiously briefed that the gesture had indeed been intended to signal Charles's disapproval, and one of the aides—Mark Bolland—backed up that allegation in the court case about the *Mail*'s publication of the Prince's Hong Kong travel journal.

For supporters, this history speaks in Charles's favor. "I think people generally feel that we're not getting leadership from politicians because we all feel they're doing deals and saying what we want them to say because then they'll get into power," says one of the Prince's informal advisers. "Whether you agree with [Charles] or not, this is a person who's got views, who's full of conviction, you know where you stand with him."

CLARENCE HOUSE'S WEBSITE ASSERTS THAT "WHEN ISSUES BECOME A matter for party political debate or the subject of Government policy, the Prince stops raising them publicly."[17] In practice Charles has snagged his foot in that fox trap more than once. Charles's views, like the brimming emotions Nicholas Soames admires him for restraining, threaten to come spilling out at any moment, in spidery memos, in meetings, and in speeches. Often he prompts debate. Sometimes he simply overpowers.

Peter Ahrends lives in a lovely Georgian town house in London. That's how, in conversation at Birkhall, Charles has said that he imagines modernist architects live, in nice eighteenth-century houses.[18] Yet Ahrends is hardly the heartless ideologue the Prince's supposition entails, surrounded by beauty and comfort while foisting soulless rat runs of plate glass and concrete on the masses. The architect and the cat that shares his home conduct themselves with the caution of the elderly to whom life has not always been kind. When Ahrends arrived in Britain as an eighteen-year-old, he had already experienced Nazi Germany as the son of a Jewish father and, after emigrating to South Africa, the first dismal clench of apartheid. Yet it would be a run-in with the establishment of his adopted homeland—and especially with the heir to its throne—that left the most obvious bruises.

After qualifying as an architect, Ahrends founded ABK, a practice with two friends, Richard Burton and Paul Koralek, tapping into the optimism of the postwar period. To idealistic architects, modernism's break from the past represented the possibility of a better future. The Prince saw only ugliness in the transformation of British landscapes in the name of progress. "I couldn't bear the physical aspect of destroying town centers and historical places, digging up all the hedgerows, cutting down trees, making terrifying prairies covered in chemicals. All that stuff. I thought this was insanity," he says.[19]

ABK won a public competition to design the extension to the National Gallery, a grand nineteenth-century building with a soaring portico entrance on the north side of London's Trafalgar Square, subject to alterations and final approvals. The design went through several iterations as the architects took on board the wishes of the client, but eventually the gallery approved the plans, submitting a planning proposal and opening the scheme to public inquiry, both routine procedures in such circumstances.

The lead architect of the extension didn't go to the 150th anniversary dinner of the Royal Institute of British Architects, RIBA, on May 17, 1984, nor did he expect a speech made at the dinner to be the first item on the *News at Ten*. Ahrends switched on his TV to discover that the Prince had used his keynote address to launch an aerial bombardment on ABK's work. Charles began by tearing into architects and planners who failed to consult sufficiently before imposing buildings on communities or neglected to pay sufficient heed to disabled access; he bemoaned the tendency to tear down old buildings rather than rehabilitating them. From there, it was but a short hop to the key note of his keynote: the damage inflicted on London in his view by modern—and in particular modernist—buildings pitched next to old ones.

"It is hard to imagine that London before the last war must have had one of the most beautiful skylines of any great city, if those who recall it are to be believed. Those who do, say that the affinity between buildings and the earth, in spite of the city's immense size, was so close and organic that the houses looked almost as though they had grown out of the earth."

The Prince was working himself up to a pitch. "What, then, are we doing to our capital city now? What have we done to it since the bombing during the war? What are we shortly to do to one of its most famous areas—Trafalgar Square? Instead of designing an extension to the elegant facade of the National Gallery which complements it and continues the concept of columns and domes, it looks as if we may be presented with a kind of municipal fire station, complete with the sort of tower that contains the siren. I would understand better this type of high-tech approach if you demolished the whole of Trafalgar Square and started again with a single architect responsible for the entire layout, but what is proposed is like a monstrous carbuncle on the face of a much-loved and elegant friend."

When Ahrends attended a scheduled breakfast the next morning with developers Trafalgar House, he believed the extension could be saved. He was still too much of a foreigner, he says, to understand the power of monarchy. The developers put him right. They knew the scheme was effectively dead, even though the planning application continued to grind on until then Secretary of State for the Environment, Patrick Jenkin, delivered a final coup de grâce some months later. "The practice suffered enormously," Ahrends says quietly. "It was a battle to survive."[20]

Other practices felt the chill too. The Prince had helped to speed a climate change that meant planners could be expected to favor safe options over statement buildings. When the National Gallery finally got its extension—the Sainsbury Wing opened in 1991—it was an undistinguished postmodern lump by architects Venturi, Scott Brown, selected over more interesting contenders during a second competition. "I am rather pleased, I must say, with the result," said Charles, by this stage a trustee of the Gallery (he served as trustee from 1986 to 1993). "It hasn't produced a rather raucous young person standing beside [the old] saying, 'Look how old and wrinkled you are,' so to speak."[21]

He had not only stimulated discussion around important issues, but polarized the debate so sharply that some of these issues submerged in rancor, especially as he continued to make inflammatory speeches. "You have, ladies and gentlemen, to give this much to the Luftwaffe," he told a Mansion House dinner in 1987. "When it knocked down our buildings, it didn't replace them with anything more offensive than rubble. We did that."[22] The specific target of that speech, a scheme by Richard Rogers for the redevelopment of Paternoster Square, next to St. Paul's, bit the dust. The architect John Simpson came up with an alternative classicist master plan, a lively pastiche with multiple shop frontages to leaven the dead weight of office buildings, supported by the Prince and the public but without developer backing. After the site changed hands, the new owners opted for a third design, influenced by Simpson but without the positives of Simpson's vision, the humdrum product of too many compromises.

Another planned development by Rogers—Lord Rogers since 1996—for Chelsea Barracks caught the Prince's attention and, as Charles wrote in a letter to Sheikh Hamad bin Jassim bin Jabr Al-Thani, the head of the Qatar Investment Authority and its property arm Qatari Diar, made his heart sink. The letter emerged in 2010 during a bustup between developers Christian and Nick Candy and the management of Qatari Diar, in partnership to build high-density accommodation on former Ministry of Defence land along the Thames embankment in Chelsea. After the Qataris withdrew the planning application for the Rogers scheme, the Candy brothers sued for breach of contract, blaming the Prince's intervention for the Qataris' change of heart.

Lawyers revealed the full content of the Prince's letter in court. He urged the Sheik to consider alternative plans drawn up by one of his favorite classicist architects, Quinlan Terry, and urged a collaboration with his own architecture foundation to achieve a "timeless approach" that "<u>enhances</u> all those qualities of neighborliness, community, human-scale, proportion, and, dare I say it, 'old-fashioned' <u>beauty</u>."[23]

The author of these rococo phrases remains unrepentant. "It just seemed to me that you have to start drawing lines in the sand about how much London is going to be mucked about with," he said. "I'd seen some of the plans and I thought, this seems insane. I just wrote a letter—a confidential letter to somebody I happen to know. I didn't do anything in public. It only came into play when they, for some reason or other, leaked my letter. Frequently, I've written letters to people that they pay no attention to at all."[24]

The Prince's communications channels with Middle Eastern royals, so keenly appreciated by the Foreign Office, had again proved their efficacy. Dominic Richards, Executive Director of the Prince's Foundation for Building Communities, reckons his boss was more catalyst than sledgehammer: "I think it was a confluence of the Prince saying what most people thought and the Qataris not wanting to do something so brutal in the heart of London that would have been a ghetto for rich people." Lord Rogers continues to seethe. "The prince always goes round the back to wield his influence, using phone calls or in the case of the Chelsea Barracks, a private letter. It is an abuse of power because he is not willing to debate," he said.[25]

That's not quite accurate—Charles often convenes architects for discussions. What he doesn't do is debate publicly, maintaining traditions of palace media management that make better sense for some models of royalty than others. The result has been a form of asymmetrical warfare between some strands of architecture and the royal knight errant. As for the wider impact on British cities, that has been mixed: on the debit side, less daring and more mediocrity of new build, but some positives too.

Many good ideas the Prince promotes go on to become mainstream: sustainability in design, better attention to the public health impacts of town planning. Planning authorities give preference to schemes that mingle income groups, "pepper-potting" social tenants and others on lower incomes with the wealthy, a practice Charles has long championed. He has also argued for more interactive planning processes. In 2011, the coalition signed off on the Localism Act and new planning guidelines, both incorporating key ideas and practice promoted by his Foundation, especially through the concept of neighborhood planning under which planning authorities must support neighborhoods that wish to pursue their own development plans. More than eight hundred such plans are in process around Britain. "My experience is if you sit down with people, local people who don't normally get sat down with, you get a remarkable consensus outlook, which frequently revolves around reintroducing local identity and tradition and human scale," says the Prince.[26]

The problem for many architects—and for them the fatal flaw in Charles's approach to architecture—is that his philosophy of harmony makes him conflate really important ideas about what makes buildings and towns livable with narrow definitions of beauty. His highest term of praise is "timeless," yet many of the buildings he lauds would have looked aggressively modern in their own eras. "It's when [the Prince] starts to engage in stylistic argument, that's when I struggle," says architect Ewen Miller. "Good architecture should be good architecture whether it's an Arts and Crafts revival building, a Classical revival building or a glass box on the side of a cliff. Good architecture should transcend the style debate."[27]

The village of Poundbury is what happened when the Prince decided that his speeches and articles and books and documentaries and letters and conversations were not enough. In his 1988 documentary and 1989 book—both entitled *A Vision of Britain*—Charles had fleshed out his thoughts about what makes for good and bad buildings and towns, asserting that in the planning and commissioning of new buildings and larger developments "we *can* do better. Our fellow citizens are demanding we do better. It is up to developers, the architects, the planners and the politicians to respond."[28] And, he might have added, princes. By creating on Duchy of Cornwall land an urban extension to Dorchester, he built a real community and a test bed for principles of community architecture.

The best-looking buildings in Poundbury are pretty cottages and a row of four white Arts and Crafts–inspired houses. One of Poundbury's least successful structures is its fire station. The magazine *Building Design* derided it as "a collection of pasty sand-coloured brick and inelegant glazing."[29] The writer and critic Justin McGuirk excoriated the structure in the *Guardian* as a "dumpy neoclassical Georgian palace with three garage doors attached to it."[30] The relish with which critics attacked may have been connected to the misplaced belief that the Prince—who had criticized ABK's National Gallery extension for resembling a "municipal fire station"—had designed Poundbury's pompous pump house.

He hadn't. Miller ruefully admits that was his doing, in an unsatisfactory collaboration with Poundbury master planner Leon Krier, a flamboyant Luxembourgeois. But the master planner works closely enough with the Prince that everything in Poundbury does bear the royal stamp. Their joint vision can be praised or blamed for streetscapes that stray from Georgian to Gothic, rustic to urban, an eclectic mix that *Building Design* called a "fruity melee of architectural costumes"—anything, in other words, but modern.[31]

Poundbury is the physical manifestation of a struggle with identity and of the tension between the old and the new. "I've always wanted to bring the baby back—that went out with the bathwater. Out went all sorts of really valuable things," says Charles.[32]

In Poundbury, he is attempting to rediscover a lost England of his imagination. The emissary from Planet Windsor arrived on earth with romantic notions about villages and towns that were not just conurbations but communities, self-regulating ecosystems in which residents of different income levels and interests could flourish. Walt Disney had a similar idea. He planned EPCOT in Florida—the acronym stands for Experimental Prototype Community of Tomorrow—as a new town, announcing the scheme at a 1966 press conference In the end, EPCOT became a theme park, an annex to Disneyworld. When Disney Corporation did develop a new town, Celebration, in Florida, critics carped about its lack of authenticity. That's a charge often leveled at the Prince's English experimental prototype community of tomorrow.

That misses the point about Poundbury: it is remarkably pleasant; its residents, who number over two thousand, enjoy living there; in many of its ambitions, Poundbury is successful. Children do play on the village green. People of diverse ages and income levels live and work alongside each other, congregate in its public spaces, take tea in its cafés, and walk along peaceful lanes to shop.

Some of Poundbury's design solutions are innovative rather than old-fashioned. There are none of the cul-de-sacs popular among the builders of new housing estates that studies suggest foster higher car use. Thoroughfares—all Poundbury roads are through roads—counterintuitively encourage people to walk or cycle because routes are more direct and therefore shorter. Traffic-calming measures in Poundbury are often subliminal and rarely rely on signage.

"First thing I did was shout 'Stop, stop the car. What is that?'" says Tim Knatchbull, describing his initial reaction to one of these measures. "There was this massive tree in the middle of the road and all the traffic was driving around the tree." The friend who brought him to Poundbury explained: "'What they found is the tree slows traffic down, it makes people make eye contact with each other, they've cut the accident rate and it's a great success.' And we went round the next corner into a square and there was a pub and people making eye contact and there was a factory just beside this pretty row of houses and although there were some things that just seemed wrong to me at first sight, that may have been because they were unusual. In any case I thought 'Wow, I would love to live somewhere like this,'" says Knatchbull.[33]

Though he is a close friend and supporter of the Prince, it was 2005, twelve years after construction started, before Knatchbull finally toured Poundbury. On the death of his grandfather Lord Mountbatten, Knatchbull had inherited part of the Broadlands estate abutting Romsey in Hampshire and for decades came under pressure from volume house-builders to let them develop housing on the land. He rejected one scheme after another, feeling, as Charles did, that social problems correlated to poor housing and planning might be alleviated by better design, but he scoffed when a friend suggested a fact-finding mission to Poundbury. "I said 'You've got to be kidding, right? You didn't make that comment seriously, did you?' Because anybody who reads the newspapers knows it's a little nonsensical, neoclassical pastiche that only somebody as influential as the Prince of Wales could possibly bring about."[34]

Knatchbull's Poundbury tour inspired him to begin developing housing at Romsey with regular input from the Prince and in collaboration with the Prince's Foundation for Building Communities and its former director, American Hank Dittmar. Sometimes seeing is the only route to believing.

CHAPTER 7

Harmonies and Disharmonies

//

C HARLES APPEARS TO BE DANCING. HE'S WEARING A DOUBLE-breasted suit the glaucous gray of a seagull's wing with a jaunty little purple flower tucked into the lapel. His brogues of ancient leather are planted on the lawn at St. James's Palace in an effortless ballet fourth as he sways his upper body. His right arm describes a large and graceful circle. Three men and four women stand in a wide arc facing him. Beyond them in the flickering shade of 140-year-old London plane trees, further groups of guests arranged in the same formations await completion by their royal host.

"It is a sad fact," the Prince observed in his foreword to a book called the *Hidden Geometry of Flowers*, "that our modern outlook does not recognize geometry as a language by which we may understand Divine order."[1] The Prince perceives naturally occurring patterns in everything, not only flowers but in the glorious architecture of Chartres cathedral and in the five-pointed orbit of Venus, and perhaps that's not so surprising. Throughout his life, aides have coaxed the people he meets into neat configurations before he arrives. The semicircle is a kinder shape than a straight line, allowing people to chat with each other until he reaches them, and affording Charles a swift exit should he avail of the opportunity, which he almost never does. The tight timetable of this event, slotted into an afternoon in June 2014 during a week of keynote speeches and the publication of his annual review and before he heads to Scotland to welcome his parents to Dumfries House, means he ought already to have moved on from this first group. He has been engrossed in conversation with members of the Swarovski family, whose business has been turning cut glass to commercial gold since the nineteenth century. Then, just as he turned to leave, Nadja Swarovski, the first female member of the company's executive board, asked him a question and he paused, midstride.

His answer involves the subject everyone has notionally gathered to discuss—the science of biomimetics—but quickly expands to encompass a philosophy that for Charles explains everything about the world, and to a befuddled world might handily explain pretty much everything about Charles. This belief system, like its exponent, is one third complaint to two thirds transfiguring faith. Its kernel is this: modern thinking—or more precisely, Modernist thinking—has disconnected us from Nature-with-a-capital-N and from the trinity of celestial essences or objective Platonic values she embodies, the True, the Beautiful, and the Good. The result is alienation and destruction. Yet there is still time—just—to reconnect—by creating "virtuous circles." It is one of these circles the Prince is so enthusiastically pantomiming for Nadja Swarovski.

Biomimeticists have recognized what "mechanistic science" overlooks, that Nature has been running her own R & D experiments from the dawn of time, rejecting poor designs and preserving only the best, he tells Swarovski. In co-opting those designs, it is possible to create things that are in sympathy with Nature and are therefore more energy-efficient to manufacture or deploy, biodegradable just as fur, scales, feathers, bones, and vegetal life are, better, cleverer, more true, beautiful, and good. Building a market for biomimetics will foster a deepening appreciation of Nature and her creations along with a recognition that the extinction of any life-form means the loss of a natural solution engineered over millennia and often more technologically advanced than anything humans might come up with on their own. Products and services based on the invisible grammar of harmony will be in demand, and so businesses providing those biomimetics-based products and services will flourish, to the mutual, sustainable benefit of all in the circle, from microorganisms and potentially endangered species to commercial organizations and consumers.

It was with another virtuous circle in mind that the Prince founded

Duchy Originals, aiming to create a market for sustainably produced goods to provide a boost to small farmers, benefit their free-ranging herds and flocks, protect the wildlife that flourishes in fields and hedgerows allowed to grow without blankets of pesticide and herbicide, and provide assurance to the consumer, who can enjoy an organic Original Oaten Biscuit, organic British Beef Meatball, or a slug of organic Old Ruby Ale safe in the knowledge that these and other Duchy Originals products are not tainted with chemicals or manufactured from the products of industrialized farming.

The Prince's Trust is based on the idea of turning vicious cycles into virtuous circles, rerouting the destructive path through childhood deprivation, behavioral problems, poor prospects, crime, drugs, and alcohol dependencies into a new circuit in which the possibility of a better life provides the motivation to do the things necessary to attain that goal.

Each virtuous circle operates inside an expanding ring of concentric virtuous circles, just as vicious cycles intersect and gain in force. In holding a reception for biomimetics, Charles is attempting to signal the promise of the science—and the dangers of ignoring Nature—and to encourage what he calls "joined-up thinking," to create what he explains to Swarovski is "an integrated picture in terms of water security, energy security, food security." He frequently worries aloud about the dangers of unsustainable population growth coupled with climate change.

Most of the mechanisms that his International Sustainability Unit proposes to mitigate climate change are based on principles of enlightened self-interest in the form of tight virtuous circles that make it more profitable to conserve than destroy. Left unchecked, industries and countries interfere with ecosystems, which the Prince sees as the most fundamental virtuous circles of all, perpetuating themselves until malign or careless development upsets their natural balance.

"At the moment we are disrupting the teeming diversity of life and the 'ecosystems' that sustain it—the forests and prairies, the woodland, moorland and fens, the oceans, rivers and streams," Charles writes in *Harmony*. "And this all adds up to the degree of 'dis-ease' we are causing to the intricate balance that regulates the planet's climate, on which we so intimately depend." He explains that his reason for writing the book—which happens to be his reason for just about everything he's done during four decades as a philanthropist and charitable entrepreneur—"is that I feel I would be failing in my duty to future generations and to the Earth itself if I did not attempt to point this out and indicate possible ways we can heal the world."[2]

He wrote the book with the BBC broadcaster Ian Skelly and Tony Juniper, a prominent environmentalist working for the ISU, but the text is phrased in the Prince's distinctive cadences, in the first person, and is clearly intended as his statement of belief. He insisted, despite the reservations of the publisher, on the title *Harmony*, and made a documentary of the same name with US filmmakers Julie Bergman Sender and Stuart Sender.

Charles's overarching quest—the motivation behind everything he does—is to restore harmony. It is a particularly cruel irony that his mission frequently plunges him into conflicts and disharmony. He feels hurt by the controversies he creates and often not a little bewildered. A fan of the British TV comedy series *Blackadder*, he identifies, says someone who knows him well, not with the scheming antihero of the title or its dumb Prince but with the hapless Baldrick, a member of the lower orders whose "cunning plans" are ridiculed but often turn out to be right. Like Baldrick, Charles sometimes reaches the right conclusions via some questionable pathways. Like Baldrick, sometimes he just gets things wrong.

In november 1948, general jan smuts sent a cable to king George: "We pray that the Prince will be a blessing to our Commonwealth and to the world."[3]

Smuts had resigned as premier of South Africa a few months before Charles's birth and would live just two more years, but his influence has permeated the Prince's life just as it continues to flow through significant streams of the conservation and environmental movement. Smuts was not only a politician and military strategist; he was also a keen amateur botanist, ecologist, and the founder of holism—or "whole-ism," as Charles prefers to spell it. Smuts set out his philosophy in his 1926 book *Holism and Evolution*. Nature tended to form wholes, he wrote. "The whole is not a mere mechanical system . . . It is more than the sum of its parts." This idea neatly served the fraying idea of Empire, and was also pressed into service to attempt to justify some dangerous ideas about race, linking into the romantic notion of the noble savage.

That is an idea Charles on occasion comes perilously close to echoing.

He is convinced that man in his natural state, Adam before the apple, is essentially good. It is the post-Enlightenment world that has interposed itself between man and his better nature. In these beliefs it's easy to detect the influence of Laurens van der Post, who had absorbed Smuts's holism at its source in his native South Africa and blended it with other strains of thought, in particular the teachings of Swiss psychiatrist Carl Jung. Van der Post advocated Jung's concept of a collective unconscious that binds human beings whether they are Kalahari bushmen or princes in palaces. The trove of shared memory and experience is sometimes accessed through dreams.

Van der Post exaggerated his achievements and dramatized and embellished his adventures. But his brilliant storytelling in books and television programs secured him a wide fan base. To a Prince condemned to the forced innocence of that chilly Eden, Planet Windsor, the warm, supportive friendship of this older man who sought to teach but not to criticize was also immensely attractive. Moreover in reworking the idea of the collective unconscious, van der Post provided Charles with the thing he most lacked, assurance of an automatic connection to people—and not only to the ermine ranks but simple, good, unspoiled people.

Thanks to Smuts and van der Post, Charles's philosophy will always carry difficult resonances. At times it can sound like a posh version of creationism, Intelligent Design but with better spelling and a wider vocabulary. When he talks or writes about the wisdoms of British hill farmers or remote tribes living in harmony with nature, he is aiming to preserve those wisdoms, but risks appearing to support a status quo that confines those farmers and tribes to the grinding poverty of subsistence. Since some of his examples are nonwhite, and because of the roots of holism, he could be mistaken for a racist, but he's no more racist (or indeed sexist) than many educated, affluent white British men, which is to say, of course, that he is by no means fully exempt from either charge. However, unlike most educated, affluent white British men, he has regular contact with people from different backgrounds, ethnic and cultural heritages. His belief system fortifies his determination to create employment opportunities for former offenders and help disadvantaged young people reach their full potential. He understands, and tries to change, some of the drivers of twenty-first-century segregation that mean that joblessness among black British men remains stubbornly double that of their white male counterparts.

But his belief system also makes it impossible for him to accept "mechanistic" approaches to life that in his view squeeze out the spiritual. Just as the sight of brutalist tower blocks crystallized his distaste for modernist architecture, so some of the uglier outcrops of technology and medicine have for him become totemic of the failure of science to admit a spiritual dimension. He wants to make room not so much for the god particle as for god.

There are many people who shy away from this approach yet share his distaste for aspects of the industrialized world. Technology once promised space-age dreams in which everyone lived in cities, in sleek skyscrapers fitted out with all manner of clever white goods, their talkative Frigidaires fully stocked with mysterious foods. These happy future folk would commute to work in flying machines, if, in these utopias, they worked at all.

A significant portion of that vision has come horribly true as the superrich overfly the sprawl of the Brazilian megalopolis Sâo Paulo in their helicopters. In nations including not only Brazil but Argentina, Australia, Belgium, Canada, Denmark, Finland, France, Norway, Sweden, the UK, and the United States, 80 percent or more of the populations are concentrated in urban areas. In China, Russia, and even in Charles's second home, Romania, more than half of the populations live in cities.[4] Yet many conurbations serve only their richest inhabitants well. A transnational apartheid has seen the affluent living longer and healthier lives than their poorer counterparts. That gap is now narrowing again but only because affluence is wreaking its own toll, with the longer life spans gifted by clean water supplies and improved medical technologies eroding as a result of what Kurt Hahn called "spectatoritis," unhealthily sedentary lifestyles, combined with smoking, excessive drinking, and calorie-rich, content-poor diets. Obesity, until recently a signifier of urban poverty, is swelling among the better off. Big Food and Big Pharma are flourishing. In July 2014, the US Centers for Disease Control and Prevention revealed that half of all Americans have at least one chronic disease, representing the main causes of poor health, disability, and death, and accounting for most health care expenditures.

The Prince has been trying to address these problems from a number of different angles over many years. His charities run programs designed to reconnect urban children with the natural environment, to encourage physical activity, and also to raise awareness of food sources. In promoting sustainable farming, he is simultaneously seeking to encourage better diets and to attack the vicious cycles of industrialized agriculture—an example he cites in *Harmony* is the US beef industry, forced to spend money on ammonia to cleanse meat of E. coli that continues to infect cattle reared not on grass but corn in feed lots. When he first entered the debate on health care provision more than three decades ago, he hoped to break another malign cycle, by encouraging policy makers to do more toward tackling the causes of chronic diseases before these diseases take hold and must be treated, incurring costs that no system can continue to sustain as more technologies and treatments become available. He has continued to warn of the folly of medicalizing every complaint and throwing pills at patients when patients and taxpayers would benefit if these problems were averted upstream.

Charles keeps making these important points and, in confronting the sway of global corporations, has been doing what few governments risk and few individuals have the access or influence to do meaningfully. Yet the manner in which he intervenes means some people find it hard to hear him. They may agree on numerous issues—as this author does—but, like this author, they may also struggle with the routes he takes to reach some of his views, in particular with the more mystical aspects of holism.

Supporters of the Prince's wider vision may also regret that his methods of delivery have a tendency to undercut his messages, whether about architecture or health. The Prince has spoken up so loudly in favor of integrated medicine—the blending of conventional and alternative approaches—that a section of his audience is permanently deafened.

HOMEOPATHY WAS THE BRAINCHILD OF A GERMAN PHYSICIAN, SAMuel Hahnemann, who postulated that "we should imitate Nature, which sometimes cures a chronic affliction with another supervening disease, and prescribe for the illness we wish to cure, especially if chronic, a drug with power to provoke another, artificial disease, as similar as possible, and the former disease will be cured: fight like with like."[5]

Britain's royals have been attempting to fight like with like ever since Queen Adelaide, German consort of King William IV, sought the services of a homeopath, a German practitioner called Johann Ernst Stapf, in the 1830s. The Queen Mother encouraged her grandson to take homeopathy seriously. The Queen still sees a homeopath.

The Prince not only trusts to homeopathy but a wider range of therapies. "He's always telling us to consult Dr. Ali," says a member of his inner circle. That's Mosaraf Ali, a doctor thanked for his contribution to *Harmony*, who according to his website is an "expert in Ayurvedic medicine and naturopathy with a holistic vision." Mosaraf's website also carries a testimonial from Charles ("Dr. Ali has done us a great favor in pointing out the way forward during the coming centuries") and includes the Prince on a list of "endorsements from famous people" that also names Morgan Freeman, Sylvester Stallone, Samuel L. Jackson, Andrew Lloyd Webber, and Kate Moss. The general practitioners who serve the royal court and accompany members of the family on their travels are not only qualified in conventional medicine but have taken time to learn about alternative therapies and to offer an integrated approach to treatment.

In December 1982, Charles delivered an incendiary address to the British Medical Association, chiding mainstream medicine for an "objective, statistical, computerized approach to the healing of the sick. If disease is regarded as an objective problem isolated from all personal factors, then surgery plus more and more powerful drugs must be the answer." He highlighted very real dilemmas involved in mass health care provision and raised very important questions about the growing muscle of the pharmaceuticals industry in determining health care policies, prescribing a more encompassing—holistic—approach to the assembled doctors: "Wonderful as many of them are it should still be more widely stressed by doctors that the health of human beings is so often determined by their behavior, their food and the nature of their environment."[6]

This was not only sensible stuff; it needed—and still needs—to be said. But Charles framed his speech in polarizing terms, opening with a complaint. "I have often thought that one of the least attractive traits of various professional bodies and institutions is the deeply ingrained suspicion and outright hostility which they can exhibit towards anything unorthodox or unconventional," he said. He added: "Perhaps we just have to accept it is god's will that the unorthodox individual is doomed to years of frustration, ridicule and failure in order to act out his role in the scheme of things, until his day arrives and mankind is ready to receive his message."[7]

Although the Prince went on to identify the "unorthodox individual" of his speech as the renowned sixteenth-century healer, Paracelsus, he clearly reflected—and anticipated—his own experience. He has endured years of frustration, ridicule, and failure, as his interventions, far from sowing harmony, open him to attack, redoubling his conviction that something needs to be done and his impulse to use his position to override criticism, encouraging him to do things that strengthen his critics. This is Charles's repeating pattern—not a virtuous circle but a vicious cycle—and Edzard Ernst, for a while, became snared in its vortex.

In 2005, Ernst, Britain's first Professor of Complementary Medicine, based at the University of Exeter, raised alarms over *Complementary Health Care*, a patient guide published by the Prince's Foundation for Integrated Health. It was, Ernst told journalists, "over-optimistically misleading." Later the same year Ernst read a draft of the *Smallwood Report*, a study conducted under Charles's aegis "to investigate the contribution which certain complementary therapies could potentially make to the delivery of healthcare in the UK."[8] Ernst had provided information to the researchers of the report, and says he offered them his own findings on twenty-seven economic evaluations of popular forms of alternative therapy that proved inconclusive. His own primary research into alternative therapies, the basis for a 2008 book he coauthored, *Trick or Treatment*, dismissed most such therapies as having, at best, a placebo effect. The draft of the *Smallwood Report* did not reflect Ernst's input, and he felt it included potentially dangerous recommendations—such as the use of homeopathy to treat asthma—so he asked for his name to be removed.

Ernst maintains that shortly before publication of the final report, he received a call from an old contact at the *Times* of London who had received a leaked copy of the report. "He said, 'I don't want you to disclose any contents of the report, but tell me a bit about it, about the methodology, why you pulled out.' And then I didn't mince my words and the next day it was on the title page of the *Times*,"[9] says Ernst. The piece quoted Ernst not only tearing into the report but suggesting that the Prince had overstepped his constitutional role. Michael Peat, then both the Prince's Private Secretary and Chairman of the Foundation for Integrated Health, wrote to the University of Exeter accusing the professor of breach of confidentiality. The university launched a thirteen-month investigation that eventually decided not to issue Ernst with a formal disciplinary notice but warned him, Ernst says, that he risked sanctions if he did anything similar in future.

This did not deter him from participating in a television documentary, *Charles: The Meddling Prince*, that aired in 2007, eliciting a seventeen-page rebuttal from Clarence House. Two years later, Ernst attacked Duchy Originals—and its founder—for selling a so-called Detox Tincture. "Prince Charles contributes to the ill-health of the nation by pretending we can all over-indulge, then take his tincture and be fine again. Under the banner of holistic and integrative healthcare he thus promotes a quick fix and outright quackery," Ernst told the *Guardian*.[10] Meanwhile, funds for Ernst's research unit at Exeter dried up. He claims he offered to retire to save the unit, but that the university instead shut it down in 2011.

The polarized ecosystem of the health care debate maintains a balance of extremes, pitting the conventional against the alternative, the power of pharmaceutical giants against the profiteers of the snake oil industry, rationalists against advocates for a spiritual dimension. There is too little room for healthy skepticism, too little research that isn't directed to creating new, marketable products. One result is that alternative therapies that Ernst concedes have benefits, such as yoga and Pilates, remain ill-regulated in many countries, with no single body ensuring that practitioners are qualified to set standards. Patients are most often the losers.

The Prince, as he usually does, has used back channels to try to promote his ideas. In Peter Hain, who served in the cabinets of Tony Blair and Gordon Brown, he found a rare ally. As Secretary of State for Northern Ireland from 2005 to 2007, Hain introduced a trial for complementary medicine in Britain's state-funded health system. "It had spectacularly good results," Hain told an interviewer in 2014. "And when [Charles] learnt about this he was really enthusiastic and tried to persuade the Welsh government to do the same thing and the government in Whitehall to do the same thing for England."[11]

Ernst responded to Hain's interview with a splenetic blog post questioning the legitimacy of the trial. "So, is the whole 'trial' story an utterly irrelevant old hat?" Ernst asks. "Certainly not! Its true significance does not lie in the fact that a few amateurs are trying to push bogus treatments into the NHS via the flimsiest pseudo-research of the century. The true significance, I think, is that it shows how Prince Charles, once again, oversteps the boundaries of his constitutional role."[12]

Such criticisms are unlikely to deflect Charles, and not only because the concept of his constitutional role is as dynamic as the natural world and its ecosystems. The Prince is implacable because he is a believer, not just in alternative and complementary medicines and the potential of biomimetics but in a larger picture that includes the unseen and the unknown. He is Prince Hamlet proclaiming more things on heaven and earth than we might dream. "We live in a culture which doesn't really believe in the soul," says Ian Skelly. "You are seen as a bit of a crank if you talk in that way, yet actually if you talk to people individually they speak in a very spiritual way about love and about feelings for things. Culturally we've put that in a corner, and it has no part to play in the mainstream economic approach to life."[13] This is not only something Charles is determined to change; it fits with the role he is expected to take on as king, as Supreme Governor of the Church of England. Yet the strength of his beliefs, far from making this future role a better fit, means that some traditionalists worry about his suitability.

ANGLICANISM IS MOST LIKELY TO GET ITSELF IN A TIZZY WHEN IT cares too visibly, in an un-English sort of way. The deepest schisms of recent times emerged in the gulf between the emotional supporters of Gene Robinson, a proudly gay man ordained in 2003 as Bishop of New Hampshire by the liberal, North American Episcopal Church, and the emotional opponents of gay clergy, noisily represented in the congregations of Africa and Asia. The General Synod is the Church of England's parliament; the ten-yearly Lambeth Conference sets wider Anglican policy. The Archbishop of Canterbury attempts, and often fails, to steer the debate rather than handing down doctrine like the Pope.

Such differences to Roman Catholicism are literally defining. The Church of England formed in opposition to the Vatican after Henry VIII broke with Pope Clement VII over the latter's inclement refusal to annul the King's marriage to Catherine of Aragon. Laws passed once the Glorious Revolution had deposed Britain's last Catholic ruler, James II, simultaneously enshrined and interlocked the dominions of the Church of England and Britain's—exclusively and explicitly Anglican—sovereigns to come, while British colonialism expanded the sway of Anglicanism and the monarchy. The Church of England is the established—state—church; its Bishops help to make the country's laws. The Coronation Oath requires the monarch to "maintain and preserve inviolably the settlement of the Church of England, and the doctrine, worship, discipline, and government thereof, as by law established in England" and to "preserve unto the Bishops and Clergy of England, and to the Churches there committed to their charge, all such rights and privileges, as by law do or shall appertain to them or any of them." The Queen serves as Defender of the Faith that defends her against interlopers and incense-wavers. This mantle was never likely to fall comfortably on her son.

The biggest revelation of Jonathan Dimbleby's 1994 documentary portrait of Charles almost got lost in the pandemonium surrounding the Prince's disclosure of infidelity. The more startling declaration came earlier in Dimbleby's film, during a discussion about the Prince's exploration of world religions and his assertion that there are "common threads that link us all in one great and important tapestry." "Does that mean that spiritually and intellectually you feel at home walking between and within all those religions and don't feel tied to the Church of England, the Protestant Church?" Dimbleby wonders. "Yes," the Prince replies. "I feel there is an enormous amount, once you begin to understand where we are linked, in common that can be immensely helpful. I'm one of those people who searches. I'm interested in pursuing a path, if I can find it, through the thickets." So saying, Charles apparently swerves straight into a clump of thornbushes.

"I personally would rather see [the role of the monarch] as Defender of Faith, not *the* Faith, because [the Faith] means just one particular interpretation of the Faith, which I think is sometimes something that causes a deal of a problem," he declares. "It has done for hundreds of years. People have fought each other to the death over these things, which seems to me a peculiar waste of people's energy, when we're all actually aiming for the same ultimate goal, I think." The future coauthor of *Harmony* begins to sketch out his nascent philosophy, mooting the idea that a monarch might be "Defender of the Divine in existence, the pattern of the divine which is, I think, in all of us, but which because we are human beings can be expressed in so many different ways." Lest there be any doubt about his message, he name-checks some of the other religions he envisages that he, as King, would be inclined to defend. "I've always felt the Catholic subjects of the sovereign are equally as important as the Anglican ones or the Protestant ones. Likewise I think that the Islamic subjects or the Hindu subjects or the Zoroastrian subjects are of equal and vital importance." In Charles's theology, all believers are equal to each other, if not necessarily to the sovereign.[14]

These musings may not have roused as much tabloid excitement as his confession of adultery, but they created consternation in Lambeth Palace. "As heir, [the Prince] has to be concerned with every citizen, regardless of creed or color," then Archbishop of Canterbury George Carey told an interviewer. "I believe that is what he intended to say."[15]

Carey suggested that tweaks to the coronation service—but not to the coronation oath—would fulfill the Prince's desire to see all faiths given the same prominence. In his biography of the Prince, published later the same year, Dimbleby rejected Carey's "minimalist interpretation" and produced the transcript of a segment of the interview with the Prince that had been cut from the broadcast. In it, the Prince returns to his theme of the shared ground among religions. "The great Middle Eastern religions—Judaism, Islam, Christianity, all stemming from the same geographical area—all have a great deal in common. . . . There are aspects of Hinduism and Buddhism . . . which are attached by very profound threads to Islam, Christianity and Judaism." Carey's attempt at fire-fighting had fanned the flames. Charles hadn't stumbled into the briars. He had made his points deliberately and with his usual determination to kindle debate. He was backed in this endeavor by his biographer. "I was really furious," says Dimbleby. "I knew what [the Prince] meant; we'd talked about it a lot. A great deal."[16]

Carey's predecessor will also have known what the Prince meant, though never could grasp quite what the Prince *meant*. Robert Runcie served as Archbishop of Canterbury from 1980 to 1991, conducting Charles's marriage to Diana and a few years later asked by the Prince to lunch with him and his unhappy wife "on the basis of 'It's been rather a lot for Diana, because religion hasn't stuck much with her. And we feel we ought to mention it to you, because you married us,'" as Runcie told his own biographer. Of Charles, Runcie said: "It would quite help if he loved the Church of England a bit more."

To Runcie, the Prince's views lacked consistency. The cleric couldn't reconcile Charles's apparent liberalism on issues such as urban poverty with his impulse to align himself with the sorts of conservatives who opposed moves to broaden the appeal of the Church by modernizing its language. Nor could Runcie understand how the Prince's mystic bent fitted into the picture. "I think he was deeply into the Laurens van der Post spirituality," said Runcie, concluding, "I don't think he took the Church of England very seriously."[17]

The Bishop of London, Richard Chartres, understands his old university friend far better. "If people can't extract from [the Prince] what they want, they invent it and with immense confidence people are saying well of course he's not going to want a Christian coronation because he is a Defender of Faith. Now he's an intelligent guy. And he is totally aware of the philosophical and spiritual incoherence of being a Defender of Faith as if you didn't have one for yourself but were looking down from some other more elevated level on the whole scene. Of course, like sensible people he recognizes that faith communities have a role in social cohesion and spreading the practice of virtue and in their local manifestation they're often very central to most volunteering in local society. He's been trying to make absolutely clear that he has immense sympathy with the world of religion, the world of faith, because he sees very clearly how it relates to a view of the world in which human beings do not play the role of oppressive dominance but understand their connectedness with the health of the whole planet and the whole human race. But the idea that he doesn't really have a faith of his own is untrue. He is a convinced Christian."[18]

Far from being inconsistent or contradictory, the Prince is true to his complex belief system. "You can be a loyal member of the Church of England and you can appreciate the extraordinary quality of the spiritual life that other people have in their traditions," says Chartres, adding that the Prince's book *Harmony* "is a very important contribution at the present moment when we are looking for a global conversation among the wisdom traditions and anybody who's involved in a religious body, as I am, ought to feel very humble indeed as we look at the comparative success of economists and scientists in developing the kind of global conversations that we need in order to confront series of promises and perils which are not to be confined to one continent or one nation."[19]

There are philosophical points of disagreement—Chartres does not elaborate—but in a broad sense he and the heir to the throne are in concert, traditionalists and radicals, of the establishment and just as liable to challenge the establishment view. They mirror each other because, longtime friends that they are, they have influenced each other's thinking over many years and collaborated on interfaith initiatives and recently on the Prince's campaign to protect Orthodox Christians in the Middle East. The Bishop praises the Prince's "energy, the hard work—we're not talking about going around occasional discourses of an anodyne kind—we're talking about the shaping of institutions to make a long-term difference in areas which when he started on them were not very obvious to the majority of opinion." Chartres cites Business in the Community and the Prince's Trust as examples. "These are institutional responses to a series of problems very profoundly understood and sustained over the long term by his commitment to them and his determination to make sure they have the funds and the wherewithal to make a difference. . . . He doesn't flit. There is a coherence about all of his interests that runs through the Temenos Academy and *Harmony* and the Prince's Trust. There is a coherent view and it is fundamentally spiritual."[20]

For all that, Chartres did not attend the April 2005 wedding of his old friend. Charles and Camilla got officially hitched in a civil ceremony at Windsor Guildhall, exchanging wedding rings of Welsh gold, in front of their children and other family members before heading to St. George's Chapel at Windsor Castle for a service of prayer and dedication. The Church of England maintains an interdict on marrying divorcées with living spouses if the marriage might be "tantamount to consecrating an old infidelity." The two consecutive ceremonies got round that problem but some potential guests spared themselves the sight of the future Supreme Governor of the Church of England entering matrimony outside the Church. The Queen and Prince Philip also stayed away from Windsor Guildhall, though they did join the happy couple afterward.

* * *

FREQUENTLY ACCUSED OF ARROGANCE BY THE PROFESSIONS HE RILES, Charles has always wrestled with insecurity. His diffidence is not assumed. He sounds most vehement when masking his fears—and that of course means when making interventions that are likely to be controversial, sometimes in self-fulfilling prophesy. He confesses to getting knots in his stomach before speeches. "I've had conversations with him—and he probably won't remember me saying so—but 'You're an elder now, you're no longer the student, you're the one who knows this stuff,'" says Ian Skelly. "I think he's always seen himself as a student at the feet of the great and wise and rather like the ugly duckling and the swan, he doesn't realize how fully fledged he is."[21]

Charles was far from fledged in the late 1970s when he met Laurens van der Post at the Suffolk house of a mutual friend, Captain Robin Sheepshanks. It seems to have been a union of mutual needs, between a Prince longing to find meaning in his existence and a storyteller who could weave apparent answers out of thin air, the one insecure but with the glossiest of social pedigrees, the other self-invented to a stupefying degree.

Throughout the 1980s and into the 1990s, van der Post plugged his protégé into a wider network of ideas and people. In the poet Kathleen Raine, the Prince discovered both a safe friendship with a substantially older woman and a repository of the ideas that fascinated and sustained him. Raine had founded a journal "devoted to the arts of the imagination," *Temenos* (the word means "sacred space"). She met Charles over dinner at Kensington Palace. "I thought, that poor young man—anything I can do for him, I will do, because he is very lonely," she said later.[22]

Van der Post died in 1996, three months after Charles's divorce came through, leaving his younger friend in a wilderness more impervious than any they had visited together. During the years of bleakness, anyone the Prince felt he could trust took on more importance to him than ever; his instinct to search for wider and higher meanings became more urgent. He made frequent visits to Raine's house in Chelsea for tea and cake and long discussions about "flowers and gardens . . . the encroaching technology and materialism of the modern world . . . art and architecture, music and poetry."[23] Always they talked about their joint project, to return the world to an awareness of ancient wisdoms.

In 1990, with Charles's encouragement, Raine set up the Temenos Academy, and for a period from 1992 ran the organization from a perch within the Prince's newly established Institute of Architecture. The founding aim of the Academy, and its journal, relaunched as the *Temenos Academy Review*, was to spread the philosophy of Perennialism—the notion of a universal truth that underpins all the major religions and is not the sole preserve of the Church of England or any Christian communion. "The arts of the imagination flourish . . . in the Temenos—the precinct of that sacred centre, be that centre temple, synagogue, church, mosque, or the invisible sanctuary within the heart," explained Raine in a statement that still garnishes the Temenos website. "Since knowledge is universal, we seek to learn from all traditions."[24]

In 2003 Charles attended Raine's small private funeral and spoke at a remembrance service held later the same year at St. James's Palace. He revealed that Raine had sympathized with him, seeing his role as heir to the throne as "the most difficult task in England." He quoted her advice: "Dear, dear Prince, don't give that riff-raff an inch of ground, not a hair's breadth; stand firm on the holy ground of the heart. The only way to deal with the evil forces of their world is from a higher level, not to meet them on their own." In closing his eulogy, he adapted a line from *Hamlet*: "May God rest her dear departed soul and may flights of angels sing her to her rest."[25]

Once as anguished as the Prince of Denmark, the Prince of Britain and the Realms through his associations with Raine and van der Post acquired a vision of the world in which everything made some kind of sense. He has continued to elaborate that vision and his confidence is growing in step with his personal happiness. "He has assumed a certainty in the time I've known him," says Skelly, these days Chairman of the Temenos Academy. "He's much more sure of himself, philosophically. He has a wisdom about him."[26] Charles remembers his mentors with fondness and gratitude. Some in the British establishment, indeed in Buckingham Palace, regard their legacy with deep mistrust.

IN *HARMONY*, THE PRINCE TRACES A "GOLDEN THREAD" OF WISDOM "from Pythagoras and Plato to Shakespeare and [fifteenth-century Italian priest Marsilio] Ficino, from [Italian Renaissance painter] Giorgione, Bach and Handel to Wordsworth, Poussin and Blake—all of these great artists were very clear that there is a harmony to the world that must be maintained."[27] He might have traced the same thread to a significant twentieth-century destination, French-Egyptian philosopher René Guénon, or onward to German-French-Swiss–US resident Frithjof Schuon, both of whom interwove strands of Islamic esoterism, in particular Sufism, into Traditionalism, a philosophical branch closely allied to Perennialism.

The Prince may not name check all of his influences in *Harmony* but he does summon up a Sufi aphorism: "Although there are many lamps, it is all the same light."[28] This is the view of religion that strikes fear into some of the functionaries of Lambeth and Buckingham palaces, gets mistaken for pick-and-mix New Ageism, and also feeds conspiracy theories about the Prince's secret conversion to Islam or to Orthodoxy. It is the fundament of the Prince's determination to be a Defender of Faith, rather than *the* Faith. Yet it is also the fundament of the Prince's faith, and that faith is Anglican, albeit higher Church and more mystically inclined than that of many of his co-confessionals. Prayer is as much a part of the Prince's late-night routine as his red boxes. In Charles the Church of England stands to gain a Supreme Governor who takes his duties, and his religion, exceptionally seriously.

Prominent among those duties, as he interprets them, is interfaith work, helping Crown and Country—and its established Church—to come to terms with an increasingly diverse population, and in turn to help that population to live harmoniously. The 2011 Census of England and Wales produced stark figures: 59.3 percent of the population identified as Christian, down from 71.1 percent at the census a decade earlier. The Muslim population, though still small by comparison, has grown from 3 percent of the total in 2001 to 4.8 percent, and in some inner-city areas is a far more significant presence—34.5 percent in the London borough of Tower Hamlets. More than 22 percent of Londoners practice a religion other than Christianity.[29] A similar proportion, slightly lower in London, slightly higher across England and Wales, has no faith affiliation.

These changes represent challenges to what politicians have taken to calling "community cohesion," most often when that spirit is lacking. At the sharp end, in areas of high unemployment and deprivation, the competition for scarce resources easily takes on sectarian and racial tones that populist movements encourage and exploit. Islamophobia is increasing; so too is the appeal to some younger Muslims and British converts of forms of Islam that are irredeemably at odds with notions of happy multiculturalism. The toll of hate crimes against religions continues to rise; the proportion carried out in the name of religion is less frequently documented, but the murder of Lee Rigby in May 2013 by two Britons of Nigerian descent who had converted to Islam became the pretext for a spate of attacks not only against Muslim targets but other faith groups. Sectarian enmities from distant conflicts also play out on British streets.

The answer, Charles believes, must be "to remind people of what we share in common," and he uses speeches, meetings, and more formalized initiatives to try to do that, as well as visiting, again and again, churches of different denominations, synagogues, mosques, and temples, in Britain and elsewhere.[30]

Many initiatives involve bringing different faith groups together. In 2006 the Prince opened St. Ethelburga's Centre for Peace and Reconciliation, established by the Bishop of London in a London church rebuilt after an IRA bomb. "You don't just sit back and say you know [all faiths] are marvelous; you engage, you create friendships, you devise methodology like scriptural reasoning where you sit down with Sikhs, with Jews, with Muslims," says Chartres. "We take as a horizon a pressing contemporary problem and we actually draw resources out of our own scriptures not arguing with one another but listening acutely and accountably speaking to one another and you always emerge from that more deeply convinced about your own Christian identity and more deeply respectful at the same time."[31]

"The royals in general and HRH in particular do interfaith better than anyone," says Jonathan Sacks.[32] At the time of the conversation in August 2013, Lord Sacks was entering his last fortnight as Chief Rabbi of the United Hebrew Congregations of the Commonwealth. He first met Charles seventeen years earlier aboard a private jet to London, after the funeral of Israel's murdered Prime Minister Yitzhak Rabin. The then leader of Britain's main opposition party, Labour's Tony Blair, also hitched a ride. As the Prince sat, nose in a book, Blair leaned over and asked him what he was reading. It turned out to be the Hebrew Bible, and soon everyone present had been drawn into a wide-ranging discussion. Sacks remembers being impressed not only by Charles's theological knowledge but his broader take on issues. "He had so carefully thought through positions," Sacks recalls. "You cannot be with HRH for very long without realising that he has thought immensely about really big vision-type issues. He thinks on a very broad canvas and he has an integrated worldview."

Such a view is often conflated with what Richard Chartres terms "upper middle class religion, taking a *bon bouche* from here and there, a bit of Californian Buddhism mixed with a bit of Sufism—a religion which deifies your tastes." This, says the Bishop, is "no good at all, unless you commit yourself seriously to a way in God's good time you will be brought to a position where you can befriend all the lovers of God. . . . You need a way that brings you to a point of unity, poised where you can love without distortions or hidden agendas, you can appreciate. That's absolutely central and anybody who really feels that they have to subject the other to withering negative criticism just shows how little progress they've made on their own way. That's a sign of spiritual immaturity. So I rejoice in the fact that the Prince of Wales loves Islam."[33]

CHAPTER 8

A Foreign Asset

//

O N A VISIT TO SAUDI ARABIA IN FEBRUARY 2014 CHARLES DONNED
a *ghutra*, the traditional cotton headdress folded over a kafiyyeh, or
skullcap, and the full-length shirt called a *thawb*, to participate in a sword
dance. "I'm a fake sheikh," he told a wide-eyed child. The ostensible reason for this display was to celebrate the Janadriyah Festival, an annual
cultural event. His footwork wasn't up to the standard that makes Emma
Thompson go into a mock swoon or over the years has enlivened Balmoral
balls, put a spring into tea dances, gingered up the Rio Carnival, and
impressed at least one Degree of the Three. Nor did it win him approval
among critics of Saudi Arabia, a kingdom ruled over by an absolute monarchy that only introduced the country's Basic Law in 1992, after the first
Gulf War, and retained its clutch throughout the Arab Spring. King Abdullah has been hailed as a modernizer, and he is—but only by the arch-
conservative standards of his predecessor and older brother, King Fahd.
Abdullah, who turned ninety in August 2014, brooks no dissent. Anyone
organizing protests or publicly criticizing the government risks prosecution
and severe penalties. "Tarnishing the reputation of the state" is defined as an
act of terrorism. So is atheism. Yet despite the country's sweeping anti-terror
laws, the oil-rich nation (it straddles almost a fifth of the world's proven oil
reserves) remains a crucible and source of funding for the kind of Salafist

jihadism that produced Osama bin Laden and continues to inspire violent Sunni organizations such as al-Shabab, Boko Haram, and the self-styled Islamic State, intent on waging a holy war.

Among the primary targets of these jihadists are other Muslims they consider infidels, including Shia Muslims, who after the death of the Prophet Muhammad in 632 made the fateful decision to follow the hereditary principle and support his descendants in the struggle to lead Islam. The Sunnis back then called for a democratically chosen Caliph, but the people who kill in the name of Sunni Islam care nothing for democracy. In addition to turning their fire on Shias, some Sunni extremists aim to oust the Saudi royals and topple enemies of the faith, including the "Great Satan," America. The term was originally coined by the Shia cleric Ayatollah Ruhollah Khomeini, who led the revolution that deposed Iran's royalty. Iran has helped to finance Shia militant groups including Lebanon-based Hezbollah and the Palestinian organization Hamas that direct their fire against Sunni and Western targets. In the intricate history of the Sunni and Shia conflict and Islam's conflict with the West, one's enemy's enemies are rarely friends.

As Charles acknowledged in a 1993 speech, the hostilities owe some of their venom and a good deal of their complexity to Western interventions over fourteen centuries. "Extremism is no more the monopoly of Islam than it is the monopoly of other religions, including Christianity," he said and set to illustrating the point with examples that, though they ignored most of the colonial adventures that drew disputed borders, highlighted the legacy of the Crusades. "To Western schoolchildren, the 200 years of the Crusades are traditionally seen as a series of heroic, chivalrous exploits in which the kings, knights, princes—and children—of Europe tried to wrest Jerusalem from the wicked Muslim infidel. To Muslims, the Crusades were an episode of great cruelty and terrible plunder, of Western infidel soldiers of fortune and horrific atrocities, perhaps exemplified best by the massacres committed by the Crusaders when, in 1099, they took back Jerusalem, the third holiest city in Islam. For us in the West, 1492 speaks of human endeavor and new horizons, of Columbus and the discovery of the Americas. To Muslims, 1492 is a year of tragedy—the year Granada fell to Ferdinand and Isabella, signifying the end of eight centuries of Muslim civilization in Europe.

"The point, I think, is not that one or other picture is more true, or has a monopoly of truth. It is that misunderstandings arise when we fail to appreciate how others look at the world, its history, and our respective roles in it. The corollary of how we in the West see our history has so often been to regard Islam as a threat—in medieval times as a military conqueror, and in more modern times as a source of intolerance, extremism and terrorism."[1]

The speech stood at odds with much mainstream Western thinking. "At that time, he was far ahead of others in coming up with the view that something needs to be done to bring about a better understanding between the Islamic world and the West," says Farhan Nizami, the founding Director of the Oxford Centre for Islamic Studies where the Prince delivered the speech. "To be calling for the Islamic world and the West to work together, to say we were almost at the crossroads, I think was remarkably prescient."[2]

Charles has been, in the words of Nizami, "a very active patron" of the Oxford institution, helping to attract a range of speakers as varied as the St. James's Palace guest list: from the icon of reconciliation, Nelson Mandela, to avatars of more repressive regimes such as Saudi Arabia's Foreign Minister Saud Al-Faisal, who told the audience that "Saudi Arabia is thrust towards assuming a position of influence and authority to maintain the moral tradition and the purity of Islam."[3] Of all these speakers, Charles made the biggest splash. His speech not only sounded radical; it was carefully strategized, made just ahead of a trip to the Gulf that the Prince feared would be a rerun of previous trips—polite, content-free meetings in air-conditioned rooms. He used the platform to draw attention to "the terrible sufferings" of Bosnian Muslims and to inveigh against Saddam Hussein's persecution of the Marsh Arabs of Southern Iraq. He also appeared to hold up Islam as an antidote to Western materialism, already betraying his concerns about post-Enlightenment Christianity and its acceptance of "mechanistic science." "At the heart of Islam is its preservation of an integral view of the universe," the Prince told his audience at the Sheldonian Theatre in Oxford. "Islam—like Buddhism and Hinduism—refuses to separate man and nature, religion and science, mind and matter, and has preserved a metaphysical and unified view of ourselves and the world around us."[4] He was describing his own holistic philosophy.

In the Gulf nations, as in the wider Muslim world, Charles's speech drew warm applause. When he arrived in Saudi Arabia, King Fahd set aside usual protocols to greet him at his guesthouse before dawn. In Britain, the heir to the throne's views on Islam, expounded in further speeches and enthusiastically demonstrated through many more visits and meetings, interfaith initiatives, and his continuing patronage of the institution run by Nizami—in receipt of funding by Saudi Arabia as well as other countries—have aroused the mixture of amusement and rancor that often attends his efforts.[5] Columnists mock him: Does he not know the penalties for adultery under sharia law? In Saudi Arabia cheating on your spouse carries a potential death sentence.

Conspiracists of all waters find in his connections with the Muslim world confirmation of his murky aims. "Prince Charles has been placed by the Queen at the head of the British-Saudi Empire terror machine, utilizing relationships he has developed over more than a quarter of a century," declare Richard Freeman and William F. Wertz Jr., the authors of an essay published by Lyndon LaRouche, an arch-conspiracist, failed US presidential candidate, and convicted fraudster. "Charles is [also] at the forefront of Queen Elizabeth's drive, through starvation, disease, war, and murder, to reduce the world's population from its present 7 billion persons to 1 billion."[6]

Dianaists posit that the Prince's interest in Islam stems from his need to compete with his former wife's Muslim boyfriends, Hasnat Khan and Dodi Fayed, ignoring not only a psychology that makes that interpretation implausible but a time line that makes it impossible. Another persistent theme insists that the Prince is a Muslim revert.

To many liberals, the Prince's tendresse for Islam equates to support for repressive interpretations of the faith and for the regimes that rule in its name, especially Saudi Arabia and its dictatorial monarchy. The book *Saudi Babylon* relates that Alan Gerson, a lawyer for the 9/11 families, asked in a 2003 meeting at New Scotland Yard if the UK authorities had "uncovered anything to show the charities run by some members of the Saudi royal family were channeling money to the terrorists." Stephen Ratcliffe, a Special Branch officer tasked with tracing terrorist money, is described as appearing "hesitant and a little sheepish" in response. "'Our ability to investigate the Saudis is very limited,' he said. He then paused, looked across at a photograph of Prince Charles on the wall, raised his eyebrows and smiled knowingly without saying a word."[7]

The Salman Rushdie affair saw Charles side with Islamic conservatives, according to Rushdie's friend and fellow author Martin Amis. Ayatollah Khomeini issued a fatwa against Rushdie in 1989 for his novel *The Satanic Verses*. The ostensible grounds for Khomeini's call to murder Rushdie was that his book had insulted Islam; the cleric's deeper aim was to position Shia Iran and not Sunni-led Saudi Arabia as the fulcrum of the Islamic revolution. The notion that Rushdie was the offender, rather than his persecutors, found some powerful allies, not just in Margaret Thatcher's government—she appears in cameo in *The Satanic Verses* as Mrs. Torture—but in Lambeth Palace. Robert Runcie let it be known he could "well understand the devout Muslims' reaction, wounded by what they hold most dear and would themselves die for."

Elsewhere blows were traded in place of words, spilling over into riots in which forty-two people died and violent attacks on those involved in publishing the book. A would-be Rushdie assassin accidentally blew himself up. The book's Japanese translator was stabbed to death. Rushdie went into hiding. In this febrile atmosphere Amis found himself at a dining table in royal company. "I had an argument with Prince Charles at a small dinner party," Amis recalled in an interview marking the twenty-fifth anniversary of the fatwa. "He said—very typically, it seems to me—'I'm sorry, but if someone insults someone else's deepest convictions, well then,' blah blah blah. . . . And I said that a novel doesn't set out to insult anyone. 'It sets out to give pleasure to its readers,' I told him. 'A novel is an essentially playful undertaking, and this is an exceedingly playful novel.' The Prince took it on board, but I'd suppose the next night at a different party he would have said the same thing."[8]

It's unlikely Charles had read *The Satanic Verses*. In their Cambridge days, Lucia Santa Cruz persuaded her friend to read *Anna Karenina*, she says, remarking that despite the false, fervid speculation that attended their platonic friendship, the novel was the only new experience she provided him. "He said he liked [the novel], but he never wanted to read another one, I don't think. He always wanted to stick to history or essays," she adds.[9]

In Rushdie's most famous work the Prince may have been surprised to find a measure of what he says he wants to foster—a serious engagement with Islam that does not shrink from criticism. In 2006, Charles used a speech at the Imam Muhammad bin Saud University in Riyadh to issue a call for a more flexible reading of scripture that was startling within the context of the deeply conservative Islamic institution.

More recently, Charles has begun to campaign for Christian communities that are being targeted by fundamentalists in Egypt, Iraq, Syria, and other predominantly Muslim countries, taking that message of concern direct to the Gulf, on the trip to Saudi Arabia, Qatar, Abu Dhabi, and Bahrain in February 2014 that produced the images of the Prince participating in the sword dance.

His critics spotted blood on the dance floor. Amnesty UK called on the Prince to raise human rights abuses with his Saudi hosts while its Twitter feed posted a link to the video. "Prince Charles's sword dance," read the accompanying tweet. "Yes, they like swords in Saudi Arabia. Including for public executions."

It did nothing to dispel dark interpretations of the Prince's mission that the British aerospace company BAE Systems announced the conclusion of a deal to sell Typhoon jets to the Saudi government the day after he left Riyadh for Doha. In the *Guardian*, defense and security writer Richard Norton-Taylor quoted Andrew Smith, spokesman for the Campaign Against the Arms Trade, CAAT: "It is clear that Prince Charles has been used by the UK government and BAE Systems as an arms dealer." The Prince's aides deny—with unusual ferocity—that the arms deal came up in any of his conversations. No matter. "It did not have to," wrote Norton-Taylor. "The Saudis must have got the message. It was the heir to the British throne's tenth official visit to the feudal monarchy. He made his trip, we are told, at the request of the Foreign Office."[10]

The Prince, so often criticized for crosscutting with ministerial work, had indeed dutifully carried out the wishes of Her Majesty's Government in traveling to Saudi Arabia, according to sources in HM Government. He went at the FCO's request and with an agenda briefed to him in advance. He raised his anxieties about Christian communities in the Gulf states and about the luxury-oriented, car-centered, energy-spendthrift cities in the Middle East that call into question his notion that Islam is naturally in sympathy with the environment. He met young entrepreneurs in Riyadh, ecologists in Doha, participated in an interfaith dialogue. Yet his government business took precedence.

Ever since the Prince's Oxford speech, he has the confidence of key contacts in the region, not least the Gulf royals who regard him not only as an equal, but a defender of Islam. "I do not know of another major Western figure anywhere who would have as high a standing in the Muslim world as the Prince of Wales," says Nizami.[11] "The value he brings to this is the value of long-term relationships, not short-term transactional ones," says an insider. "That is immensely reassuring to his interlocutors."

This has made the Prince an effective asset for the Foreign Office and the British intelligence community in certain key regions, able to transmit the British viewpoint to major players and to glean information that may not be so readily divulged to a minister of state or diplomat. Sources say these missions always take account of the constitutional limits to his role: he would not be asked to negotiate or conclude deals, whether political or commercial, but to advise and warn, promote and listen. A source close to the Prince says he doesn't like being used to market weaponry and now sidesteps such activities where possible. That wasn't always the case. In Jonathan Dimbleby's 1994 documentary, Charles defends his appearance at the Dubai arms fair on the basis that he is boosting British trade, arguing that the arms will likely be used as a deterrent and if the UK doesn't sell them, someone else will. If he has changed his mind, why doesn't the dissident Prince speak up? One answer, according to insiders, is that he has done so, in—thus far—private communications. If he is uncomfortable with his itineraries, he will say so, in terms, black ink with underlinings.

Another answer is that any noisy protests on his part would diminish his usefulness in the Gulf. Some of the objectives of his recent trip to Saudi Arabia relied on that vanishing commodity: secrecy. All of them relied on his close skein of relationships in the region. "It's soft, it's track-five diplomacy, under über-Chatham House rules," says a source. As the Prince put on his headdress, picked up his sword, and set to dancing, London harbored deepening fears that Saudi support for the Syrian insurgency had not only failed in the objective of toppling President Assad, but continued to strengthen jihadi groups that draw many of their fighters from radicalized youth from outside Syria. The conflict has also displaced millions of refugees. At private meetings with the King and other Saudi royals, including Abdullah's youngest brother and subsequently anointed heir Prince Muqrin bin Abdulaziz, the Prince discussed how the Saudis could best target humanitarian aid and articulated the risk of blowback as battle-hardened militants returned home—whether to Saudi Arabia or the UK. The Prince also communicated British worries about wider regional stability and in particular the capture by the group then calling itself ISIS of the Iraqi city of Fallujah.

There must be questions about any initiative that gives succor to the Saudi regime or attempts to appease the unappeasable. At the time, Britain aimed to do both. Less than two months after Charles's visit, Prince Bandar bin Sultan, Saudi Arabia's intelligence chief and driver of the misfired Syria policy, stood down. The choice of his successor, Interior Minister Mohamed bin Nayef, signaled closer strategic and intelligence cooperation between Saudi Arabia and its Western allies just as the crisis in the region sharpened, with ISIS forces sweeping into Iraq. The Saudis are deeply problematic allies, says a source. British and US foreign policy is in disarray but for now there is no alternative to trying to work with the Saudis. The Prince's discussions, while not conclusive, "may well have aided clear thinking in exalted [Saudi] circles," the source adds.

SERVICE TO QUEEN AND COUNTRY OFTEN GOES UNRECOGNIZED, AS Charles knows, and not only from direct experience. As heir to the throne and in his duties representing the Queen, he receives regular briefings from intelligence officials and has made private visits to the headquarters of MI5, MI6, and GCHQ. "You can usually ensure a moment when large numbers of staff gather round a central atrium," says an aide. Charles has also met teams in Northern Ireland and farther-flung locations. "The Prince's visits are greatly appreciated by staff," says a statement from the organizations provided for this book. A former field operative remembers such a visit as "slightly unreal but [it] cheered everybody up."

In 2012 the Prince took on a formal role with the services at their request, becoming their first royal patron. He and Camilla also attended the premiere of the James Bond movie *Skyfall*, asking that monies raised should benefit charities helping former and serving members of the intelligence services. He held the first annual Prince of Wales Intelligence Community Awards a year earlier. It had been his idea to find a way to celebrate achievements by members of the intelligence services; the three agencies then got together to agree to the criteria. The lunchtime ceremony is held every year in the St. James's Palace State Apartments. "His Royal Highness has often commented that due to the secret nature of the three agencies' work, their successes often remain unrecognized and unreported," says the statement from the intelligence services. "The awards complement the public honors and recognize staff for their outstanding efforts to keep the country safe."

Many royal engagements are announced in advance. These awards are only reported a day after the event, to maintain confidentiality. The attendees, numbering around two hundred, include friends and family, the services heads and the ministers with oversight of the services. Citations are given to whole teams, and are directed not just to field agents but also for excellence in administration, management, and what in a corporate setting might be termed information technology. Charles conducts the ceremony with the same high formality as he doles out public honors. "The Prince's appreciation of the work of the intelligence agencies came across very strongly and it was great to hear how much he values what we do. . . . We were really proud to receive the award," says one 2014 recipient. "It was fantastic to see the Prince appreciate the work that goes into joint operations," says another. "His questions showed just how interested he is in our work."

Most people employed in intelligence are unable to tell any but those closest to them how they spend their days and then only in circumscribed form. To outsiders, spies often describe themselves as "consultants," deflecting curiosity by pretending to specialize in areas so boring or abstruse as to discourage further inquiries. The awards offer a rare chance to operate in daylight. "I was delighted my parents could glimpse into my world." "Our work being recognized by the Prince of Wales in front of our colleagues and family made me very proud, and my mum more so." "There are not many occasions where you can speak so openly about our work; this is one." "Being in the shadows, it was extraordinary to be at St. James's Palace talking to the Prince about our work."

That positive reinforcement is all the more welcome in the changed and rugged landscape spies refer to as "Snowdonia." In 2013, former CIA systems administrator Edward Snowden leaked thousands of classified documents obtained during his work as an outside contractor to the US National

Security Agency (NSA), a conjoined sibling of Britain's GCHQ. The documents revealed that the United States and UK in concert with other countries were scooping up huge amounts of data from electronic communications of all kinds, snooping on allies in their efforts to contain terrorism, and circumventing restrictions against spying on their own citizens by sharing data between them. A core group of five countries—Five Eyes—jointly operating many of the surveillance programs originally came together during World War II when Britain reunited with its former Anglophone colonies, the United States, Australia, Canada, and New Zealand, to plan for the postwar world and continued their cooperation into the Cold War era and beyond.

Snowden's leaks disrupted relations with friendly countries that found they had been targeted and damaged the reputations of the intelligence agencies involved—and, according to those agencies, compromised active operations and operatives as well as future capacities. They also raised questions almost as bottomless as the NSA archives, about privacy versus security and accountability versus secrecy.

The backwash is engulfing public and corporate life, urging new safeguards for individual privacy and greater institutional transparency. The arguments don't hinge simply on ethics but also on the practical difficulties of blocking the spread of information in a porous world. It is a struggle neither Charles nor the palace apparatus yet grasps, even though they often find themselves directly impacted.

Four of the Five Eyes are countries for which Charles is likely to serve as head of state. Australia, Canada, and New Zealand still bend the knee to the Crown, but it is the Crown, eager to retain their loyalty, that pays court to them, with regular visits. Charles's May 2014 visit to Canada wasn't an unalloyed success.

CAMILLA SMILES ON THE PODIUM. SHE'S WEARING A BLUE THAT'S more cobalt than royal, designed to tone with her Nova Scotia tartan collar and scarf, and beginning to accessorize with her fingers on this unseasonably frigid morning. The Duchess of Cornwall has adjusted smoothly to many of the oddities of being a royal, but she wasn't born with the Windsor metabolism. She feels the cold, unlike her poikilothermic husband and in-laws, and finds foreign trips grueling. It doesn't help that the Prince demands jam-packed schedules that allocate no slots to lunches or quiet lie-downs, irrespective of the time zones overflown. Then there are the endless ceremonials. She's often required to spend more time being welcomed and waved off than actually looking at a place.

On the first day of the Canada trip, that's probably a good thing. She has been spared the freezing run-through of Nova Scotia's welcoming ceremony on Halifax's Grand Parade. A choir of schoolchildren shivered in harmony as their adult overlords wrapped up against the cold. No matter: everyone was excited. The authorities had deployed a guard of honor and a platform full of movers and shakers including Justice Minister Peter MacKay, sent to Canada's federal parliament by the voters of a Nova Scotian constituency. A military band, perplexingly, played "What Shall We Do with the Drunken Sailor?" until MacKay moved to the microphone to check sound levels, announcing his pleasure in welcoming "the Princess of Wales" to his country—the title by which Diana was known. By the time he delivers his speech, MacKay has corrected his mistake, but it's a foretaste of a trip during which avidity for the spectacle of royalty masks a deeper confusion about who the visitors are and what they're doing in Canada.

Some of that confusion is stirred by the ghost who already hovered above the proceedings before MacKay inadvertently named her. Charles and Diana routinely drew crowds in the tens of thousands on their first trip to Canada in 1983. Charles and Camilla's whistle-stop tour to Halifax, Pictou County, Charlottetown, and Winnipeg never commands big attendances, but everywhere they go, the couple is greeted by small numbers of well-wishers propelled onto the streets by the impulse to breathe the same air as royalty. "Just look at the smiles," says Shelly Glover, federal Minister for Canadian Heritage. "They just love the Prince and the Duchess. . . . The media here and in the UK are very different in outlook. I see media here covering the royal visit with smiles. The Canadian media are just as excited as the rest of us."[12]

That isn't much of an exaggeration. The state broadcaster CBC streams every event live. Other channels confect royal specials and dust down archival footage from the Prince's previous sixteen trips to his future kingdom. Local newspapers splash the visit on their front pages and shower the royals with praise. When Charles feeds sandwiches to a polar bear called Hudson at a Manitoba zoo, Canadian journalists clap like seals offered particularly tasty mackerel.

Britain's fourth estate couldn't have cared less. At first only one story from Canada makes it into the British newspapers and then barely scraping onto two or three inside pages. After the welcome ceremony in Halifax, Charles and Camilla visit a local resource center for military families where the couple chats with a trio of volunteers costumed as a carrot, a bunch of grapes, and a banana as part of a drive to promote healthy eating. In the UK, the image inspires a gag as inevitable as some of the Prince's own punch lines: that he has moved on from talking to plants to holding conversations with fruit.

But an encounter later the same day will create a volume of coverage back in Britain that surpasses even Diana's high-water mark or the Cambridges' overseas missions. At a tea for World War II veterans and war brides at the Canadian Museum of Immigration at Pier 21, Charles and Camilla meet eighty-seven-year-old Marianne Ferguson. A volunteer at the museum, Ferguson, née Echt, first arrived at Pier 21 aboard a ship called the *Andania* in February 1939, three months before King George and Queen Elizabeth landed on Canadian shores. She was a Jewish refugee from Danzig, who had witnessed the brutality of Nazism.

How much of her story she revealed to Charles in the few minutes they spent in each other's company—or what, exactly, he said in response—remains unclear. Neither the Prince nor his aides would comment on the "private conversation," but according to the *Daily Mail* a remark made by the Prince was "heard by several witnesses. Mother-of-three Mrs. Ferguson said: 'I had finished showing him the exhibit and talked with him about my own family background and how I came to Canada. The Prince then said, "And now Putin is doing just about the same as Hitler." I must say that I agree with him and am sure a lot of people do. I was very surprised that he made the comment as I know [members of the Royal Family] aren't meant to say these things but it was very heartfelt and honest.'"[13]

British politicians tripped over themselves in the rush to slap down the Prince or to defend him. "If Prince Charles wants to make controversial statements on national or international issues he should abdicate and stand for election," tweeted Labour MP Mike Gapes. Russia hit back too.

State-funded broadcaster Russia Today accused the Windsors of susceptibility to Nazism, summoning as evidence the family's German antecedents, the infamous 1937 visit paid by the Duke of Windsor—as Edward VIII became on abdication—to Hitler, and for good measure reminding viewers of Prince Philip's SS brother-in-law and the swastika armband Prince Harry once wore to attend a costume party. Putin weighed in, riposting that Charles's alleged comment did not live up to standards of "royal behavior"—a criticism that provoked snickering in the Foreign Office given the fate of the Romanovs—but the Russian President downplayed the seriousness of the diplomatic spat. "I think that if our partners in Great Britain, just as I am, are guided by national interests rather than some other considerations, then all this will pass quite quickly and we'll continue to co-operate as we have done before," he pronounced magisterially.[14]

The world hadn't shifted on its axis. The fracas confirmed the Prince's critics in their analysis that he is dangerously outspoken but endeared him to another constituency that is tired of political platitudes. Despite the churning coverage, it wasn't really a big deal. But Charles, for all that he assumed a brave face for his last duties in Canada, flew back to Britain demoralized. He had traveled with an agenda and a higher purpose, as a representative of Canada's head of state and as the nation's presumed next head of state, not only to shore up support for the monarchy but also to showcase its potential future form. His program of activities made little distinction between head-of-state functions and the Prince's promotion of various causes. In this blurring of lines, he had the support of his hosts. "The Canadian government sees his charities as being an important element in the relationship with the Crown and part of its value," said a well-placed source.

THE PRINCE MAY BE BRITAIN'S MOST PROLIFIC PHILANTHROPIST BY many measures, but that's not how Britons see him. His image farther afield, clouded though it is by memories of Diana, more often acknowledges the scale of his charitable work. "Coming from somewhere other than here, I saw the Prince as a leader," says Hank Dittmar.[15] "I didn't come with a lot of other baggage British people have about the system." Another of Charles's

American-born advisers, Dame Amelia Fawcett, lauds the Prince as an unsung hero. "In the United States he would be lionized," she says. "The sniping, the envy, the 'how-dare-he,' 'he's-too-privileged,' no one would think like that. They'd think, 'Wow, look at what he's doing; here's a man who has got everything, who is wealthy and privileged, who doesn't need to do anything, but he's doing so much for so many.'"[16]

America might well share Britain's conflicted attitudes to wealth, privilege, and the Crown had the nation not shaken off the colonial yoke—and the British Crown—in 1776. Australia, Canada, Jamaica, New Zealand, and the other far-flung Commonwealth Realms never made a full break and retain some of the symptoms of adolescence as a result. Australia, in particular, is often truculent toward the royals, then screams like a kid at a pop concert when they pay a visit. As Charles contemplates the relationship between the House of Windsor and the Realms, wondering how to get it onto a more mature footing, or mulls his possible future role as head of the wider Commonwealth, the lessons of history carry both comfort and warning. The monarchy may appear sturdy and adaptable, but empires, countries, the solid-looking world, and social orders have all proved friable.

The growth of the British Empire reflected the nation's military strength, entrepreneurial spirit, and sense of destiny. It crumbled with those defining characteristics and as the ideological, commercial, and strategic logic of the British brand of colonialism failed. The brutality deployed to retain dependencies tore away the fig leaf of the Empire's moral purpose and jarred with the very notion of Britishness. The costs of fighting global wars eventually far exceeded the revenues from distant territories. In 1947, Charles's great-uncle Mountbatten as the last Governor-General of India declared the partition of India and Pakistan. Both nations became independent republics. Two years later, UK Prime Minister Clement Attlee agreed that India could remain a member of the Commonwealth of Nations, up to that point an association of countries ruled directly or indirectly by Britain. Over the years more countries joined, former colonies and others without historical ties, all hoping for diplomatic advantage from the association.

The Commonwealth, in turn, has attempted to promote democracy, human rights, and the rule of law. Its inability to bring to heel members in flagrant breach of these values raises questions about how long the association will endure. Then there's the small matter of what happens when the Queen dies. There is no automatic guarantee that her son will be welcomed to the role. The Palace is leaving as little as possible to chance. In a piece of theater so significant that the Queen rose from her sickbed to attend, Commonwealth Secretary-General Kamalesh Sharma used the signing of a new Commonwealth charter in March 2013 to firm up Charles's candidacy. "You have carried forward with untiring dedication and conviction the task laid upon you of following your father as Head of the Commonwealth," he told the Queen. "Throughout the Commonwealth's existence, the Crown has symbolized the free association of our nations and our peoples, promoting the right and proper purpose of assembly and dialogue. The ties forged between the people and communities of the Commonwealth have been reinforced by the care which you have taken to visit and meet so many of them over more than 60 years. The support given to you in this endeavor by the Prince of Wales and other members of the Royal Family deepens the Commonwealth's links to the Crown."[17]

That support often takes the form of visits designed to project the deathless continuity of those links. Yet many of the destinations on such trips spark intimations of their mortality too, as Charles's 2014 Canada itinerary showed. There have been forced migrations: arrivals like Ferguson's at Pier 21 and the 187 Scots, sent in search of a new home by the Highland Clearances, who in 1773 disembarked in Pictou from the ship *Hector*, and ragged exoduses of indigenous peoples and Acadians, the descendants of French colonialists, persecuted and expelled in Britannia's name. Europeans had made landfall on the American continent in the seventeenth century, first the French, then the British, and fought across the landmass, battling for territory and in proxy for their wider imperial conflict, deploying soldiers and corporate entities such as the Hudson's Bay Company to secure their claims. France ceded its Canadian lands to Britain in the 1763 Treaty of Paris but then weighed in against its old foe in the American War of Independence.

Canada itself is only a century and a half old, formed by the melding of British colonies into a dominion with a significant degree of autonomy. In 1931 it gained formal independence, though for another fifty years Westminster would retain residual powers to amend the Canadian constitution.

From some perspectives, the apparatus of monarchy looks like a similar piece of historical detritus, as picturesque as the replica of *Hector* that Charles and Camilla stopped to admire during their visit to Pictou—and about as seaworthy.

Supporters of the Canadian monarchy rehearse the standard arguments for the institution, starting with its unifying function in a sprawling federation of provinces and three territories that encompasses First Nations peoples, Inuit and Métis, and a variety of Anglophone and Francophone populations distributed across a landmass that stretches from temperate British Columbia to the tundra of Nunavut. Then there are the constitutional functions anchored by royalty plus, of course, the overarching guarantee that a monarch provides in safeguarding democracy. The Monarchist League of Canada trots out an additional argument too, a peculiarly Canadian spin on the interplay between the monarchy and national identity—the Windsors represent a bulwark against US cultural imperialism.

Opinion polls in Canada broadly mirror trends in the other realms: a falling off in support for the monarchy during the 1990s and first decade of the twenty-first century, followed recently by a revival in interest in the younger generations and especially William and Kate and baby George. A 2013 Forum Poll for the *National Post* rated William almost three times more popular than his father and produced some confusing data on the appeal of the monarchy in general, with a majority of respondents in favor of keeping the Crown—48 percent compared to 37 percent for abolition—but 63 percent also saying the head of state should be Canadian and reside in Canada.[18]

The blizzards of polls and flurries of disputes between committed monarchists and ardent republicans that accompany royal visits succeed like a good Canadian dump of snow in disguising the significant features of the landscape. There's a broad, flat plain of apathy out there—Canadians who really don't care very much either way—and the electric fence that encircles the institution of the monarchy means they're right not to waste too much energy on the issue. The patriation of Canada's constitution in 1982, though symbolic of its independent nationhood, entrenched the overseas monarchy more firmly at its heart, requiring any constitutional amendment affecting the Crown to secure the unanimous support of the federal and provincial governments, about as likely as catching a tan in the Nunavut winter.

The solidity of the constitutional arrangements might be assumed to place Canada low on the priorities of the Windsors when other Realms and voting populations could far more easily mobilize the tumbrels. That would be to misunderstand the sense of duty—and destiny—shared by the Queen and her son that compels them to render the service they believe themselves born to fulfill. Both, in their own distinctive ways, believe in adding value to their roles. In return—and though the Queen disguises this impulse far better than her thin-skinned son—they want to be wanted.

Though Charles's chief focus has been on turning his existing position to meaningful use, he has been thinking about the longer term, too, for many years and now with increasing urgency. In Canada he is developing another test bed for his ideas, a virtual Duchy Home Farm or Poundbury. In devising a new model of monarchy for the Realms, the Prince hopes to defeat their new model armies of republicanism. Canada, with small but committed forces on either side and larger phalanxes of don't-knows and couldn't-cares, makes a good testing ground.

CHAPTER 9

Happy and Notorious

//

A MOMENT IN CANADA SPEAKS TO THE NATURE OF THE RELATION-ship between the Prince and his Duchess. On the first full day of the trip, the royal convoy has split into two, with Charles going to Halifax Public Gardens to perform one of the standard gestures of royalty, "planting" a sapling by ceremonially dumping a scoop of soil. In 1939, King George VI carried out the same symbolic act at the base of one of the trees that now towers over his grandson. Camilla has been chauffeured to a rougher part of Halifax, to speak to women who have escaped abusive partners with the help of a charity called Alice Housing.

The schedule carefully plotted by Canadian officials and royal aides envisages the Prince making quick work of his tree planting and going on to Seaport Farmer's Market to tour the stalls before reuniting with his wife for the first of several displays of Scottish dancing Nova Scotia lays on for them. But Charles always runs late. During a walkabout in the park, he stops and speaks to everybody, doesn't just say hello and move down the line but is drawn into conversations, inevitably delaying his segment of the convoy. Camilla, though she engages with people—and at this stop listens intently to difficult stories of spousal violence—tends to keep to the timings she has been given. As a result, she arrives at the covered farmer's market ahead of her husband and takes the opportunity to shelter, briefly, in a side room, recharging the batteries that in people not raised to royal life easily run low during long days of glad-handing.

After ten minutes, she feels refreshed enough to be a Duchess once again and she embarks on her own tour of the market stalls. Charles, unaware that Camilla has beaten him to this destination, makes his own royal progress along the aisles. He feels rough—he will generously share British cold germs with the peoples of Canada on this trip—but nevertheless he again becomes absorbed in the royal job, talking to stallholders, sampling their jams and cakes and cordials. He doesn't spot his wife until their parties converge. As he catches sight of Camilla, he stops, surprised, and then another expression transfigures his pallid face: joy. "Oh," he says, enchanted. "You."

HOLD ON TO THAT IMAGE. IT'S NOT EASY TO DO SO AMID A CLAMOR of competing pictures and multiple narratives, many of them sulfurous. That is not to say the other versions of Charles and Camilla are all without merit. The Rashomon effect—the way one reality observed by different individuals may produce equally valid, yet apparently contradictory, histories—has proved especially potent in their case.

It doesn't help that any truths about a couple whose love for each other destroyed their first marriages lie buried beneath a man-made lithosphere of nonsense. Many of the most preposterous stories emanate from sources thousands of miles from their protagonists. The First Amendment of the US Constitution protects the right of individuals to express themselves through publication and dissemination of information, ideas, and opinions without interference, constraint, or prosecution by the government. The noblest of clauses has spawned the strangest of phenomena—supermarket tabloids. These are sensationalist magazines that are even odder than the stories they purport to cover. They occasionally break real news: The *National Enquirer* ran the Squidgygate transcript before the British media dared to do so. Supermarket tabloids have also published photographs of heaven, reported alien invasions, and declared Elvis alive almost as often as they've announced the Duchess of Cambridge's pregnancy. Diana conspiracies are a perennial.

Among 2014 headlines the *Globe* designed to grab attention at the checkout was this, in March: "DIANA'S KILLER HIDING IN RUSSIA—HAND HIM OVER, WILLIAM RAGES."

A glimmer of internal logic illuminated the tall tale. Russia had refused to surrender Edward Snowden to the US authorities, so surely it would refrain from sending Diana's assassin for trial in England—should such a person exist. There was no love lost between the Russian President and the British royals, the tabloid stated with accidental prescience. (Less than two months later, Charles's critical commentary on Putin's Crimea adventures would make world headlines.)

By July, the *Globe* had devised a fresh and even further-fetched angle on the conspiracy: "CAMILLA SHOCKS KATE: CHARLES MURDERED DIANA—AND I'M NEXT!" A cover flash provided a clue to the Prince's supposed motive: "$350M DIVORCE TURNS UGLY." This followed up on an issue earlier the same month that claimed the Queen had ordered him to divorce Camilla. The same issue revealed that "POPE FRANCIS IS DYING."

In ages past, the majority of people fortunate enough to live in democracies retained some faith in the authorities to tell the truth. Everybody read magazines like the *Globe* understanding that this was entertainment, not news. These days consumers trust nothing and everything, getting much of their information from the Internet and sources less credible than supermarket tabloids, increasingly unable to distinguish virtual junk food from something more nourishing. So it is that an immeasurable but significant contingent of the burgeoning global population assumes Charles to be heading for the divorce courts for a second time, possibly at the bidding of the Queen, or only refraining only from doing so because Camilla holds dirt on the royals (another popular Internet meme).

Does it matter that a prince who mistrusts the legacy of the Enlightenment should suffer under an encroaching Endarkenment? Certainly not as much as the Endarkenment itself matters, but its miasma does help to obscure what Charles does and why, especially in combination with mainstream coverage, itself riven by old allegiances and half-forgotten resentments. As for Camilla, if the punishment for her double adultery in an earlier century might have seen her immobilized in stocks for passersby to scoff and spit at, her latter-day humiliation has been no less public and almost as brutal.

From the moment of her exposure as the Prince's illicit lover, the British press held her up not just for scorn but ridicule. "Trundling a trolley round Sainsbury's yesterday, [Camilla] hardly looked like a woman at the centre of a royal love scandal," reported the *Daily Mirror* in 1993.[1] "But as Camilla faced the world for the first time in weeks, she did supply the answer to a frequently posed question—'what DOES Prince Charles see in her?' In her outsize headscarf and unfussy clothes, she was a dead ringer for HM . . . His Mum." Here's an excerpt from the *Daily Express* of the same period: "Women in particular, who tend for some extraordinary reason to be much more bitchy than men in assessing female attributes, have been astounded at the thought that Prince Charles would choose the equine-faced Camilla over the fashion plate Diana, unless it had something to do with his passion for horses."[2] The barrage of articles reported public disapproval and reinforced it. An oft-quoted story that Camilla had been pelted with bread rolls in a supermarket car park by angry supporters of Diana seems to have been pure invention. In Clarence House there is a suspicion that a Camilla look-alike was hired to stage this and other stunts.

Camilla endured her notoriety in silence. "People say she's tough," says Lucia Santa Cruz. "She's not tough. She's amazingly strong, which is different. She is a solid person. She had a very good family background. She's got very good parents, she's got a sister that she's close to. She has the strength that people from very, very solid families tend to have, and she's very resilient. She is very dignified, which in a way made all this so much worse for her. It was the worst kind of public bullying. [There was] nothing she could do to get out of her situation. She never opened her mouth; she never defended herself."[3]

She did get some help. Mark Bolland, on the Prince's staff from 1996 until his less-than-happy departure in 2002, worked after Diana's death to gain acceptance for the royal mistress. One strand of the strategy saw Charles and Camilla begin to appear together instead of always sidestepping cameras. Their January 1999 unveiling, on the steps of the Ritz hotel after the fiftieth birthday party of Camilla's sister, Annabel Elliot, attracted "up to 200 photographers and journalists . . . to witness the occasion, having set up 60 ladders lined three-deep in anticipation outside the hotel," the BBC reported. "Television satellite vans were parked in side streets alongside the London hotel, and bright TV lights illuminated the scene.

Alongside the media throng was a crowd of members of the public several hundred strong."[4] Their first public kiss—a peck on the cheek—took place at another birthday party, marking the fifteenth year of the National Osteoporosis Society in June 2001.

The second strategic strand proved more controversial within the palace system. Other members of the Windsor family suspected Bolland leaked negative stories about them in order to make Charles look better by comparison. It's an allegation Bolland appeared to accept in a 2005 interview. "It was all about Camilla," he told Sholto Byrnes of the *Independent*. "All about the refusal of the Queen and Buckingham Palace to take the relationship seriously and assist the prince in reaching a conclusion. That underpinned everything."

"It seems extraordinary for royal servants to be briefing against other members of the reigning family," Byrnes writes. " 'The team that was there probably cared too much and got too emotional about it at times,' concedes Bolland. 'We got in a sort of Prince of Wales bunker within the House of Windsor. But to an extent that reflected him.' "[5]

Charles and camilla plighted their troth on april 9, 2005, a day later than originally planned. The death of Pope John Paul II on April 2 necessitated the short-notice change when the Prince agreed to stand in for the Queen at the funeral in Rome. Segments of the media reported this as a sign from above that the union was jinxed.

Though technically Princess of Wales since the marriage, Camilla has abjured the title and its unhappy resonances. Nevertheless, divorce rumors have circulated pretty much from the first day of the royal honeymoon at Birkhall, given credence by publications that, unlike America's supermarket tabloids, consider themselves journals of record and by journalists with histories of procuring real royal scoops. Diana was so fond of the *Daily Mail*'s Richard Kay that she gave him substantial insights into her life; her trust was repaid after her death, when Kay declined to write a tell-all biography. "I was very close to her and I felt that one of the reasons I never wrote a book was that she'd got a raw deal. Mostly by people who worked for her or were her friends. And they all rushed to get their memoirs out as quickly as possible and I always felt my great difficulty would be not what to put into a book but what to leave out," he says.[6] In 2010, five years into the Prince's second marriage, Kay and his colleague Geoffrey Levy published a long piece entitled "Why Charles and Camilla Are Now Leading Such Separate Lives."

Their article described "a very strange marriage" made under duress, in anticipation of the Prince's accession. In this version of events, not to marry Camilla represented a greater barrier to Charles's eventual kingship than marrying her, but neither partner wanted to do it. Some accounts suggest a different reality. The night the engagement was announced Camilla was "excited like a young girl," says Robin Boles, the Chief Executive of In Kind Direct, one of the Prince's organizations, which redistributes surplus goods from companies to charities.[7]

Kay and Levy wrote that Charles and Camilla's staff routinely clashed. The couple's habits clashed too, the Prince's "obsessional neatness" offended by the Duchess's "renowned domestic untidiness." An "aged dowager who has known Camilla all her life" provided a pithy commentary: "When a woman's been a man's mistress for 30 years and then marries him, the relationship is bound to change. They still love each other, I have no doubt of that, but life as a married couple is difficult for two such independent spirits, who have always enjoyed the physical aspects of life. There's a certain electricity about sex between lovers which is bound to dissipate after several years of marriage."

A "seasoned royal aide" gave another possible reason for the supposed chill in the heir: "Camilla absolutely adores having her grandchildren around her and is always talking about them, but Charles simply cannot stand the noise and mess that small children make." As a result, the authors explained, the Prince preferred splendid isolation in his own houses, while the Duchess entertained her grandchildren at Ray Mill, her bolt-hole in Wiltshire since she divorced Andrew Parker Bowles in 1995. Adding to the disaffection, the Duchess apparently resented her royal duties. "For now," the article concluded, "theirs is not a marriage in actual 'difficulties,' because it is an arrangement that both appear to be content with. And yet—who would ever have imagined that the older woman for whom a crown prince dumped a young and beautiful wife now chooses to spend so much time away from him in a world of her own?"[8]

The authors were wise to hedge. By April 2014, with the couple nine years married and the Prince's delight in his own grandson palpable, Kay and Levy wrote a second long article on the state of the relationship. "From 'That Wicked Woman' to Her Majesty's Secret Weapon" described Camilla's "remorseless" and "inexorable royal progress," adding that she seemed "to have settled comfortably into the royal role that arrived late in life." There is a negative: Camilla's ascendancy in the Queen's affections has alienated Charles's young brothers and their wives. "Edward is furious that Sophie now has to curtsey to Camilla. . . . Through all this, the former *maîtresse en titre* glides effortlessly beside the Prince of Wales, soothing his brow one moment, cajoling him the next. If she is eventually crowned Queen Camilla, will it be his triumph, or hers?"[9]

"The thrust of the [first] piece, that their relationship works when they are not on top of each other, still holds true," e-mails Kay. "Camilla does prefer being at Ray Mill with her grandchildren around her while the Prince likes the familiarity of Highgrove, where he prefers to work without being disturbed by noisy step-grandchildren. . . . On their relationship, if anything it seems now that they somehow strengthened the union between them."[10]

This is the Rashomon effect in action. From some angles, the time Camilla and Charles spend apart is easily interpreted as a symptom of dysfunction. From others, it's a sign of stability, in the relationship and the psyches of both parties to it. The Prince will never be carefree but he has figured out the ingredients he needs to maintain an even keel: Camilla, his family, his gardens, his faith, his sanctuaries, and—possibly even above all—his work. When I asked him the standard feature writer's question, "what gives you joy?" he embarked on a long answer about being able to put back together again and heal things that have otherwise been abandoned or allowed to become derelict or destroyed. His aide Kristina Kyriacou, with evident amusement, prompted him: "your grandson, Sir." He laughed and happily proffered a more traditional—and entirely heartfelt—answer: "Having a wonderful wife. And of course now a grandson."[11] "All his friends have been on our knees saying, 'Won't you just slow down?'" says Emma Thompson. "I now think it would be very bad for him. I think he'd unravel in some way."[12]

Camilla, too, needs the space to pursue her own interests. "She's got much more of a world of her own than people suspect," says Lucia Santa

Cruz. "She's very happy on her own. She's an amazing reader; she's very well read. Every time I discover a new author and I say 'have you read?' she's read them all. Very difficult to give her a book. She loves what she calls pottering in the garden so she's very happy on her own and that means she's got a lot of internal life. Which I think also is her protection. She could flit off and be on her own, by herself and happy. She loves being in her house on her own."[13]

Together, the Prince and Camilla belie the reports of friction. They share secret jokes and mirror each other's body language (though Camilla has yet to adopt the Windsor habit of holding her hands behind her back). "She's terrific, so down-to-earth, so good for him," says Patrick Holden.[14] Ben Elliot reckons this cuts both ways: the Prince is good for his aunt. "He really loves her. They're so affectionate to each other. Some couples when they've been together that long . . ." Elliot trails off, then continues. "He's so sweet to her."[15]

There are long-standing niggles. Camilla likes plain food, grilled fish, steamed vegetables. Charles has a taste for suet puddings and game. There are potentially more explosive issues. Camilla doesn't entirely buy into the princely philosophy and sometimes challenges his views, but if other people disagree with him, that's another matter. "She is entirely loyal to his likes and dislikes," says Lucia Santa Cruz. "We argue about organics, the solution to world problems, the extent of ecology versus the needs of huge populations and she will always say 'but he is right about this.' "[16]

A Clarence House insider credits Camilla with giving the Prince his most secure line yet to Planet Earth: "She's a caring and considerate mother and she's never lost sight of the importance of family, the importance of having them close and keeping them around. That keeps her grounded and that gives her a practicality that perhaps she might otherwise forget. It gives her an anchor. I'm always surprised at how savvy she is. . . . It's clear she's not in a bubble."

The couple has developed an effective working partnership too, often appearing as a double act. She has acquired the usual range of respectable royal involvements, as patron or president, from animal charities, garden trusts, veterans' associations, and the Royal Voluntary Service to Maggie's Cancer Caring Centre, hospices and hospitals, opera societies and orchestras. Some patronages, such as the Charleston Trust, are "arty, literary, she loves that; Ditchling museum, again something very arty, it touches the rather bookish side of her nature," says Amanda Macmanus, one of Camilla's two part-time Assistant Private Secretaries and a woman who appears as jolly as the Duchess herself.[17]

Camilla's good humor cloaks the resilience Santa Cruz describes that enabled her to withstand the backlash against her role in the breakup of the Prince's first marriage. In 1995, at the height of the backlash, the then Mrs. Parker Bowles agreed to become the patron of the National Osteoporosis Society after watching her mother die from the condition that crumbles bones. "We watched in horror as she quite literally shrank before our eyes," Camilla recalled later. "My mother's GP was kind and sympathetic, but he was able to do little to alleviate the pain she was in."[18] The charity's CEO took a gamble that at the time seemed risky: that Camilla's association would bring the right kind of attention to the brand.

More recently the Duchess has also quietly developed a range of campaigning interests distinct from her husband's and other members of the royal family, grappling with issues that in palace terms could seem edgy. She promotes credit unions—nonprofit financial cooperatives—seeking to draw attention to the problems of debt and rip-off loans that affect lower-income demographics most severely. She works with several organizations supporting victims of rape and sexual abuse. She has given her backing to a campaign against the practice of female genital mutilation.

From a privileged background, but an earthy one, tempered by the flames of contempt, the Duchess is no shrinking violet. At a reception, she spotted her friend, Australian novelist Kathy Lette, maneuvering through the crowd on crutches. "What did you do to yourself?" Camilla asked. "I fell off my toyboy," Lette replied. Camilla roared.

Her behavior could rarely be described as queenly, yet as Richard Kay and Geoffrey Levy hinted, the assumption in Clarence House as in Buckingham Palace and in wider royal circles is that Camilla will one day sit enthroned alongside her King not as "Princess Consort"—the designation mooted by aides during the early days of her rehabilitation—but Queen. Nobody doubts this is what Charles wants. "I think she's very good for him," says Robin Boles. "She should be Queen. There's nothing in the law that stops her from being Queen. I'd put my money on it."[19]

That isn't quite as safe a bet as it looks. People who meet Camilla generally warm to her. She has authenticity, as Nicholas Soames explains with his characteristic exuberance. "There's not one bit of side to the Duchess of Cornwall. She's what-you-see-is-what-you-get. She's what my father would have called 'a bloody good egg.' She's terrific, she's great, and people respond to that. What they most respond to is people being themselves. She's just a really good girl, good-natured, she likes people. Exactly like the Prince's grandmother was, who grew up in grand surroundings and was good with what the press, in their patronizing way, are pleased to call 'ordinary people.'"[20]

The problem is that most of those "ordinary people" haven't met Camilla, and many of them remember her predecessor. Opinion polls are moving in favor of Charles. A May 2013 poll showed a narrow majority expects him to make a good king. There is diminishing support for the idea of the crown passing straight to William. But the same poll revealed Camilla as the only member of the royal family judged to have made a negative contribution to the monarchy; 46 percent of respondents argued that she should be relegated to consort status, with only 16 percent backing the idea of Queen Camilla.[21] Another poll at the start of 2014 echoed these findings.

During the infamous Camillagate discussion, Charles told his then lover, "I'm so proud of you." "Don't be silly. I've never achieved anything," Camilla demurred. He insisted, she protested. Then he uttered a line often construed as proof of his self-absorption: "Your greatest achievement is to love me." "Oh darling," she said, "easier than falling off a chair." His next sentence gives an insight into their reality at the time: "You suffer all these indignities and tortures and calumnies." "Oh darling," she replied. "Don't be so silly. I'd suffer anything for you. That's love. It's the strength of love."

Loving Charles continues to be an achievement, a test of strength that she keeps winning. For the Prince her victories couldn't be more important, and not only because he has known what love means for more than four decades. "He's absolutely a whole other person now. He was desperately unhappy. He's not any more," says Emma Thompson.[22]

ALWAYS LOOK ON THE BRIGHT SIDE OF LIFE. THE PRINCE OF WAILS has proven himself conspicuously bad at following this advice, but twice cameras have captured him intoning it. In Jonathan Dimbleby's 1994 documentary, a tentative Charles affects to join in as the rock musician Phil Collins leads a chorus of young jobless. "When you're chewing on life's gristle / Don't grumble, give a whistle / And this'll help things turn out for the best / And always look on the bright side of life!" The lyrics gained an unexpected poignancy in the mouths of Prince's Trust clients and a Prince at a low ebb.

Written by Monty Python alumnus Eric Idle, the song originally garnished the final sequence of *Monty Python's Life of Brian* in which the hero, a reluctant Jewish messiah in Roman-occupied Judea, is crucified. As Brian hangs amid rows of prisoners condemned to die in the same way, Idle, splayed on an adjacent cross, begins to sing and soon everybody takes up the refrain. Protestors accused the film of blasphemy at its 1979 release and launched pickets. Other jurisdictions banned the movie altogether. Aberystwyth—the town in Wales where Charles spent a lonely university term—took thirty years to lift its prohibition.

On November 12, 2008, during the final year of Aberystwyth's ban, Idle again performed the ditty, clad in a white tutu and feathered headdress, emerging from a gaggle of ballerinas during an excerpt from *Swan Lake*. His appearance marked the finale to "We Are Most Amused," a London gala in aid of the Prince's Trust and celebrating its founder's imminent sixtieth birthday. Once again the cameras sought out Charles in the audience and this time found him cantillating with gusto.

Much had changed since his last sing-along with the Prince's Trust fourteen years earlier. The song had gained a new audience and some additional lyrics as part of *Spamalot*, a hit musical loosely based on another movie by the Pythons, *Monty Python and the Holy Grail*. The Annual Greenhouse Gas Index had registered an increase of as much as 30 percent. Humans had reproduced in unprecedented volumes, adding 1.1 billion to the global population. Britain alone had provided Her Majesty with 4 million new subjects, swelling to a population of 61 million. Digital technology had taken hold throughout Her Realms and far beyond, laying waste some industries and creating others, changing how people communicated and the nature of their communications. World wealth had risen but some of it was illusory. The once mighty Lehman Brothers filed for bankruptcy less than two months before the gala. Trust in most institutions was failing. The monarchy and its heir, by contrast, were undergoing something of a renaissance. Flanked on one side by Camilla, now HRH the Duchess of Cornwall and his dearest wife, and on the other by his younger son, Harry, Charles radiated cheer, convulsing with laughter at words Idle unexpectedly inserted into this special rendition. "If '*Spamalot*' is hot and you like it or p'raps not / A bunch of knights in search of holy grails / When you're sixty years of age and your mum won't leave the stage / It's good to know that you're still Prince of Wales!"

In his seventh decade, Charles still pursues his grails. His mum remains on the stage, but he knows that the moment of her exit is drawing inexorably closer. That is not a prospect he relishes, since any coronation must follow a funeral. "Always look on the bright side of death," Idle continued. "Just before you draw your terminal breath / For life's a piece of shit, when you look at it / Life's a laugh and death's a joke it's true / You'll see it's all a show. Leave 'em laughing as you go / Just remember that the last laugh is on you."

The Prince will never be able to treat mortality with such insouciance— his mother's, his own, anybody's. It's tricky enough to look on the bright side of life. But with Camilla at his right hand and Harry at his left, William happily married and with a son and heir of his own, Charles's world is more benign than he has ever known it.

CHAPTER 10

Kings to Come

//

W HEN CHARLES LEADS A TOUR OF HIS PSYCHE, IT'S BEST TO BRING Wellingtons or borrow a pair from the storeroom at the side entrance to Dumfries House. Even on clement days—and in this neck of Scotland the weather systems cycle as suddenly as the princely moods—the going can get boggy. In other respects a considerate host, the Prince waits for no man and no woman in Louboutins either. One of his guests realizes her spindly heels won't survive the terrain and returns to the Palladian mansion. The rest of the party sloshes on, at the clip set by the royal mountain goat. Most are younger than he is, but only his estate manager, Oliver Middlemiss, easily keeps pace. At his back, Charles hears time's winged chariot. Before him lie deserted fields, crumbling outbuildings, vast eternities of potential to change lives, in practical, measurable ways and also in a less tangible sense, by reconnecting people to Nature and the past. If *Harmony* is Charles's manifesto, the Dumfries estate has become its physical manifestation, a map of his soul complete with funny little gazebos.

Among the guests exploring these twisting pathways is the group of "Bond villains"—wealthy donors and potential donors to the Prince's charities—who on the previous evening joined the Prince at Dumfries House for a meal of Walled Garden Pea and Broad Bean Risotto with a

Soft Poached Hen's Egg, Pan-Seared Wild Sea Bass, Pommes Écrasés and Hand-Picked Dumfries House Vegetables (exactly the sort of dish Camilla enjoys), and Autumn Plum Crumble with Vanilla Custard (more Charles's thing), served with Puligny-Montrachet Les Meix Olivier Leflaive 2010, Sarget de Gruaud Larose Saint-Julien 2006, and Laurent Perrier Rosé. At the end of this repast, a piper, in full ceremonial uniform—kilt, tunic, sporran, full plaid, and a feather hat—marched twice around the long oval table, playing a medley of traditional Scottish music that included the "Skye Boat Song," the story of Bonnie Prince Charlie, "the lad that's born to be king."

Conversations ranged widely during the meal, at predinner drinks in the Tapestry Room and over digestifs and coffee in the North Drawing Room. Should anyone have asked about the concept behind the ongoing project to renovate the stately home and transform its grounds, Charles, Camilla, and Fiona Lees, Chief Executive of the local East Ayrshire council, were on hand to explain, along with key members of the Dumfries House Trust including its Chief Executive, Michael Fawcett. The plan—inevitably—is to establish a virtuous circle, by saving the timeless—if period-specific—glories of Dumfries House, luring tourists to the estate and the wider area, and in so doing helping to fund the restoration and maintenance of the one and the revival of the other.

The most important surviving early work of architect Robert Adam, Dumfries House was built between 1754 and 1759 for the widower William Crighton-Dalrymple, the 5th Earl of Dumfries, who hoped it would persuade a particularly nubile young woman to marry him. She spurned his advances even though the Earl kitted out his love nest with a stupendous four-poster bed and matching furniture made by a fashionable cabinet-maker of the day, Thomas Chippendale. The lovelorn aristocrat married a cousin instead, dying without an heir eight years after moving in. The house went on to witness further sore disappointments as well as heady excitements. Successive owners splurged care and money, in the nineteenth century installing the first generation of the fully flushable mod-cons Britons like to call "thrones" (pioneered by another famous Thomas C., Thomas Crapper) and adding a wing to the building. The resources to pay for such luxuries eventually became stretched, and in April 2007 Dumfries House and estate came on the market, its collection of Chippendales shrouded in bubble wrap for the journey to Christie's salesrooms in London. Then Charles intervened.

This was a characteristic intervention, triggered by passion and instinct, an idea in search of a practicable framework, unfunded, unformulated, seemingly unfeasible, controversial, and also visionary. His starting point was the conviction that the house and furniture must not be separated but should be preserved intact and ensemble for the nation. Without having visited the property, he swiftly convened a consortium that lodged the winning bid of $71.5 million, including a $31.8 million loan secured against his charitable foundation and based on the assumed development value of a corner of the estate earmarked for a Poundbury-style housing enclave called Knockroon.

At the opening of the newly restored Walled Garden in July 2014, Charles gave a brief speech. "As anyone who saw this garden before work started will know, the challenge posed in restoring the site has been considerable. It's always nice to have statistics, so, since 2011, the project has required 47,000 handmade bricks, 37,000 concrete blocks, 9,500 tonnes of hardcore for paths, 5,000 tonnes of soil, one mile of coping stones and four miles of vine wire," he said.[1] He omitted sharper statistics: five zones of Auchinleck and Cumnock are among the poorest in the whole of Scotland; 18 percent of people in the area are officially rated as deprived; soaring unemployment is slowed only by shrinking populations.[2] Against these figures, he might have invoked the fifty full-time and twenty part-time seasonal jobs created in the house and grounds or the courses in trades and crafts, free to participants, run on the Dumfries estate that are designed to help the long-term unemployed into work, such as Get Into Hospitality, five weeks of intensive training in the Dumfries House kitchens. Some 70 percent of alumni head straight into paid work. Sarah-Jane Clark, twenty-three, from nearby Kilmarnock, had been jobless for almost eighteen months before she enrolled. "I wasn't too sure about the cooking side. Once I got a shot in the kitchen I knew. . . . It was the first time I felt confident in a job," she says.[3] She's now employed as an apprentice chef and planning a career in catering.

The Prince—who switches to another of his many titles, Duke of Rothesay, when in Scotland—has summoned several of his charities to see what they can do in and for the surrounding area. One of the first schemes involves the renovation of the town hall in New Cumnock, a conurbation even harder hit by the downturn than its older namesake. The revamped building will offer meeting spaces, IT suites, a stage, arts and crafts rooms, nothing lavish in some contexts but a significant bonus for a place far more used to closures than openings. Gette Fulton, a local resident and one of the directors of New Cumnock's most unexpected facility, an outdoor public swimming pool (it operates for just three months a year), says Charles's arrival in the area has lifted spirits. She is impressed by the Knockroon development. "Have you been in the houses there? It just shows what can be done. . . . People are going to say the area is up-and-coming." Fulton first visited the Dumfries estate recently; previous lairds built walls to keep out commoners. "We were discouraged from going," she says.[4] Charles is building to attract visitors, not to repel them, and to establish outposts of benign influence in the community.

This is the strange, compelling geography he lays out for his Bond villains: a work in progress he doesn't expect to see completed in his lifetime; an arboretum that at this muddy early stage of its existence looks like a slough of despond but actually represents his optimism; capsules of many of his charities and initiatives; a mini Poundbury; an outdoor center imparting Gordonstounian principles of rugged communal problem solving; workshops where young men and women learn crafts that have already been deployed on the estate to build rustic follies. School parties roam the kitchen garden, children too urban to have ever seen a vegetable in its natural state encouraged to get their hands dirty. At the center of everything sits a perfect exemplar of eighteenth-century architecture and a unique collection of furniture, cherished again.

These are small groins set against prevailing tides, but they make a difference to people watching helpless as livelihoods and communities are swept away. None of this would be possible without donations from people like David Brownlow, one of the dinner guests, as impeccable as any Bond villain but, like Charles, keen to talk about good works rather than plotting the downfall of the planet. Brownlow, who is British and a self-made recruitment tycoon, reckons he has contributed around $5.5 million and given an additional three or four days a month of his time to secure Dumfries House since the Prince first met and wooed him into supporting his charities in 2005. His largesse helped to dig the Dumfries project out of an early crisis, when land prices, and confidence, dropped as the banking crisis unfolded. Knockroon appeared stillborn and has been slow to disprove doubters, though the families living in its white-rendered homes seem as contented as Poundbury's residents. Critics accused the Prince of endangering his charitable empire through his recklessness. Yet by the autumn of 2011, the loan had been paid off and soon cafés, a restaurant, and a bed-and-breakfast on the estate had added fresh revenue streams. Still, these are small beer against the costs of the project and of Charles's wider and deeper ambitions.

So Charles continues to tap wealthy individuals and potential corporate donors, aiming not only to entice funds for individual facilities but also to create an endowment that will generate regular income in years to come. Similar efforts are under way in relation to any of the Prince's charities and initiatives likely to struggle in a future that will deprive them of their founder's attention by elevating him to a higher place, be it the throne or the afterlife that his faith—his Anglican faith—reassures him he will find. In the financial year ending 2014, his charities raised $208 million in private and corporate donations in addition to their income from public sources and endowments.

"He's on a constant fundraiser, constant," says Ben Elliot, who has gained an appreciation of what such efforts involve since setting up his own charity, the Quintessentially Foundation. Elliot came to the September 2013 Dumfries House dinner bringing a member of the Polish aristocracy who was curious to see whether the model the Prince is pioneering might translate to his family's own estates. "[The Prince] has got so many things he cares about that this machine, whether it's Dumfries House or any one of his other projects, takes enormous energy to feed."[5]

But the machine also feeds Charles and in July 2014 brought him emotional sustenance from a rare quarter indeed. The Queen and the Duke of Edinburgh traveled to the Dumfries estate to attend the opening of the Walled Garden. Throughout Charles's life, his mother has conferred on him medals, orders, and titles with a generosity that she would never think appropriate to match in sappy sentiment. This time, he was able to return the favor, naming the garden in her honor. Moreover, if the Duke has previously seemed unimpressed by some of his son's achievements, on this occasion he mirrored the weather system that settled over East Ayrshire for the key hours of the visit: dry, a little gusty, but warm.

Fiona Lees accompanied the royals as they toured the estate. "Thousands of people are benefiting from HRH's work . . . we could not ask for a better hand up for regeneration and there cannot be a better example of heritage led regeneration," she e-mailed later. "A light has been shone on our communities and they are bursting with pride."[6] So, on that day, was the Prince.

Asbestos. gm foods. a question about whether he sees echoes in Tony Blair's "Stakeholder Society" or in David Cameron's minor reworking, the elusive "Big Society," of the kind of community involvement he has championed for years sets Charles on a different tack, listing technologies developed to provide solutions that have created problems instead. As is often the case, at least half of his assertions are incontrovertibly right; the other half could easily be debated until the genetically modified dairy cows come home. "What I'm saying is you have to look at things, each one, and not imagine it's the quick fix these things appear to be," he says.[7] The left corner of his mouth veers downward.

The time frames of a prince—especially one who has spent more than sixty years in constitutional limbo—are not those of ordinary humanity and certainly not of politicians. He commits to projects such as Dumfries that stretch into the unforeseeable long term and believes in formulae that have proven their worth over centuries, even millennia: the golden mean in architecture, natural designs observed and reverse-engineered by biomimeticists, traditional breeds of cattle and, of course, sheep. He trusts to the value of painstaking group problem solving, the benefits of convening different constellations of people to reason slowly through options, try out ideas, and sometimes fail, gaining from the process as well as from its ultimate success. This is a technique he learned at Gordonstoun and has incorporated in many of the programs run by the Prince's Trust and his other charities. Participants in team-building exercises at the Tamar Manoukian Outdoor Centre on the Dumfries estate work together to fill with water a pipe riddled with thirteen holes in order to float a rubber duck to the top and retrieve a message attached to it. Sometimes it's a note of congratulations. Often, it's just a clue about what to tackle next.

In April 2013 William and Kate attended the opening of the center, named after a member of the prominent Armenian family that funded it. "Make it brief," William told his father as Charles cleared his throat to give a speech. He spoke in jest but with Kate carrying the weight of their unborn child and a sharp bite to the spring air, this wouldn't have been the best moment for one of Charles's more discursive efforts.

William anyway tends to be as clipped as his father is expansive. He has given a few interviews in which his emotions break through; answering questions about his mother and once visibly choking as he watched footage of a rhino injured by poachers and bleeding to death. The segment was filmed soon after George's birth, for a documentary aimed at raising awareness of the plight of endangered wildlife. "The last few weeks for me have been a very different emotional experience—something I never thought I would feel for myself," said the new father. "I find, even though it's only been a short period, that a lot of things affect me now—when I see a clip like that there's so much emotion and so much feeling wrapped up into conservation and environment. It's just so powerful. You'd think something that big and that's been around so long, would have worked out a way to avoid being caught and persecuted, but they really don't. I do feel anger, but I also feel really great hope that we will overcome this as a human race. The more we raise the issue and the more education there is . . . I wouldn't be here right now if I didn't think there was a chance it could be successful. Poaching is now probably the worst I've ever known it, but I am not the kind of guy to give up."[8]

In that moment he sounded like his father, albeit without the same level of verbal dexterity or any leavening humor. For the most part William reveals little to journalists, radiating a contempt for the increasingly endangered species at least as heartfelt as his concern for rhinos. The royal rat pack assumes this must be because William blames the press for his mother's death, forgetting that he surely remembers enough of his boyhood to blame the press for what it did to her life. Yet William's terseness is also a function of a process Charles himself went through. In defining himself against his parents, Charles became the man he is. In defining himself against his father, William has become more like his royal grandmother, closed and cautious, comfortable with actions rather than words.

William has also become his own man. Until comparatively recently,

Clarence House advisers clung to a vision of transition that would see Charles pass his charitable empire to his sons when he assumed the Crown. The Prince's Trust would simply move its apostrophe one space to the right. "It would be nice to see the continuum," says a palace insider. But neither of "the boys," as the thirtysomething William and Harry are still known among palace staff, shows an inclination to get involved with the Trust or to take on the rest of the sprawl. They dutifully turn up for Prince's Trust events or occasions such as the opening of the outdoors center at Dumfries House and joined their father at a February 2014 conservation conference, but otherwise they are focused on their own careers, establishing their own organizations, and demonstrating their independence in other ways too.

This sometimes means they make their own mistakes. The conservation conference was overshadowed by revelations that the boys were newly returned from a hunting trip in Spain. They hadn't slaughtered endangered creatures, just wild boar and stag, but the juxtaposition of killing and conference wasn't ideal. Kensington Palace aides were caught on the hop. The boys had not informed them of their plans and if they had, says a source, "we'd have advised them not to go and they'd have ignored us." The Princes' determination to plow their own furrows recalls the young Charles. The furrows, however, are distinct.

From the spring of this year, William embarks on an experiment that will see the second in line to the throne trying to hold down a civilian job, as an air ambulance pilot, albeit with more flexibility in his schedule than his colleagues so that he can continue to carry out royal duties. He plans to donate his salary to charity, illustrating the larger anomaly of a royal seeking a slice of normal life. Kate, meanwhile, has started flying solo in her own way, representing the Queen. She was supposed to undertake her first overseas engagement without William in September 2014, a trip to Malta, but William stood in for his wife after severe morning sickness temporarily clipped her wings.

That same month Harry celebrated his thirtieth birthday in the afterglow of the Invictus Games, a sporting competition for injured service personnel from thirteen nations that he staged at London's former Olympic Park. Newspaper coverage was benign. The British tabloids like Harry— for now. "He's the *Sun* readers' favorite royal," says the newspaper's royal photographer Arthur Edwards. "They think he's like them and that's the highest compliment. He's a larrikin."[9] A celebrity wheelchair rugby match at the Invictus Games featured Harry, his first cousin Zara, and her husband, Mike Tindall, a recently retired professional rugby player, raising the specter of "The Grand Knockout Tournament" and a previous generation's pratfalls only to banish it again. The Games provided a platform for the disabled competitors rather than the cavortings of royals. Yet the event's success doesn't solve Harry's larger existential conundrum any more than his current tabloid popularity will shield him against a future narrative of redundancy, as one of the spares, not the heir. (Since the birth of his nephew George, Harry stands fourth in line to the throne.)

Nor has Harry yet solved the problem of how to find a partner who is grounded and sane, yet not so sane that the prospect of life on Planet Windsor sends her in retreat. It took his brother almost a decade and a public rupture with Kate before he felt secure in taking the decision to marry. It took his father far longer to find contentment. Diana never did.

That history still shapes her sons' decisions. "William seems to have chosen to live up in Norfolk [as his country retreat], and yet his father has spent so long building [Highgrove] that I'm sure he would love one of his sons to inherit. It's a father's expression of immortality," says an insider. "It embraces his commitment to sustainable farming and to the world of the botanical, the natural world, and then he's got his Islamic garden there so it's an expression of his interests."

Highgrove also carries echoes of a difficult past. This is the place the boys spent some of their best times and the most confusing. Ill-equipped as Charles was to cope with his first marriage or its collapse or the sudden challenge of parenting children whose resentment at his rejection of their mother had now been layered with grief and more anger at her death, he made a miraculously good job of the last of these. At Diana's funeral, her brother delivered a eulogy that included a barely disguised swipe at royal parenting. "I pledge that we, your blood family, will do all we can to continue the imaginative way in which you were steering these two exceptional young men so that their souls are not simply immersed by duty and tradition but can sing openly as you planned," said Earl Spencer. The Prince's biographer Anthony Holden judged that Diana's influence had already been erased when, less than three months after her death, Harry stood along-side his father at a charity concert in South Africa attended by Nelson Mandela and featuring the Spice Girls. In balmy temperatures, listening to pop, Harry, aged thirteen, wore a suit and tie.

There is no question that Charles raised his sons to an awareness of duty and tradition—and an appreciation for a well-cut suit, though the boys tend to prefer single- to double-breasted—but he nurtured them too. He has always been keen to give them, in place of the tough love favored by his own parents, something more enveloping; he determined with Diana that they should be as protected from the public gaze as possible and spend as much time with their parents as possible, and when the time came they would not attend Gordonstoun but the softer Eton, right on the doorstep of Windsor. He resisted the temptation to denigrate Diana while she lived and afterward encouraged the boys to think and talk about her and maintain contact with her friends. The relationships between father and sons are not without stresses and complexities, but they are stronger as a result. Unsurprisingly, these bonds are most easily visible in a shared sense of humor, says Ben Elliot, "them ridiculing him, him ridiculing them, that joshing that often goes with good relationships. Not just about a lack of hair or those kinds of things. I've seen with his younger son them almost just like frolicking with one another in a really lovely way."[10] "They are so, so loving," says Emma Thompson.[11]

When he married and started a family, William shifted the dynamic, presenting the idealized family unit that used to be monarchy's specialty. Yet in appearing to secure the future of the Windsor dynasty, a potential future King happily married to his future Queen and already blessed with an heir (and a spare on the way), unblemished by scandals, unburdened by failures, the Cambridges have attained a popularity that threatens to undermine the first in line to the throne. "People admire the Queen so much because she's impeccable—she shows no emotion—and they also say Prince William is a modern royal, but somehow Prince Charles is in the middle and gets criticized from both sides," says Patrick Holden. "But in his own way he's also defining the new role of the monarchy and, in my opinion, doing it brilliantly well."[12]

Holden says the media narrative of princely jealousies is overdone.

He has heard Charles comment ruefully on his sons' and daughter-in-law's ability to draw crowds and headlines but has witnessed far more often the Prince's boundless pride in the younger generation. He is always learning from his children, the Prince remarks during predinner conversation at Dumfries House. He is constantly amazed by what they know about the world—and what he doesn't. In return, he has tried to do as the Queen Mother did for him, introducing them to arts and culture, at any rate those corners of art and culture that resonate for him.

He also takes an obvious pleasure in instructing his boys in the stage-craft necessary to carry off royal ceremonial. "The role is a role and it's something that has to be played to the hilt all the time," says Emma Thompson.[13] The metaphor is apt, if somewhat alarming. In September 2013, Charles and his elder son spent hours closeted at Birkhall practicing how to conduct investitures ahead of William's debut doing it for real. For the rehearsal they used a sword dispatched from London to ensure William got the hang of the tricky maneuver that involves touching the blade on the shoulders of those receiving knighthoods without inflicting injury.

As father and son rehearsed, Camilla and Kate enjoyed the tranquility of the Balmoral estate, at least during the periods George left it unpunctuated. His birth has drawn a close family closer. The boys not only accept Camilla but are affectionate toward her, seeing how much she lifts their father's spirits. Diana has not been forgotten but she no longer divides and conquers. "HRH said something in connection with his grandson the other day which I thought was incredibly revealing, about how the most important thing is to have a heart that's open," says Patrick Holden.[14]

Hearts are open. Harmony reigns. The question remains: Will the Prince, his eldest after him, and, after William, George? Part of the answer lies beyond royal control, in social and economic developments that may enhance the residual value of the monarchy or shred it. But a larger responsibility for their fate lies with the royals themselves and in particular with the next sovereign. The Queen has kept the throne safe, if not warm. Should her son live long enough to succeed her, he is unlikely to live long enough to secure his legacy through the kind of slow, careful change management that served his mother so well. His greatest challenge will be to stand for continuity while redefining the monarchy, remaking it in his own image while buttressing it for his heirs. He has already embarked on that project, unrolling a potential new model of kingship that melds the ceremonial aspects of the role with a much more active beneficence than the old formula of charitable patronage.

After touring the grounds of Dumfries House with his Bond villains, the Prince returns to the house for a private meeting with Fiona Lees, the Chief Executive of East Ayrshire council, also attended by Kristina Kyriacou. In a small upstairs sitting room the three hunch together, strategizing ways to deal with the most urgent problems confronting the area, stimulating a sluggish economy and dealing with the abandoned open-cast mines that litter the landscape, filling with contaminated water. "We need people to help us think about this," says Lees. The Prince agrees. "If you get a whole lot of people in one room, they make connections. Much of the time this never happens in some extraordinary way," he says.[15]

Conclusion

///

Until philosophers are kings, or the kings and princes of this world have the spirit and power of philosophy, and political greatness and wisdom meet in one, and those commoner natures who pursue either to the exclusion of the other are compelled to stand aside, cities will never have rest from their evils—nor the human race, as I believe—and then only will this our state have a possibility of life and behold the light of day.

Republic, Plato

IN APRIL 2014, A BROADCASTER ASKED ME TO PARTICIPATE IN A SURreal exercise, recording an interview as part of a preprepared obituary to run if the Prince should die without being so courteous as to give news organizations prior notice of the event. In an upstairs room of a London pub called the Peasant—the producers chose the location without intended irony—I answered questions posed by a journalist designed to help me sum up Charles and his impact. I found it tricky to do this in sound bites, and even at the luxury of book length, it has been a struggle to draw a balanced assessment. So much is written and said about the Prince, but so much is also distorted for one reason or another. This book should hopefully have highlighted those reasons and stripped away some of the distortions. I have no doubt its publication will also be taken as license to create fresh mischaracterizations and caricatures of its subject.

That Charles is the victim of such distortions does not exonerate him and his extended court from a share of the responsibility for them. He is always making connections—between people and ideas, the past, present, and future, the material and the spiritual, golden threads that bind. This is one of his greatest talents. What he doesn't always spot are key connections between what he does, or is done in his name, and how this impacts perceptions.

One frequent charge against the Prince, that he does too little, is obviously untrue. Another—that if he were not doing the things he does, as activist and charitable entrepreneur, other such entrepreneurs would fill the breach—seemed increasingly dubious as I delved into the detail and scope of his activities. The Prince's Trust and his other charities and initiatives are near-perfect reflections of the Prince. He has been misrepresented and misunderstood, in ways anatomized in this book. But sometimes when Charles gets bad press, it's because he deserves it or an aspect of his organization warrants it, or because people harbor legitimate disagreements that they cannot directly debate with him or easily voice except by attempting to make as much noise as he does.

Courtiers too often tell him what they think he wants to hear rather than what he needs to hear. He isn't always given the opportunity to understand the full dynamics of a situation. He is surrounded by individuals who will try to hearten him, and sometimes to gain favor by playing princely trigger points that everybody in palace circles knows how to locate. Charles has long been a Defender of Faith—faith in Nature and perennial wisdoms as well as Christianity—and thus will never accept alternative philosophies or movements such as Modernism that to him appear as kryptonite. He doesn't grasp that many of the people he has run up against over the years are as passionate as he is, as driven and well meaning as he is.

There is no point in arguing that he should jettison the belief system he has spent a lifetime constructing. He would no more be capable of doing that than I, an atheist, can subscribe to that belief system. I may not be fully in harmony with *Harmony*, but I have witnessed the benign outcomes of the princely philosophy, the virtuous circles Charles is capable of creating.

He sometimes sparks vicious cycles too, and in drawing to a conclusion, I will aim to highlight ways in which he might guard against that tendency in future, for his own benefit and the benefit of the institution he represents.

I do so not as a monarchist but as a pragmatist. I believe all humans are born equal except for the natives of Planet Windsor, who arrive in the world at a huge disadvantage to the rest of us, burdened with expectation and duty. If I were designing a country from scratch, it would be a republic. I was born into such a country, but for most of my life I have lived in the United Kingdom of Great Britain and Northern Ireland, and have come over the years not only to appreciate the public service that some—not all—royals perform, and the pageantry—and comedy—they supply, but also to understand the upheaval their replacement would represent. Monarchy doesn't make sense but the system still, mostly, works quite well. "If you chuck away too many things," says the Prince, "you end up discovering there was value in them."[1]

Republicans are convinced that the point of transition from the Queen to her son—if and when this comes—will be the moment of maximum danger to the Crown. They are not wrong. But some British republicans also argue that the transition from Crown to elected head of state could be quick and painless, a matter of crossing out "Her Majesty the Queen" or, far more likely, "His Majesty the King" and writing in "President." The overseas Realms already have inbuilt structures to deputize for the nonresident sovereign. Their national identities are not so intricately interwoven with the Windsor brand. Despite the William and Kate effect, it seems likely that Australia or Jamaica or New Zealand may begin to disentangle themselves from the hereditary system after the Queen has died, perhaps even before that. The Commonwealth faces questions in the longer term not only about its titular head but its purpose.

If Britain begins to unwind its constitutional settlement, the process will surely be messier. "If you get rid of the Crown, you have to write a new constitution," says Graham Smith of the UK campaign group Republic. "The key point of the constitution is that the people are sovereign and all power starts with them so if the constitution doesn't assign power to the sovereign then it has to stay with the people. We could say, 'Look, there are certain powers which were with the Crown which are now with government, certain powers which are now with parliament, some powers are now with the head of state and everything else is just not there.' You can have it however you want it."[2]

I remain skeptical about this. Big constitutional changes are difficult and lengthy and absorb energies that may be better deployed elsewhere. They also risk unintended consequences, so must be thoroughly thought through and minutely plotted. There are, as the Prince observes, no quick fixes. The reason British politicians continue to squabble about how to reform the House of Lords—and since Scotland's referendum, about how to devolve more powers across the UK—is not only that vested interests have impeded progress. It is that in replacing self-evidently flawed systems such as an upper chamber stocked with the beneficiaries of naked political patronage and still (ye gods) with a rump of hereditary peers, entitled by accident of birth to make, revise, and reject laws, the architects of reform instead threaten to introduce self-evidently flawed replacements.

The current House of Lords, for all its weaknesses, complements the House of Commons. Its members need not seek election and so their time horizons are extended. They are more independent of party affiliations and bring a wider range of experiences to bear than MPs. "The thing about being here for life is that you are not so bound to your party," says Labour peer Tony Berkeley. "Because over a time of thirty years some people are here, each party changes its policies. They all do. And the older people say, 'Hang on, you're all doing it wrong' and they have ways of expressing their view, they don't vote so often. They abstain. Or they speak their minds a bit more."[3]

Fully or partly elected alternatives risk eroding these useful differences. Representative democracies are precious things, but not every one of their constituent parts must always entail direct elections for the systems to be truly democratic.

At Republic's annual general meeting in May 2014, Graham Smith quoted from the final speech made by the famous Labour firebrand Tony Benn ahead of his retirement as a Labour MP. Benn renounced his hereditary peerage to sit in the Commons and returned to the reasons for his decision in his parliamentary valedictory, listing five questions for any governing institution: "What power have you got? Where did you get it from? In whose interests do you exercise it? To whom are you accountable? And how can we get rid of you?" Benn concluded: "If you cannot get rid of the people who govern you, you do not live in a democratic system."[4] The current House of Lords is not directly accountable to voters but it is subject to reform and even abolition as and when MPs coalesce around a workable plan. What the debates at Republic's AGM fail to acknowledge is that the monarchy is in a similar position, even if the sovereign is consulted on legislation and would be expected to provide the last signature on any law abolishing the throne. If that day comes, no Windsor monarch is likely to withhold his or her signature or barricade the palace gates.

Graham Smith doesn't really hold out hope of stopping the coronation but expects King Charles to make the argument for republicans once installed on the throne. "People couldn't imagine David Cameron being Prime Minister until he was. And I think the same will happen with Charles, and the other thing that will come is 'Well, hang on a minute, we've just changed our head of state and I didn't get a vote.' And that's quite a big thing as well and I think that people kind of talk in theoretical terms saying well we don't need to vote for them but when they've actually seen it change in front of their eyes without ever being asked that might change the way people feel about it."[5]

The secret to galvanizing opposition against the monarchy, Smith says, is to get people angry. He thinks the presumed future King will annoy the hell out of his subjects. Here are some thoughts about how Charles could make himself more loved than loathed.

NICCOLÒ MACHIAVELLI, RENAISSANCE ITALY'S MOST CELEBRATED political philosopher, declared that sheep and royalty don't mix. In his famous treatise *The Prince*, he tells the story of Emperor Maximinus, who earned the disdain of his subjects by keeping flocks. The cautionary tale is unlikely to chime with a twenty-first-century, sheep-promoting Prince, but Machiavelli also offers more apposite advice. "It makes him contemptible when he is considered fickle, frivolous, effeminate, mean-spirited, irresolute, from all of which a prince should guard himself as from a rock; and he should endeavor to show in his actions greatness, courage, gravity and fortitude; and in his private dealings with his subjects let him show that his judgments are irrevocable, and maintain himself in such reputation that no one can hope either to deceive him or get round him," he wrote.[6] Apart from the injunction against effeminacy, this must count as timeless a piece of wisdom as any perennialist prince could hope to follow.

There's another nugget the heir to the throne might usefully take on board: Machiavelli counsels princes to keep their servants and soldiers in check. The ranks of Charles's servants and soldiers—his courtiers and the ground forces implementing his vision through his charities and initiatives— include some of the most talented and dedicated individuals I've ever met, as passionate about the Boss as he is in his activism. The more he is criti- cized, the more they band together in a protective ring, lowering their lances at the outside world. This tendency has been reinforced as Buckingham Pal- ace attempts to lead a restructuring to prepare the monarchy for the tran- sition that actuaries looking at the Queen's age and the longevity of her mother might predict still to be ten or twenty years away. A regency may be more imminent.

In either case, this is a time to prepare, to listen and learn with an open- ness that a siege mentality impedes. The Prince must ensure that everybody working for him brings him bad news as well as good and never seeks to slay perceived dragons on his behalf. The fire-breathers may just have a point the Knight of the Realms would benefit from hearing. If not, he's skilled enough at wielding his own sword and, if anything, rather too ready to use it.

There is widespread irritation in Clarence House at some of the efforts to root around in the Prince's affairs. Aides suspect that the declared motive of such missions—a push for more transparency and accountability—masks a desire to get rid of the monarchy, or at least its heir. The *Guardian*'s Alan Rusbridger makes no bones about his republican agenda. Investigations by other news organizations more often look to a smaller prize: a scoop. The opacity of the royal palaces means that even small details carry a journal- istic value.

"It is riveting how much inventiveness exists. People create scenarios and write scripts for strange almost-plays, I find, which bear no relation to reality, no relation to the way I view things or do things or think about things," Charles complained to Jonathan Dimbleby more than twenty years ago. "Everyone is saying there's a right to know everything. I don't agree. There isn't a right to know at all."[7] Even back then, before Edward Snowden but after Andrew Morton—and supposing the Prince hadn't been unbur-

dening himself to a biographer as part of a project he himself had initiated—
the Prince's yen for greater privacy was never likely to be fulfilled. Daylight
had started to permeate the Windsor courts in ways that damaged the monarchy, strengthening the aversion of "that Dracula family" to sunshine when
they might have benefited from unlocking some of the shutters before
others prized them open.

This is not to suggest that the royals should pander to the revised definition of public interest as anything and everything that interests the public. The Windsors are entitled to conduct their personal lives in private. Nor
is this an argument for every communication being automatically subject to
scrutiny. There are missions the Prince undertakes, for example, during his
Middle East trips, that would be compromised if conducted in the full gaze
of the world. It is harder to see why he should enjoy a higher level of protection under Freedom of Information laws than a government minister. Bagehot's dictum about the mystery of monarchy no longer applies in Snowdonia.
Its mystery causes strife. We must let in daylight upon magic, which after all
can be more impressive up close, as the Prince's Trust alumnus Dynamo
frequently demonstrates.

Clarence House sources say the Prince never sought his battle with
the *Guardian* and long ago would have preferred to publish his memos
than to fight over them, not least because he and his advisers are privately
far from confident that the Supreme Court will rule in his favor. Whatever the outcome, there's nothing to stop him asking the government that
comes to power in Britain's May 2015 elections to look at bringing the
rules relating to his correspondence in line with those covering other
public officials and bodies.

A royal insider argues that the royal households cannot be the advocates of public policy on disclosure because the Queen has been stoically
doing her job for more than sixty years. A release of documents from earlier
stages of her reign might not properly account for the way in which attitudes have evolved, inside the royal palaces as well as outside their walls.
That argument might hold true for the retrospective release of letters and
memos. There's little sign that Prince Philip has imbibed the rules of political correctness or grappled with the issues that underlie them, but his son
has done a better job of moving with the times, sometimes falling behind
but just as often jumping ahead of them.

Charles now has another opportunity to show leadership, in redrawing and clarifying the boundaries between the private and public spheres of palace life. His views on most things are already in the public domain, laid out in *Harmony* and in his collected speeches. His courtiers gain nothing in downplaying these views or concealing his philosophy. The quality most prized in this trust-free era is authenticity.

The Prince might do well to offer up more access to the work he does—whether royal work or charitable work, especially as the two blend and merge. He might even consider beginning not only to speak for himself but to answer for himself. He leaves it to aides such as his Principal Private Secretary, William Nye, to present his Annual Review and to make his case to the House of Commons Public Accounts Committee. Yet, as I have seen at first hand, Charles can be the most fluent and persuasive of advocates for his own causes.

He should also take an open-minded look at what Tony Berkeley is doing. Berkeley—a rare creature, both a life peer and a hereditary; his full title is Anthony Fitzhardinge Gueterbock, 18th Baron Berkeley and Baron Gueterbock—in 2011 introduced a Private Member's Bill on marine legislation, only to receive a letter from the clerk in the House of Lords bill office: "Dear Lord Berkeley, The marine navigation bill that you introduced on 5 July would affect the Prince of Wales's interests and so will require the Prince of Wales's consent for its consideration by parliament. . . . The government whips office in the Lords and the parliamentary branch of the Department of Transport are aware of what is required."[8] An arcane constitutional convention gives Charles a veto over any proposed legislation deemed to impact on "the hereditary revenues, personal property or other interests" of the Duchy of Cornwall, and given the wide-ranging nature of its business, this is potentially quite a considerable power. What is less obvious is whether he has ever used it to block or amend a bill. That information remains confidential under the same convention.

Understanding the Duchy isn't easy. It operates like a corporation but isn't taxed like one. "If it looks like a duck and quacks like a duck and swims like a duck you sort of assume it's a duck," said Nick Smith, Labour MP for the Welsh constituency of Blaenau Gwent, at a July 2013 hearing of the House of Commons Public Accounts Committee. "Given the Duchy of Cornwall looks and behaves like a corporation with income from complex investments and quacks like a corporation with a council including the great and good from banking, on the face of it many of my constituents would say the Duchy should pay corporation tax and capital gains tax. Aren't my constituents being reasonable?"

No, said William Nye, one of three witnesses to appear. "The Duchy is a very unusual organization. It is a private estate; it is not a corporation. It is a private estate in many respects like other private estates, but in one or two respects not like a private estate. Some of the things that you have high-lighted, Mr. Smith, still do not make it a corporation. There is a council. It is an advisory council that advises the Duke of Cornwall. . . . Essentially it is a set of properties that belong to the Duke of Cornwall. The fact that it is a large set of properties and is worth a lot of money does not, per se, make it a corporation. The memorandum of understanding [on royal taxa-tion, agreed in 1993] establishes that it is not a corporation and not subject to corporation tax."

The Public Accounts Committee had already attempted—and failed—in an April 2005 hearing to get to grips with Prince Charles's tax status and the nitty-gritty of the Duchy. Again it floundered, even after Nye essayed another definition of the Duchy. "It is a bit like a trust in some respects, although it is not formally, legally speaking, a trust. It is a little bit like a family business in some respects, but it is not solely a business. It is an estate, which has a sort of entail in it, although it is a slightly complex entail. It has aspects of social enterprise, in that although it is commercial, it is able to take a long-term stewardship view of what is in the interests of the Duchy overall, meaning the assets for the Duke [of Cornwall] and future dukes, and of the communities and the tenants. To that extent, it has aspects of social enterprise."

As the hearing drew to a close, Richard Bacon, Conservative MP for South Norfolk, made a final stab at comprehension. "If it looks like a pri-vate ducal estate set up to provide an income to the heir to the throne, and it quacks like a private ducal estate set up to provide an income to the heir to the throne, can one assume that it might just possibly be a private ducal estate set up to provide an income to the heir to the throne?" "I think that must be possible," deadpanned Nye. Britain's unwritten constitutional arrangements, built on precedents and conventions that may have been eas-ily graspable in earlier times, can now seem wilfully obscure.

The committee called for changes to drag the Duchy into the twenty-first century. "Greater transparency is needed," said its 2013 report. "The Duchy enjoys an exemption from paying tax even though it engages in a range of commercial activities. This tax exemption may give it an unfair advantage over its competitors who do pay corporation and capital gains tax." Its recommendations show no signs of being adopted, and that means the fact of the Duchy and the privilege it represents continues to overshadow some of the extraordinary things it has enabled Charles to do.

Berkeley responded to the letter by introducing another Private Member's Bill into the House of Lords intended to iron out inconsistencies between the Prince's status under British law and the position of other subjects of Her Majesty and to make the system more easily understandable as well as bringing the Duchy in line with the other entities with which it competes commercially. Berkeley says he knows the bill needs further work and anyway has no chance of becoming law without government backing, but he is using the process to generate debate. "What I'd really like to see is the Duchy making these changes voluntarily," he explains. "Either a government does it or the Duchy will have to do it proactively to get the laws changed."

It will always go better for the Windsors to initiate reform rather than to have reform imposed. The small numbers of avowed republicans in Parliament belies the speed with which sentiment could turn. Misty patriotism—and that is all that sustains many parliamentarians' support for the monarchy—would evaporate in the heat of sustained public rage.

The most obvious locus of public neuralgia, especially at a time of economic uncertainty and straitened budgets, is around the expense of maintaining royals in their palaces, in their carriages, on walkabouts, in helicopters, on their private train. Even for those who believe monarchy still matters, the contribution royalty makes must always be balanced against debits.

The $405,000 bill for flying Charles to Nelson Mandela's funeral and back in December 2013—a figure released in the annex to Buckingham Palace's *Annual Report and Accounts 2013–2014* along with other journeys costing more than $16,000 in that period—looks venal if you assume the Prince might have used ordinary scheduled airlines for the journey. His aides insisted at the press conference for his own Annual Review that the short notice and complexity of getting to Qunu in Kwazulu Natal made private charters the only practicable option. Staffers who made the journey say he was not traveling in style. My own overseas jaunts with royals, including the May 2014 trip with Charles and Camilla to Canada, have not been luxurious. The nose section of the Canadian air force jet contained a cramped private cabin but everyone apart from the royal couple rode in conditions familiar to economy class fliers—in the 1980s. (Journalists and photographers reimbursed the Canadian government C$1,800 [US$1,592] apiece for this no-frills transport.)

Aides maintain that security in part dictates the manner of royal travel and swells the size of retinues. Convoys expensively deploy skilled police drivers to recce the routes in advance as well as moving the retinues around once the visit begins. Charles and Camilla travel with valets, assistants, a hairdresser, and extensive wardrobes as part of the pageantry of such visits, to project majesty and protect dignity.

There are nevertheless clear arguments for finding ways to project majesty and protect dignity more cheaply. In 1994, a high-water mark of royal turbulence, John Major decided that the forty-one-year-old royal yacht *Britannia* should not be recommissioned when the next major repair bill fell due. Like the royals, the yacht presented an image of Britain to the world; like the royals, that image was becoming increasingly dilapidated. "You had to judge whether it was worth spending fifty million pounds on it, or, to be more accurate, whether it would have been a good idea to spend fifty million pounds on it in the middle of a deep recession, with a public mood deeply aggrieved," he says.[9]

During the 1997 election campaign, the Conservatives pledged a replacement for *Britannia*. Labour won power and swiftly scrapped the yacht instead, consigning the vessel to a new life in Edinburgh as a tourist attraction. The stoical Queen was seen to shed tears at the decommissioning ceremony. She may have cause to weep over the royal train after Britain next goes to the polls: as expensive as if it ran on gilded rails, the nine-carriage train is an obvious target for any incoming government keen on finding quick savings. The Public Accounts Committee has already recommended that it be scrapped. In 2014 Buckingham Palace told the committee that the train will stay in service "for as long as the rolling stock is working, which it believes will be for another five to ten years. However, it has not yet developed alternative options or a replacement to a royal train, which it considers provides safe and secure transport, particularly for overnight travel to early-morning royal engagements."[10]

The Prince's aides make a similar point, insisting this form of travel is better value for money than the cost of individual journeys suggests; Charles uses the train not to undertake solo travel but as a mobile hotel and conference facility. A former Cabinet minister enthuses that the train, like the monarchy itself, is an asset, a touch eccentric but ineffably British. To many people, though, the Prince, in taking the train, simply appears on the wrong track. A two-day trip to York and Harrogate in northern England added $36,900 to his travel bill in July 2013; a regional tour to the Midlands the previous month cost $31,113. His sons, by contrast, have not only both opted for commercial flights for private travel, but in May 2014 Harry arrived in Estonia on budget airline EasyJet for a two-day official visit to the country, and in December William caught the US Airways shuttle from New York to Washington to meet President Obama at the White House.

MANY OF HIS OPPONENTS ASSUME CHARLES STANDS FOR THE STATUS quo. In fact he already purposes to make some significant changes. As King, he intends to preside over a monarchy that is smaller.

For all that the Prince is more inclined to conserve than cut, for all that he dislikes the pain of rationalizing and restructuring, he is also focused on distant horizons. His activism is aimed at benefiting populations not yet born. In performing his royal role, he has not only formulated a model for his own potential kingship but is intent on securing the monarchy for the future. He knows that he and his kith must continue to adapt to survive and that part of this process must involve streamlining the Windsor family firm, reducing its seventeen-person, four-generation team by pasturing older and more marginal members. He is also pondering ways better to preserve the heritage of royal residences and retain their capacity as venues for state occasions while opening them up to more public access and for other uses.

None of this will happen during the reign of the Queen, who has always commanded her son's allegiance, or the lifetime of her consort, who still inspires his love, fear, and respect in equal measure. But after the coronation of the new King—conducted by the Archbishop of Canterbury and with a form of words that reflects the value the sovereign places on all faiths, whether or not this is directly signaled by a change to the coronation oath—his siblings, nieces, nephews, and cousins are likely to recede further into the background. At the court of King Charles III and Queen Camilla, immediate family will be easily adequate in skills and numbers to fulfill the toe-scrunching aspects of the royal job, smiling through presentations and speeches, pinning medals, cutting ribbons, cracking bottles against the hulls of ships, exchanging pleasantries, on an endless shuttle through Britain and the Realms.

The King's Trust can expect to continue to benefit from its founder's input, even if his time to raise funds or present achievement awards to graduates of Trust programs is more limited. Most of his charities and initiatives will survive in some form; a few are likely to struggle and fade.

Charles will never be neutral, just as he will never be party political. For better or for worse—in my final analysis, more often for better than for worse—the Prince is a man with a mission, a knight on a quest. His overarching goals—saving his adopted planet and the monarchy—underpin pretty much everything he does and are sometimes at odds with each other. He accepts that he will not be able to campaign from the throne room as he has campaigned from its antechamber, but if he no longer speaks up quite so often, or intervenes quite so vigorously, he'll have his weekly audiences with the Prime Minister instead. Whether he uses those audiences to lobby for additional reforms of the monarchy and health-giving transparencies will depend on his ability to emulate his mother, not by being like her, but by keeping Planet Windsor in close orbit to Earth.

If he never becomes king, he has already achieved a substantial legacy and left a huge trail. In researching this book I have waded through morasses of material—books, clippings, pamphlets, documents. I've pored over pretty much everything he's written that's in the public domain and every speech he's delivered that I could get my hands on. I've perused the odd black spider. I have interviewed many people who have been party to multiple stages or segments of Charles's highly variegated life, seeking to look beyond the competing claims of his proponents and his critics, while listening intently to both fragmented camps. I have observed him as closely as he and Clarence House permitted, and in doing so come to admire his achievements, regret the missteps that undermine them, shake my head over parts of his philosophy. I agree with some of his views, recoil from others. I have laughed with him and, not infrequently, at him, and almost every day stifled laughter at situations that brewed up around him. His planet is the funniest place I have ever visited, and the strangest. I like the Prince. I feel sorry for the child he once was. I am gladdened that in resolving the tensions of his personal life, Charles appears coming closer to reconciling the different strains and duties of his position, closer to seizing the grail he most often describes but rarely has glimpsed: harmony.

He and his aides are understandably frustrated that some of the best things he does go unrecognized. This book has shone light into those corners, but also caught in its beam some things that Clarence House might perhaps have preferred to keep in darkness. My aim throughout has been to portray the Prince fairly and accurately, without fear or favor, and to provide fresh insights. I have also done my best to clarify the transactional relationship between monarch and subjects so that these subjects can better judge whether they're getting enough out of the transaction and how the calculation might alter—because it would alter—under King Charles III. Two years of trailing the Prince—and they have been long years; "I can't wait to stop thinking about you," I once told the bemused focus of my attentions—have increased my appreciation for the positives he has brought to his role and my understanding of how he might invest the monarchy with fresh meaning. But research has also heightened my awareness of existing negatives and how this process could go wrong.

Like Don Quixote and Hamlet, the Prince faces tangible opponents but also just as frequently tangles with shadows and specters. A frivoling Prince would never have fought so many battles, polarized opinion, or roused such passions. The man who would be King of Hearts has never been able to take the path of least resistance. "I like to think that it's no accident that a man who feels such a profound sense of service and stewardship should be in his position on our planet at this time," says Patrick Holden. "He's a visionary, he's a remarkable human being."[11] "The thing that I would say about him is that he's genuine," says Fiona Reynolds. "It's all felt in a really deep way and I think that's the thing that above all I admire. Heavens, if he'd wanted an easy life he wouldn't have gone the route he has, but because he cares so passionately he's backed these sometimes very unpopular causes, but done so out of genuine conviction."[12] "I would much rather have a monarch who is concerned and interested and tries to do something to help people than someone who is completely disinterested and simply deals with the ceremonial and doesn't care," says John Major.[13] Emma Thompson gives a trenchant summation: "All of the movements that he's spearheaded and supported for years that have slowly become more mainstream are an example of how difficult it is for the press in this country to support anything the royal family does that isn't being nice to children or small furry animals. He wouldn't have had any shit from the press if he had been looking after donkeys or dogs."[14]

Prince Charles hasn't done much for donkeys or dogs. Some professions will say he hasn't done much for them either; indeed that he has actively harmed them. There will always be critics who take him for a parasite, an eccentric, a plant whisperer. He knows what he's trying to achieve but it's hard enough to make his aims understood, much less to capture his grails. "It's everybody else's grandchildren I've been bothering about," he says, sadly. "But the trouble is if you take that long a view, people don't always know what you're on about."[15]

Notes

//

PREFACE

1. Estelle Shirbon, "Prince Charles in No Hurry to Become King—*Time* magazine," Reuters, October 25, 2013.
2. Natalie Evans, "Prince Charles Fears Becoming King Will Be Like 'Prison,'" *Mirror*, October 25, 2013.
3. "Prince Charles 'Prison' Claim Denied," BBC online, October 25, 2013.
4. Catherine Mayer, "Heart of a King," *Time*, November 4, 2013.
5. Catherine Mayer, "Exclusive: Prince Charles, Born to Be King But Aiming Higher," Time.com, October 24, 2013.
6. Author's interview with Emma Thompson, September 16, 2013.
7. Rebecca English, "Pictured: The Encounter That Plunged Charles into a Global Storm When He Compared Putin to Hitler in Conversation with Jewish Refugee," *Daily Mail*, May 24, 2014.
8. Jeremy Paxman, *On Royalty*, Chapter 12: "The End of the Line?" (Viking, 2006).
9. Author's interview with Elizabeth Buchanan, Central London, March 5, 2014.
10. Valerie Elliott, "Royals Jet Off into a Storm of Protest as They Leave George at Home During Maldives Getaway," *Daily Mail*, March 8, 2014.
11. E-mail from Kate O'Donovan, April 1, 2014.
12. Author's interview with Alan Rusbridger, *Guardian* office, Central London, March 31, 2014.
13. *Cumberland Evening Times*, August 22, 1962.
14. Anthony Holden, *Charles: A Biography* (Bantam Press, 1998).
15. Anthony Holden, *Charles: A Biography* (Weidenfeld & Nicolson, 1988).
16. Ipsos-MORI, "Monarchy/Royal Family Trends: The Next Monarch," July 2013.
17. Diana's interview with Martin Bashir for *Panorama*, first broadcast BBC, November 20, 1995.
18. Ibid.

INTRODUCTION

1. *Panorama*, first broadcast BBC, November 20, 1995.
2. Author's interview with The Hon. Timothy Knatchbull, West London, February 18, 2014.
3. Author's interview with Emma Sparham, August 7, 2013.
4. Author's interview with Ben Elliot, Central London, May 27, 2014.

5. Author's interview with Ian Skelly, Central London, April 16, 2014.

6. Author's interview with Chief Rabbi Jonathan Sacks, North London, August 20, 2013.

7. Author's conversation with the Prince of Wales, Birkhall, Scotland, September 26, 2013.

8. Author's interview with Lucia Santa Cruz, March 25, 2014.

9. Author's interview with Chief Rabbi Jonathan Sacks, North London, August 20, 2013.

10. Author's conversation with the Prince of Wales, Birkhall, Scotland, September 26, 2013.

11. Author's interview with Emma Thompson, September 16, 2013.

12. On-the-record briefing, St. James's Palace, June 25, 2014.

13. Professor Dr. Herman Matthijs, "De Kostprijs van de Monarchie in Europa," University of Ghent and Free University of Brussels, April 2012.

14. From the Prince's website, http://www.princeofwales.gov.uk/the-prince-of-wales/promoting-and -protecting/raising-issues.

15. The Prince of Wales with Tony Juniper and Ian Skelly, *Harmony: A New Way of Looking at Our World* (Blue Door, HarperCollins, 2010).

16. *Charles: The Private Man, the Public Role*, documentary presented and coproduced by Jonathan Dimbleby for ITV, first screened June 30, 1994.

17. The Prince of Wales, *Harmony: A Vision for Our Future* (HarperCollins, 2010).

18. Author's interview with Patrick Holden, Central London, August 6, 2013.

19. Author's interview with Emma Thompson, September 16, 2013.

20. Alan Bennett, *The Madness of King George III* (Faber and Faber, 1995).

21. CVM/Don Anderson poll, March 2012.

22. Simon Wong, "Key: NZ Becoming a Republic 'Inevitable,'" 3 News Online, April 8, 2014.

23. Ipsos-MORI Almanac, 2012.

24. British Social Attitudes 30, NatCen Social Research 2013.

25. AAP wire, April 16, 2014.

26. Letter to the editor of the *Times*, from Gerald Vinestock, in Lancaster, published April 17, 2014.

27. *The Diamond Queen*, BBC 1, Episode 1, written and presented by Andrew Marr, first broadcast February 6, 2012.

28. Author's conversation with the Prince of Wales, Birkhall, Scotland, September 26, 2013.

29. Interview by J. F. O. McAllister and Catherine Mayer for *Time*, 2006.

30. *The Prince of Wales: Up Close*, documentary presented by Trevor McDonald, first screened on ITV on May 16, 2006.

31. Office of National Statistics. Poverty calculated as living below 60 percent of median incomes before housing costs.

32. *The Prince of Wales: Up Close*, documentary presented by Trevor McDonald, first screened on ITV on May 16, 2006.

33. Michael Elliott, "Why the Royals Miss Diana," *Time*, November 17, 2002.

34. Author's interview with Elizabeth Buchanan, Central London, March 5, 2014.

35. Walter Bagehot, *The English Constitution*, Book No. III (*The Monarchy*) (n.p., 1867).

36. Author's conversation with the Prince of Wales, Birkhall, Scotland, September 26, 2013.

37. Author's interview with Elizabeth Buchanan, Central London, March 5, 2014.

CHAPTER 1

1. Author's interview with Julia Cleverdon, Clarence House, July 25, 2013.

2. Author's interview with The Hon. Timothy Knatchbull, West London, February 18, 2014.

3. Author's conversation with the Prince of Wales, Birkhall, Scotland, September 26, 2013.

4. Andrew Alderson, "Prince Charles: Wind Farms Are Horrendous," *Sunday Telegraph*, August 8, 2004.

5. Memo to Oliver Everett quoted in Jonathan Dimbleby, *The Prince of Wales: A Biography*, Chapter 13 (Little Brown & Company, 1994).

6. Author's interview with Elizabeth Buchanan, Central London, March 5, 2014.

7. From the Prince's own website as of May 2014, http://www.princeofwales.gov.uk/the-prince-of -wales/royal-duties.

8. Letter from Sir Michael Peat to *Dispatches*, Channel 4, March 5, 2007.

9. *In Private in Public*, presented by Alastair Burnet, produced by Stewart Purvis for ITV, 1986.

10. Anthony Sampson, *The Changing Anatomy of Britain*, Chapter 1: "Monarchy: The Surviving Tribe" (Book Club Associates, 1982).
11. *Elizabeth R: A Year in the Life of the Queen*, directed and produced by Edward Mirzoeff, BBC, first broadcast February 6, 1992.
12. *In Private in Public*, presented by Alistair Burnet, produced by Stewart Purvis for ITV, 1986.
13. Author's interview with Patrick Holden, Central London, August 6, 2013.
14. Author's interview with Fiona Reynolds, Central London, May 29, 2014.
15. Jonathan Dimbleby, *The Prince of Wales: A Biography*, Chapter 22.
16. Author's conversation with the Prince of Wales, Birkhall, Scotland, September 26, 2013.
17. Author's interview with Clive Alderton, September 17, 2013.
18. Author's interview with Emma Thompson, September 16, 2013.
19. Sampson, *The Changing Anatomy of Britain*, Chapter 1.
20. Quoted by an aide.
21. Dimbleby, *The Prince of Wales: A Biography*, Chapter 20.
22. Author's interview with Sir John Major, Vauxhall, London, October 2014.
23. Speech by the Prince of Wales at the Prince's Accounting for Sustainability Forum, December 12, 2013.
24. Speech by the Prince of Wales at the Prince's Charities Investor Engagement Event, June 27, 2013.
25. Speech by the Prince of Wales to Lincolnshire Young Farmers Club, Riseholme Agricultural College, November 29, 2011.
26. The Prince of Wales with Juniper and Skelly, *Harmony: A New Way of Looking at Our World*.
27. Dimbleby, *The Prince of Wales: A Biography*, Chapter 3.
28. Author's conversation with the Prince of Wales, Birkhall, Scotland, September 26, 2013.
29. Author's interview with Emma Thompson, September 16, 2013.

CHAPTER 2

1. Author's interview with Sir John Major, Vauxhall, London, October 2014.
2. Vernon Bogdanor, *The Monarchy and the Constitution*, Chapter 4: "The Appointment of a Prime Minister" (Oxford University Press, 1995).
3. Graham Smith, "Election 2010: The Queen Could Write Herself Out of the Script," *Guardian*, May 4, 2010.
4. *The Cabinet Manual: A Guide to Laws, Conventions and Rules on the Operation of Government*, 1st ed., October 2011.
5. Author's interview with Sir John Major, Vauxhall, London, October 2014.
6. Author's interview with Sir John Major, London, October 2014.
7. "Nigel Farage Attacked over Romanians 'Slur,'" BBC Online, May 18, 2014.
8. Author's interview with the Bishop of London, the Old Deanery, April 23, 2014.
9. Helen Mirren, *The Diamond Queen*, BBC 1, Episode 1, written and presented by Andrew Marr, first broadcast February 6, 2012.
10. Robert Barr, "Lockerbie Begins Burial after Flight 103 Service," Associated Press, January 5, 1989.
11. Anthony Sampson, *The Changing Anatomy of Britain*, Chapter 1: "Monarchy: The Surviving Tribe" (Book Club Associates, 1982).
12. Anthony Holden, *Charles: A Biography*, Chapter 2: "No, Not You Dear" (Bantam Press, 1998).
13. Author's interview with Prince Andrew, Beijing, April 2004.
14. *Elizabeth R: A Year in the Life of the Queen*, directed and produced by Edward Mirzoeff, BBC, first broadcast February 6, 1992.
15. William Shawcross, *Queen Elizabeth, the Queen Mother: The Official Biography*, Chapter 13: "The Queen at War" (Macmillan, 2009).
16. *A Jubilee Tribute to the Queen by the Prince of Wales*, BBC, first broadcast June 1, 2012.
17. Author's interview with Sir John Major, Vauxhall, London, October 2014.
18. The Queen, speech at Guildhall, November 24, 1992.
19. Gordon Rayner, "Queen's Treasurer Accused of 'Shocking Complacency' over Crumbling Palaces by MPs," *Daily Telegraph*, October 14, 2013.
20. *Elizabeth R: A Year in the Life of the Queen*, directed and produced by Edward Mirzoeff, BBC, first broadcast February 6, 1992.

21. Ben Pimlott, *The Queen: Elizabeth II and the Monarchy*, Diamond Jubilee ed., Chapter 1 (Harper Press, 1996).

22. "Hacking Trial: Police 'Told to Leave Queen's Nuts,'" BBC Online, December 12, 2013.

23. Robert Lacey, *The Life and Reign of Elizabeth II* (Free Press, 2002).

24. Interview recorded in 2011 for *The Diamond Queen*, BBC 1, written and presented by Andrew Marr, first broadcast February 6, 2012.

25. Philip Ziegler, *Mountbatten: The Official Biography*, Chapter 24: "Post-Surrender Tasks" (Collins, 1985).

26. Ibid.

27. William Boyd, *School Ties*, Introduction (Penguin, 1985).

28. Robert Skidelsky, *English Progressive Schools* (Penguin, 1969).

29. *The Duke: Portrait of Prince Philip*, presented by Trevor Macdonald, Back2Back Productions for ITV, first broadcast May 12, 2008.

30. Ibid.

31. Jonathan Dimbleby, *The Prince of Wales: A Biography*, Chapter 20 (Little Brown & Company, 1994).

32. Author's interview with The Hon. Timothy Knatchbull, West London, February 18, 2014.

33. Ibid.

34. Ibid.

35. Timothy Knatchbull, *From a Clear Blue Sky* (Hutchinson, 2009).

36. Author's interview with The Hon. Timothy Knatchbull, West London, February 18, 2014.

CHAPTER 3

1. Author's conversation with the Prince of Wales, Birkhall, Scotland, September 26, 2013.

2. Alan Titchmarsh, "Birkhall, Balmoral Estate, Aberdeenshire," *Country Life*, November 14, 2013.

3. John Vidal, "Charles Designs 'Healing Garden,'" *Guardian*, May 16, 2002.

4. Ibid.

5. Author's conversation with the Prince of Wales, Birkhall, Scotland, September 26, 2013.

6. *Plato's Republic*, trans. Benjamin Jowett (Internet Classics Archive).

7. Jonathan Dimbleby, *The Prince of Wales: A Biography*, Chapter 5 (Little Brown & Company, 1994).

8. Anonymous pupil quoted in Ross Benson, *Charles: The Untold Story*, Chapter 3 (St. Martin's Press, 1993).

9. "Kurt Hahn—An Efficacious Educator," translation of: "Kurt Hahn—ein wirkungsmächtiger Pädagoge," *Pädagogisches Handeln: Wissenschaft und Praxis im Dialog* 5, no. 2 (2001): 65–76.

10. Author's conversation with the Prince of Wales, Birkhall, Scotland, September 26, 2013.

11. BBC Radio 4, March 1, 1969.

12. *The David Frost Show*, Episode 1, Series 1, Group W Productions, first broadcast July 7, 1969.

13. Author's interview with Lucia Santa Cruz, March 25, 2014.

14. Author's interview with Timothy Knatchbull, West London, February 18, 2014.

15. William Shawcross, *Queen Elizabeth: The Queen Mother: The Official Biography*, Chapter 23: "Poetry and Pain 1981–1999" (Macmillan, 2009).

16. Author's interview with Sir Nicholas Soames, Portcullis House, February 11, 2014.

17. Quoted in Philip Ziegler, *Mountbatten: The Official Biography*, Chapter 51: "The Shop-steward of Royalty" (Collins, 1985).

18. Ibid., letter from Mountbatten to the Prince, April 21, 1979.

19. Dimbleby, *The Prince of Wales: A Biography*, Chapter 14.

20. Author's interview with Emma Thompson, September 16, 2013.

21. Author's interview with the Bishop of London, the Old Deanery, April 23, 2014.

22. Author's interview with Elizabeth Buchanan, Central London, March 5, 2014.

23. Author's interview with Andrew Wright, Clarence House, August 2, 2013.

24. Author's interview with Clive Alderton, September 17, 2013.

25. Sir Alan Lascelles with Duff Hart-Davis, *King's Counsellor: Abdication and War: The Diaries of Sir Alan Lascelles* (Weidenfeld & Nicolson, 2006).

26. Prince Harry interviews: Key extracts, BBC Online, January 21, 2013.

27. Lee Aitken, "Edward Goes His Own Way," *People*, January 26, 1987.

28. Dimbleby, *The Prince of Wales: A Biography*, Chapter 12.
29. Andrew Morton and Mick Seamark, *Andrew: The Playboy Prince*, Chapter 1: "Andymania" (Corgi Books, 1983).
30. Author's interview with Prince Andrew, Beijing, April 2004.
31. Author's interview with Sir Nicholas Soames, Portcullis House, February 11, 2014.
32. Gaby Hinsliff and Burhan Wazir, "Word by Word, Sophie Digs Herself Deeper into Trouble," *Observer*, April 8, 2001.
33. Lee Aitken, "Edward Goes His Own Way," *People* Magazine, January 26, 1987.
34. Andy Beckett, "It's a Royal Cock-up," *Guardian*, March 5, 2002.
35. *The Grand Knockout Tournament*, BBC North West, Knockout Ltd., first screened August 12, 1987.

CHAPTER 4

1. Author's interview with Sir Nicholas Soames, Portcullis House, February 11, 2014.
2. Ibid.
3. Jonathan Dimbleby, *The Prince of Wales: A Biography*, Chapter 12 (Little Brown & Company, 1994).
4. Ibid.
5. Author's interview with Lucia Santa Cruz, March 25, 2014.
6. Entry in the Prince's naval journals, dated March 25, 1974, quoted in Jonathan Dimbleby, *The Prince of Wales: A Biography*, Chapter 12.
7. Author's interview with Lucia Santa Cruz, March 25, 2014.
8. Author's interview with Emma Thompson, September 16, 2013.
9. Author's interview with Lucia Santa Cruz, March 25, 2014.
10. Angela Rippon and Andrew Gardner, *Interview with Diana Spencer and the Prince of Wales*, first broadcast by the BBC and ITN July 28, 1981.
11. Andrew Morton, *Diana: Her True Story—In Her Own Words* (Michael O'Mara Books, 1997).
12. Author's interview with Lucia Santa Cruz, March 25, 2014.
13. Author's interview with The Hon. Timothy Knatchbull, West London, February 18, 2014.
14. Humphrey Carpenter, *Robert Runcie: The Reluctant Archbishop*, Chapter 12: "What the Job Is" (Hodder & Stoughton, 1996).
15. Andrew Morton, *Diana: Her True Story—In Her Own Words* (London: Michael O'Mara Books Limited, 1992).
16. Marion Crawford, *The Little Princesses*, Chapter 6: "The Outbreak of War" (St. Martin's Press, 2003).
17. Stephen Fry, *More Fool Me: A Memoir* (Penguin, 2014).
18. Tim Clayton and Phil Craig, *Diana: Story of a Princess*, Chapter 10: "Secret Squirrel" (Coronet, Hodder & Stoughton, 2001).
19. Squidgygate transcript, thought to have been recorded December 31, 1989.
20. Camillagate transcript, thought to have been recorded December 18, 1989.
21. *Review of Press Self-Regulation*, by Sir David Calcutt QC, cm 2135, HMSO, presented to Parliament by the Secretary of State for the Department of National Heritage, January 1993.
22. Squidgygate transcript, thought to have been recorded December 31, 1989.
23. Author's interview with Anthony Holden.
24. *Diana—Her True Story: The Book That Changed Everything*, documentary, Sky Arts, first broadcast September 23, 2012.
25. *Princess Diana: Behind the Panorama Interview*, documentary, BBC, first broadcast November 8, 2005.
26. Author's interview with Jonathan Dimbleby, London, March 28, 2014.
27. Ibid.
28. Author's interview with Jonathan Dimbleby, London, March 28, 2014.
29. *Charles: The Private Man, the Public Role*, documentary presented and coproduced by Jonathan Dimbleby for ITV, first screened June 30, 1994.
30. E-mail from Jonathan Dimbleby November 15, 2014. Clayton and Craig, *Diana: Story of a Princess*, Chapter 6: "Mood Swings" (Coronet, Hodder & Stoughton, 2001).
31. Author's interview with the Bishop of London, the Old Deanery, April 23, 2014.
32. *Panorama*, BBC, first broadcast November 20, 1995.

33. Author's interview with Sir Nicholas Soames, Portcullis House, February 11, 2014.
34. "Princess Dismisses Bulimia Reports with Joke," *Scottish Herald*, November 5, 1993.
35. *Panorama*, BBC, first broadcast November 20, 1995.
36. Author's interview with Emma Thompson, September 16, 2013.
37. Chris Logan and Andrew Alderson, "Diana 'Took Charles to Cleaners' in Divorce, Says His Banker," *Sunday Telegraph*, July 25, 2004.
38. "Minister Denies Row over Diana," *Scottish Herald*, March 5, 1997.
39. Author's interview with Sir Nicholas Soames, Portcullis House, February 11, 2014.

CHAPTER 5

1. Author's interview with Andrew Wright, Clarence House, August 2, 2013.
2. Author's interview with Elizabeth Buchanan, Central London, March 5, 2014.
3. Sir Michael Peat and Edmund Lawson QC, *Report to His Royal Highness the Prince of Wales*, March 13, 2003.
4. David Leigh, "Royals Deny Rumours About Prince Charles," *Guardian*, November 7, 2003.
5. Andrew Alderson, "Prince Charles 'Set to Sue' Palace Aide over Scandal," *Sunday Telegraph*, November 9, 2003.
6. Mary Riddell, "Blackadder Bites Back," *British Journalism Review* 15, no. 2 (2004).
7. "Charles' School Comments Defended," BBC Online, November 18, 2004.
8. "Prince Hits Back in Memo Row," *Daily Mail*, November 23, 2004.
9. Peter Foster, "Has the Puppet-Master of St. James's Finally Pulled One String Too Many?" *Daily Telegraph*, December 1, 2001.
10. Riddell, "Blackadder Bites Back."
11. Richard Kay and Geoffrey Levy, "Camilla and the Blonde Private Secretary Who's Paid the Price for Being Too Close to Prince Charles," *Daily Mail*, June 13, 2008.
12. Author's interview with Elizabeth Buchanan, Central London, March 5, 2014.
13. Author's interview with Emma Thompson, September 16, 2013.
14. J. D. F. Jones, *Storyteller: The Many Lives of Laurens van der Post*, Chapter 37: "My Prince" (Scribner, 2001).
15. Ibid.
16. Dan Davies, *In Plain Sight: The Life and Lies of Jimmy Savile*, Chapter 45: "Am I Saved?" (Quercus Editions, 2014).
17. Squidgygate transcript, thought to have been recorded December 31, 1989.
18. "Jimmy Savile: The Power to Abuse," *Panorama*, BBC, first broadcast June 2, 2014.
19. *Queen and Country*, documentary series written and presented by William Shawcross, BBC, first broadcast May 1, 2002.
20. Author's interview with Sir Nicholas Soames, Portcullis House, February 11, 2014.
21. "Diana Inquest: Queen Ordered Palace to Be Swept for Bugs over Spy Fears," *Mail* Online, February 12, 2008.
22. Richard Palmer, "Tories Blocked Royal Phone-Tapping Probe," *Daily Express*, February 13, 2008.
23. Tom Bower, *Fayed: The Unauthorized Biography*, Chapter 17: "The Last Blonde" (Macmillan, 1998).
24. Louise Radnofsky and agencies, "Nazi Philip Wanted Diana Dead, Fayed Tells Inquest," *Guardian*, February 18, 2008.

CHAPTER 6

1. Author's conversation with the Prince of Wales, Birkhall, Scotland, September 26, 2013.
2. Author's interview with Sir William Castell, Wellcome Trust, London, March 19, 2004.
3. Author's interview with Martina Milburn, Prince's Trust headquarters, July 30, 2013.
4. Author's interview with Julia Cleverdon, Clarence House, July 25, 2013.
5. Hattie Collins, "The Ace in the Pack," *Guardian*, April 1, 2006.
6. Author's interview with Tom Shebbeare, Central London, July 9, 2014.
7. Author's interview with Martina Milburn, Prince's Trust headquarters, July 30, 2013.
8. Ibid.
9. Prince of Wales quoted in the *International Herald Tribune*, November 18, 1978.
10. Author's conversation with the Prince of Wales, Birkhall, Scotland, September 26, 2013.

11. "Somerset flood delay a 'tragedy,' says Prince Charles," BBC online, February 4, 2014.

12. Jim Waterson, "21 Pictures of Politicians in Wellies Staring at Floods," BuzzFeed, February 11, 2014.

13. Paul Flynn, "King Charles Doomed," *Read My Day* (Flynn blog), December 18, 2009.

14. Author's interview with Sir John Major, London, October 2014.

15. Author's interview with Sir Nicholas Soames, Portcullis House, February 11, 2014.

16. Author's interview with Emma Thompson, September 16, 2013.

17. From the Prince's own website, as of May 2014, http://www.princeofwales.gov.uk/the-prince-of-wales/promoting-and-protecting/raising-issues.

18. Author's conversation with the Prince of Wales, Birkhall, Scotland, September 26, 2013.

19. Ibid.

20. Author's interview with Peter Ahrends, North London, May 2, 2014.

21. Thomas Hine, "New Wing Vindicates Prince Charles," *Philadelphia Inquirer*, July 10, 1991.

22. A speech by HRH The Prince of Wales at the Corporation of London Planning and Communication Committee's Annual Dinner, Mansion House, London, December 1, 1987.

23. Stephen Adams, "Prince of Wales's Emotional Chelsea Barracks Letter Revealed," *Daily Telegraph*, June 24, 2010.

24. "Exclusive: Prince Charles on the Environment, the Monarchy, His Family, and Islam," *Vanity Fair* (abstract of Bob Colacello profile), October 6, 2010.

25. Robert Booth, "Prince Charles's Meddling in Planning 'Unconstitutional,' Says Richard Rogers," *Guardian*, June 15, 2009.

26. Author's conversation with the Prince of Wales, Birkhall, Scotland, September 26, 2013.

27. Author's interview with Ewen Miller, September 10, 2013.

28. HRH the Prince of Wales, *A Vision of Britain: A Personal View of Architecture*, Introduction (Doubleday, Transworld, 1989).

29. Amanda Baillieu, "Liverpool Ferry Terminal Wins Carbuncle Cup 2009," *Building Design*, August 28, 2009.

30. Justin McGuirk, "Prince Charles's Poundbury Fire Station Is a Daft Mess," *Guardian*, March 31, 2009.

31. Oliver Wainright, "Poundbury Houses at St. John's Way by Francis Roberts Architects," *Building Design*, July 4, 2012.

32. Author's conversation with the Prince of Wales, Birkhall, Scotland, September 26, 2013.

33. Author's interview with The Hon. Timothy Knatchbull, West London, February 18, 2014.

34. Ibid.

CHAPTER 7

1. From the Foreword by HRH the Prince of Wales to Keith Critchlow, *The Hidden Geometry of Flowers* (Floris Books, 2011).

2. Author's conversation with the Prince of Wales, Birkhall, Scotland, September 26, 2013.

3. "The Empire and the World Rejoice," *Melbourne Argus* correspondent and AAP, *Melbourne Argus*, November 16, 1948.

4. World Bank 2013.

5. Quoted in William F. Bynum and Vivian Nutton, eds., *Essays in the History of Therapeutics* (Editions Rodopi, 1991).

6. "Complementary Medicine," a speech by the Prince of Wales, The British Medical Association, London, December 14, 1982.

7. Ibid.

8. Christopher Smallwood's report on integrated health, press release issued by Clarence House, October 16, 2005.

9. Author's interview with Edzard Ernst, Suffolk, March 3, 2014.

10. Sarah Boseley, " 'Make-believe and Outright Quackery'—Expert's Verdict on Prince's Detox Potion," *Guardian*, March 11, 2009.

11. Quoted in *The Royal Activist*, BBC Radio 4, first broadcast June 29, 2014.

12. Edzard Ernst, "How Prince Charles Disrespects His Constitutional Role," http://edzardernst.com/, 30 June 2014.

13. Author's interview with Ian Skelly, Central London, April 16, 2014.

14. *Charles: The Private Man, the Public Role*, documentary presented and coproduced by Jonathan Dimbleby for ITV, first screened June 30, 1994.

15. Quoted in Jonathan Dimbleby, *The Prince of Wales: A Biography*, Chapter 26 (Little Brown & Company, 1994).

16. Author's interview with Jonathan Dimbleby, London, March 28, 2014.

17. Humphrey Carpenter, *Robert Runcie: The Reluctant Archbishop*, Chapter 12: "What the Job Is" (Hodder & Stoughton, 1996).

18. Author's interview with the Bishop of London, the Old Deanery, April 23, 2014.

19. Ibid.

20. Ibid.

21. Author's interview with Ian Skelly, Central London, April 16, 2014.

22. Janet Watts, "Obituary of Kathleen Raine," *Guardian Books*, July 8, 2003.

23. Philippa Bernard, *No End to Snowdrops: A Biography of Kathleen Raine*, Chapter 11: "Temenos" (Shepheard-Walwyn, 2009).

24. http://www.temenosacademy.org/temenos_home.html.

25. Bernard, *No End to Snowdrops*, Chapter 12: "India."

26. Author's interview with Ian Skelly, Central London, April 16, 2014.

27. The Prince of Wales with Juniper and Skelly, *Harmony*.

28. Ibid.

29. *Religion in England and Wales, 2011 Census, Key Statistics for Local Authorities in England and Wales*, Office for National Statistics, released December 11, 2012.

30. Gordon Rayner, "Prince of Wales 'Abused and Ridiculed' over His Attempts to Promote Inter-Faith Dialogue," *Daily Telegraph*, April 6, 2011.

31. Author's interview with the Bishop of London, the Old Deanery, April 23, 2014.

32. Author's interview with Chief Rabbi Jonathan Sacks, North London, August 20, 2013.

33. Author's interview with the Bishop of London, the Old Deanery, April 23, 2014.

CHAPTER 8

1. "Islam and the West," a speech by HRH The Prince of Wales, The Sheldonian Theatre, Oxford, October 27, 1993.

2. Author's interview with Farhan Nizami, Central London, August 22, 2013.

3. Robin Simcox, *A Degree of Influence: The Funding of Strategically Important Subjects in UK Universities*, The Centre for Social Cohesion, 2009.

4. "Islam and the West."

5. E-mail from Farhan Nizami, August 8, 2014.

6. Richard Freeman and William F. Wertz Jr., "Charles of Arabia: The British Monarchy, Saudi Arabia, and 9/11," *Executive Intelligence Review* 41, no. 21 (May 23, 2014).

7. Mark Hollingsworth with Sandy Mitchell, *Saudi Babylon: Torture, Corruption and Cover-Up Inside the House of Saud*, Chapter Two: "Caught in Al-Qaeda's Wave of Terror" (Mainstream Publishing, 2005).

8. Martin Amis quoted in Paul Elie, "A Fundamental Fight," *Vanity Fair*, May 2014.

9. Author's interview with Lucia Santa Cruz, March 25, 2014.

10. Richard Norton-Taylor, "The Future British King, Saudi Princes, and a Secret Arms Deal," *Guardian*, February 24, 2014.

11. Author's interview with Farhan Nizami, Central London, August 22, 2013.

12. Author's interview with Shelly Glover, Winnipeg, May 21, 2014.

13. Rebecca English, "'Putin Is Behaving Just Like Hitler,' says Charles. Prince's Controversial Verdict on Russian Leader's Invasion of Ukraine," *Daily Mail*, May 20, 2014.

14. "Vladimir Putin Condemns Prince Charles's 'Nazi' Remarks," BBC Online, May 24, 2014.

15. Author's interview with Dominic Richards and Hank Dittmar, Central London, August 21, 2013.

16. Author's interview with Amelia Fawcett, September 25, 2013.

17. Speech by Commonwealth Secretary-General Kamalesh Sharma, Commonwealth Day Reception, Marlborough House, London, March 11, 2013.

18. Josh Vissier, "Prince George Boosts Popularity of the Monarchy in Canada (Provided Charles Isn't King): Poll," *National Post*, July 25, 2013.

CHAPTER 9

1. Harry Arnold, "It's Camilla, Looking Just Like One's Mum," *Daily Mirror*, March 6, 1993.
2. Heather McGlone and Rosemary Carpenter, "Why Camilla Has Such a Hold on Charles," *Daily Express*, January 16, 1993.
3. Author's interview with Lucia Santa Cruz, March 25, 2014.
4. "Charles and Camilla Go Public," BBC Online, January 29, 1999.
5. Sholto Byrnes, "Mark Bolland: Marital Aide," *Independent*, March 30, 2005.
6. Author's interview with Anthony Holden and Richard Kay, Central London, April 17, 2014.
7. Author's interview with Robin Boles, In Kind Direct headquarters, August 21, 2013.
8. Richard Kay and Geoffrey Levy, "Why Charles and Camilla Are Now Living Such Separate Lives," *Daily Mail*, June 29, 2010.
9. Richard Kay and Geoffrey Levy, "From 'That Wicked Woman' to Her Majesty's Secret Weapon: Camilla's the Only One Who Stops Charles Sulking About Kate and George's Popularity," *Daily Mail*, April 18, 2014.
10. E-mail from Richard Kay, July 22, 2014.
11. Author's conversation with the Prince of Wales, Birkhall, Scotland, September 26, 2013.
12. Author's interview with Emma Thompson, September 16, 2013.
13. Author's interview with Lucia Santa Cruz, March 25, 2014.
14. Author's interview with Patrick Holden, Central London, August 6, 2013.
15. Author's interview with Ben Elliot, Central London, May 27, 2014.
16. Author's interview with Lucia Santa Cruz, March 25, 2014.
17. Author's Interview with Amanda Macmanus, Clarence House, April 9, 2014.
18. Emma Soames, "Camilla's Dearest Cause," *Daily Telegraph*, November 20, 2006.
19. Author's interview with Robin Boles, Central London, August 21, 2013.
20. Author's interview with Sir Nicholas Soames, Portcullis House, February 11, 2014.
21. YouGov/Sunday Times survey, sample size: 1945 GB Adults, fieldwork: May 9–10, 2013.
22. Author's interview with Emma Thompson, September 16, 2013.

CHAPTER 10

1. A speech by the Prince of Wales at the opening of the Queen Elizabeth Garden, Dumfries House, July 2, 2014.
2. Scottish Index of Multiple Deprivation 2012.
3. Author's interview with Sarah-Jane Clark, Dumfries estate, January 21, 2014.
4. Author's interview with Gette Fulton, Cumnock, January 20, 2014.
5. Author's interview with Ben Elliot, Central London, May 27, 2014.
6. E-mail from Fiona Lees, July 7, 2014.
7. Author's conversation with the Prince of Wales, Birkhall, Scotland, September 26, 2013.
8. Jane Treays, "Prince William on Why Conservation and Africa Are Burning Passions He Was Born to Pass On," *Radio Times*, September 15, 2013.
9. Conversation during Canada tour, May 2014.
10. Author's interview with Ben Elliot, Central London, May 27, 2014.
11. Author's interview with Emma Thompson, September 16, 2013.
12. Author's interview with Patrick Holden, Central London, August 6, 2013.
13. Author's interview with Emma Thompson, September 16, 2013.
14. Author's interview with Patrick Holden, Central London, August 6, 2013.
15. Fiona Lees and Kristina Kyriacou, Meeting with the Prince of Wales, September 13, 2013.

CONCLUSION

1. Author's conversation with the Prince of Wales, Birkhall, Scotland, September 26, 2013.
2. Author's interview with Graham Smith, Central London, May 29, 2014.
3. Author's interview with Lord Berkeley, House of Lords, April 3, 2014.
4. Hansard Debates for the House of Commons, March 22, 2001.

5. Author's interview with Graham Smith, Central London, May 29, 2014.

6. Niccolò Machiavelli, *The Prince*, Chapter 19: "That One Should Avoid Being Despised and Hated" (Wankeep Publishing, 2013; first distributed 1513, first published 1532).

7. *Charles: The Private Man, the Public Role*, documentary presented and coproduced by Jonathan Dimbleby for ITV, first screened June 30, 1994.

8. Robert Booth, "Prince of Wales: A Private Individual's Effective Veto over Public Legislation," *Guardian*, October 30, 2011.

9. Author's interview with Sir John Major, Vauxhall, London, October 2014.

10. House of Commons Committee of Public Accounts, The Sovereign Grant, Thirty-ninth Report of Session 2013–14, January 2014.

11. Author's interview with Patrick Holden, Central London, August 6, 2013.

12. Author's interview with Fiona Reynolds, Central London, May 29, 2014.

13. Author's interview with Sir John Major, Vauxhall, London, October 2014.

14. Author's interview with Emma Thompson, September 16, 2013.

15. Author's conversation with the Prince of Wales, Birkhall, Scotland, September 26, 2013.

Select Bibliography

//

Anker, Peder. *Imperial Ecology: Environmental Order in the British Empire, 1895–1945*. London: Harvard University Press, 2001.

Arbiter, Dickie. *On Duty with the Queen*. London: Blink Publishing, 2014.

Bartlett, Mike. *King Charles III*. London: Nick Hern Books, 2014.

Bedell Smith, Sally. *Diana: The Life of a Troubled Princess*. London: Aurum Press Ltd., 1999.

Benson, Ross. *Charles: The Untold Story*. New York: St. Martin's Press, 1993.

Bernard, Philippa. *No End to Snowdrops*. London: Shepheard-Walwyn Ltd., 2009.

Bogdanor, Vernon. *The Monarchy and the Constitution*. Oxford, UK: Clarendon Press, 1995.

Bower, Tom. *Fayed: The Unauthorised Biography*. London: Macmillan, 1998.

Boyd, William. *School Ties*. London: Penguin Books, 1985.

Bradford, Sarah. *Diana*. London: Penguin Books, 2007.

———. *Queen Elizabeth II: Her Life in Our Times*. London: Viking, 2012.

Brandreth, Gyles. *Breaking the Code: Westminster Diaries*. London: Orion Publishing, 2000.

———. *Charles & Camilla*. London: Arrow Books, 2006.

Brown, Tina. *The Diana Chronicles*. London: Century, 2007.

Burden, Peter. *News of the World?: Fake Sheiks and Royal Trappings*. London: Eye Books, 2008.

Burrell, Paul. *A Royal Duty*. London: Penguin Books, 2004.

Campbell, Alastair. *Diaries*. Vol. 1, *Prelude to Power, 1994–1997*. London: Hutchinson, 2011.

———. *Diaries*. Vol. 2, *Power and the People, 1997–1999*. London: Hutchinson, 2011.

———. *Diaries*. Vol. 3, *Power and Responsibility, 1999–2001*. London: Hutchinson, 2012.

Cannadine, David. *Class in Britain*. London: Penguin Books, 2000.

Carpenter, Humphrey. *Robert Runcie: The Reluctant Archbishop*. London: Hodder & Stoughton Ltd., 1996.

Clayton, Tim, and Phil Craig, eds. *Diana: Story of a Princess*. London: Hodder & Stoughton Ltd., 2001.

Cohen, David. *Diana: Death of a Goddess*. London: Arrow, 2005.

Cohen, Nick. *You Can't Read This Book*. London: Fourth Estate, 2012.

Crawford, Marion. *The Little Princesses*. London: Orion Publishing, 2012.

Critchlow, Keith. *The Hidden Geometry of Flowers: Living Rhythms, Form and Number*. Edinburgh: Floris Books, 2011.

Davenport-Hines, Richard. *An English Affair: Sex, Class and Power in the Age of Profumo*. London: HarperPress, 2013.

Davies, Dan. *In Plain Sight: The Life and Lies of Jimmy Savile*. London: Quercus, 2014.

Davies, Nick. *Hack Attack*. London: Chatto & Windus, 2014.

Dimbleby, Jonathan. *The Prince of Wales: A Biography*. London: Little, Brown & Company, 1994.

Duffel, Nick. *The Making of Them: The British Attitude to Children and the Boarding School System*. London: Lone Arrow Press, 2000.

Goodall, Sarah, and Nicholas Monson, eds. *The Palace Diaries: Twelve Years with HRH Prince Charles*. London: Mainstream Digital, 2012.

Gottlieb, Anthony. *The Dream of Reason*. London: Penguin, 2000.

Hardman, Robert. *Our Queen*. London: Hutchinson, 2011.

Heywood, Colin. *A History of Childhood*. Cambridge, UK: Polity, 2001.

Hoey, Brian. *Mountbatten: The Private Story*. London: CB Creative Books, 2013.

Holden, Anthony. *Charles: A Biography*. London: Bantam Press, 1998.

———. *Of Presidents, Prime Ministers & Princes: A Decade in Fleet Street*. London: Weidenfeld & Nicolson, 1984.

———. *Prince Charles: A Biography*. New York: Atheneum, 1979.

———. *A Princely Marriage: Charles and Diana, the First Ten Years*. London: Bantam Press, 1991.

Hollingsworth, Mark, and Sandy Mitchell, eds. *Saudi Babylon: Torture, Corruption and Cover-up Inside the House of Saud*. London: Mainstream Digital, 2012.

HRH The Prince of Wales. *Harmony: A New Way of Looking at Our World*. Edited by Tony Juniper and Ian Skelly. London: Blue Door, 2010.

———. *Harmony: A Vision for Our Future*. London: HarperCollins, 2010.

———. *The Old Man of Lochnagar*. London: Picture Puffin, 1991.

———. *A Vision of Britain: A Personal View of Architecture*. London: Doubleday, 1989.

Hutchins, Chris, and Peter Thompson, eds. *Diana's Nightmare: The Family*. London: Christopher Hutchins Ltd., 2011.

Jephson, Patrick. *Portraits of a Princess: Travels with Diana*. London: Sidgwick & Jackson Ltd., 2004.

Jobson, Robert. *William and Kate: The Love Story*. London: John Blake Publishing Ltd., 2010.

Jones, J. D. F. *Storyteller: The Many Lives of Laurens van der Post*. London: Scribner, 2002.

Joseph, Claudia. *Kate: The Making of a Princess*. London: Mainstream Publishing, 2010.

Jung, Carl. *Man and His Symbols*. London: Pan Books Ltd., 1978.

Junor, Penny. *Prince Harry: Brother, Soldier, Son*. London: Hodder & Stoughton, 2014.

Kear, Adrian, and Deborah Lynn Steinberg. *Mourning Diana: Nation, Culture, and the Performance of Grief*. London: Routledge, 1999.

Kelley, Kitty. *The Royals*. New York: Warner Books, 1997.

Knatchbull, Timothy. *From a Clear Blue Sky*. London: Hutchinson, 2009.

Knevitt, Charles. *From Pecksniff to the Prince of Wales: 150 Years of Punch on Architecture, Planning and Development, 1841–1991*. London: Polymath Publishing, 1991.

———. *One's Life: A Cartoon Biography of HRH The Prince of Wales*. London: Penguin Books, 1988.

Lacey, Robert. *A Brief Life of the Queen*. London: Gerald Duckworth & Co. Ltd., 2012.

Levine, Tom. *Die Windsors*. Frankfurt Am Mein: Campus Verlag, 2005.

Lorimer, David. *Radical Prince: The Practical Vision of the Prince of Wales*. Edinburgh: Floris Books, 2004.

Machiavelli, Niccolò. *The Prince*. London: Waxkeep Publishing, 2013.

Marr, Andrew. *The Diamond Queen*. London: Macmillan, 2011.

———. *The Real Elizabeth: An Intimate Portrait of Queen Elizabeth II*. New York: Henry Holt & Company, 2012.

Mayer, Catherine. *The Royal Family: Britain's Resilient Monarchy Celebrates Elizabeth II's 60-Year Reign*. New York: Time Books, 2012.

Mckinnon, Don. *In the Ring: A Commonwealth Memoir*. London: Elliot and Thompson Ltd., 2013.

Morton, Andrew. *Diana: Her True Story*. London: Simon & Schuster Books, 1992.

———. *William and Catherine: Their Lives, Their Wedding*. London: Michael O'Mara Books, 2011.

Paxman, Jeremy. *On Royalty*. London: Penguin Books, 2007.

Peat, Sir Michael, and Edmund Lawson, QC, eds. *Report to His Royal Highness the Prince of Wales*, March 13, 2003.

Pimlott, Ben. *The Queen: A Biography of Elizabeth II*. London: HarperCollins, 1996.

———. *The Queen: Elizabeth II and the Monarchy*. London: HarperPress, 2012.

Price, Lance. *Where Power Lies*. London: Simon & Schuster, 2010.

Republic Campaign Ltd. *How to Win the Argument: Challenging Common Arguments Made in Favour of the Monarchy*. London: Republic, 2010.

———. *60 Inglorious Years: A Provocative Reassessment of the Queen's Record*. London: Republic, 2012.

Richards, Jeffrey, Scott Wilson, and Linda Woodhead, eds. *Diana: The Making of a Media Saint*. London: I. B. Tauris & Co., 1999.

Routledge, Paul. *Gordon Brown: The Biography*. London: Simon & Schuster, 1998.

Sampson, Anthony. *The Changing Anatomy of Britain*. London: Book Club Associates, 1982.

Sedgwick, Mark J. *Against the Modern World: Traditionalism and the Secret Intellectual History of the Twentieth Century*. Oxford, UK: Oxford University Press, 2004.

Shawcross, William. *Queen Elizabeth: The Queen Mother*. London: Macmillan Publishers, 2009.

Singh, Simon, and Edzard Ernst. *Trick or Treatment?* London: Transworld Publishers, 2008.

Snell, Kate. *Diana: Her Last Love*. London: Granada Media, 2013.

Spicer, Michael. *The Spicer Diaries*. London: Thomas Dunne Books, 2012.

Starkey, David. *Crown and Country: A History of England Through the Monarchy*. London: HarperPress, 2010.

Straw, Jack. *Last Man Standing: Memoirs of a Political Survivor*. London: Macmillan, 2012.

Stubbs, David. *The Prince Charles Letters: A Future Monarch's Correspondence on Matters of the Utmost Concern*. London: Aurum Press, 2011.

Thatcher, Margaret. *The Downing Street Years*. London: HarperCollins, 1993.

Turner, Alwyn W. *Crisis? What Crisis?: Britain in the 1970s*. London: Aurum Press, 2008.

Turner, Graham. *Elizabeth: The Woman and the Queen*. London: Macmillan Publishers, 2002.

Van der Kiste, John. *Childhood at Court 1819–1914*. Stroud, UK: Sutton, 2003.

Voltaire. *Candide*. New York: Boni & Liveright, 1918.

Watson, Tom, and Martin Hickman. *Dial M for Murdoch*. London: Penguin Books, 2012.

Wharfe, Ken, and Robert Jobson, eds. *Diana: Closely Guarded Secret*. London: Michael O'Mara Books Ltd., 2003.

Whittle, Peter. *Monarchy Matters*. London: The Social Affairs Unit, 2011.

Wilson, Christopher. *A Greater Love: Prince Charles's Twenty-Year Affair with Camilla Parker Bowles*. London: Headline Publishing, 1995.

———. *The Windsor Knot: Charles, Camilla and the Legacy of Diana*. London: Pinnacle Publishing, 2002.

Wright, Peter. *Spycatcher*. London: Viking Penguin, 1987.

Ziegler, Philip. *Mountbatten*. London: Collins, 1985.

Acknowledgments

//

It is said that two Eds are better than one and I cannot but agree. *Born to Be King* owes its birth to the two best Eds in the publishing business: my agent, Ed Victor, and Ed Faulkner, Ebury's publishing director, who commissioned the book in London. Stephen Rubin, president and publisher of Henry Holt, understood that Britain's royals are not exclusively reserved for Britons' enjoyment and brought the book to the US. Many thanks also to John Sterling, who helped me to refashion the text for American readers— and to bring out the comedy as well as the pathos, grandeur, and substance of the subject.

Hannah McGrath proved to be not only an indefatigable researcher but also an invaluable sounding board. Friends and colleagues gave me all sorts of useful tips and in several cases surprised me by revealing hitherto unsuspected connections to royalty.

Writing is an antisocial process, and I am lucky that my husband, parents, step-parents, sisters, step-sisters, elective sisters, nephew, godchildren, and delightful friends continue to tolerate me. Sara Burns coaxed me out for regular walks. Nicola Jennings spurred me on by regularly updating me on the progress of her own doctoral thesis—reminding me how many hundreds of thousands of words she had banked before I even started—then invited me to join her in France on a writing break.

I finished my first draft under her roof, a little before she handed in her own manuscript.

Michael Elliott makes a cameo appearance in these pages, at a lunch with the Prince. Mike and I have known each other since meeting at *The Economist* in the 1980s. Later, as *Time*'s Deputy Managing Editor, he urged me to keep pushing for access to Charles. Several other *Time* editors played key roles in nursing the 2013 cover story that led to this book, in particular Radhika Jones, Bobby Ghosh, and the brilliant and lovely Jim Frederick, who died suddenly in July of this year, at only forty-two. Another death, in April, of an elective family member who was just twenty-five years old, and like Jim a supernova, for a few days made me question whether to stop writing and pay more attention to the people I love. Instead, the process enabled me to forget, for hours at a time. Now I would like to remember. I have no garden in which to erect shrines, as the Prince does. These few words must serve.

There are many people at Clarence House, Buckingham Palace, and Kensington Palace, working for Charles's charities and among his friends, staff, and acquaintances—even some of his "Bond villains"—to whom I owe a weighty debt of gratitude. All have tolerated me hanging around and bugging them with questions over a long period of time. Some are named in the text; others chose to remain anonymous. Getting to know these people was one of the most enjoyable byproducts of researching this biography. A special mention must go to Kristina Kyriacou for making impossible things possible.

Of course, if Prince Charles were not such an endlessly fascinating character there would be no book. My final and biggest thanks, therefore, goes to him. This is not an authorized biography and he by no means welcomed my efforts, but he didn't pull up the drawbridge.

Finally, an apology to my crestfallen goddaughter: I'm sorry this book is about *the* Prince, not Prince. Next time.

Index

About the Author

//

CATHERINE MAYER is Editor at Large at *Time* magazine. In three decades of covering European and international current affairs, she has profiled the leading figures in many fields, including royals, presidents and prime ministers, and cultural and business leaders.